Fashion and Cultural Studies

Fashion and Cultural Studies

Susan B. Kaiser

London · New York

English edition
First published in 2012 by
Berg
Editorial offices:
50 Bedford Square, London WC1B 3DP, UK
175 Fifth Avenue, New York, NY 10010, USA

Berg is an imprint of Bloomsbury Publishing Plc.

Library of Congress Cataloging-in-Publication Data

A catalogue record for this book is available from the Library of Congress.

British Library Cataloguing-in-Publication Data

A catalogue record for this book is available from the British Library.

ISBN 978 1 84788 565 4 (Cloth)
978 1 84788 564 7 (Paper)
e-ISBN 978 0 85785 430 8 (ePDF)
978 0 85785 431 5 (epub)

Typeset by Apex CoVantage.
Printed in the UK by the MPG Books Group.

www.bergpublishers.com

Contents

List of Illustrations

Acknowledgments

Fashion studies, cultural studies. This book reflects my long-term interest in bridging these fields, and I have many people to thank for their contributions to this journey. Faculty, students, and staff in the Division of Textiles and Clothing (TXC) at the University of California, Davis, have offered a collegial home/ space for interdisciplinary exploration and risk taking, and I am extremely grateful. Students in my TXC undergraduate course, Style and Fashion Studies, have read (and tactfully critiqued) earlier drafts of many chapters. They have been an ongoing source of inspiration, critically and creatively challenging me as they have done their best to keep me current. I especially want to express my deep gratitude to the remarkable graduate teaching and research assistants with whom I have had the pleasure to "connect the dots" between fashion and cultural studies over the years: Sara Bernstein, Elise Chatelain, Yin-San Chen, Kadie Corless, Ely Estoesta, Anthony Freitas, Denise Green, Carol Hall, Tania Hammidi, Karyl Ketchum, Ryan Looysen, Sarah McCullough, Linda Matheson, Norah Sorensen, Nan Turner, and Yuchen Zhao. Their creative ideas for assignments and cultural resources, suggestions on earlier drafts, and ongoing enthusiasm and intellectual passion have been ever inspiring and sustaining. These and other former graduate students continue to be wonderful colleagues.

I am also very fortunate to have terrific colleagues across the UC Davis campus. I would like to express my deep gratitude to Joan Chandler for her friendship and ongoing support and inspiration. Thanks to Susan Avila and other faculty and students in Design for the intellectual stimulation you have provided. I am also very grateful for my dynamic exchanges with in the Cultural Studies Graduate Group; these exchanges have, for more than a decade, contributed greatly to my interdisciplinary thinking across the humanities and social sciences.

In particular, I am indebted to the Women and Gender Studies faculty and students at UC Davis for teaching me so much about the very meaning of collegiality, as well as intersectionality. Thanks for offering such a warm and stimulating home for interdisciplinary exploration. Collaborations with Judith Newton helped me to embrace feminist cultural studies as a field. Anna Kuhn has offered enduring support and friendship, for which I am most appreciative. She and Maxine Craig and Amina Mama read and offered constructive suggestions on portions of this manuscript. Many thanks, as well, to Liz Constable, Rosa Linda Fregoso, Gayatri Gopinath, Wendy Ho, Suad Joseph, Caren Kaplan, Luz Mena, Kimberly Nettles, Leslie Rabine, and Juana Rodriguez for all that I have learned from you in the time our paths have crossed.

I am so fortunate to have so many fashion studies friends and colleagues around the world: thanks especially to Janet Hethorn, Carol Tulloch, Joe Hancock, Heike Jenss, Mary Lynn Damhorst, Linda Arthur, Chris Breward, Patrizia Calefato, Jo Paoletti, and Efrat Tseëlon for the stimulating interactions and encouragement that have meant so much to this project.

Everyone at Berg has been enthusiastic about this project from the beginning and throughout its (extended) life. Thanks to Joanne Eicher and to Kathryn Earle for their intellectual leadership in the Dress, Body, Culture series. I have had wonderfully supportive and thoughtful editors and staff: Hannah Shakespeare, Julia Hall, Anna Wright, Sophie Hodgson, and Emily Johnston. All have exhibited the perfect blend of professionalism and patience. I also deeply appreciate the insightful analyses of the reviewers.

I could not have completed this book without the inspiration and support of my family. Thanks to my sisters Linda, Jeanette, and Pam, and to the memory of our parents, who taught us to imagine the future. Many thanks to Nathan and Christina for providing ideas, sharing references and popular cultural tips from sports to novels, and contributing to the photo collage of Sienna and, of course, for bringing her into our lives. Thanks, Sienna, for your fresh and humorous way of seeing and being in the world. Carolyn, P. K., and Chase have also provided a lot of spark, inspiration, and encouragement that have helped to keep me going—many thanks! And last, but not certainly not least, I am indebted to Mark for being the best muse, as well as cook and confidante, whom one could ever imagine.

Fashion and Culture: Cultural Studies, Fashion Studies

Fashion is not a thing or an essence. Rather, it is a social process of nego-tiation and navigation through the murky and yet-hopeful waters of what is to come. Fashion involves *becoming* collectively with others. When and where does this happen, and who gets to decide what constitutes fashion? Fash-ion materializes as bodies move through time and space. Time and space are both abstract concepts and contexts: the process of deciphering and expressing a sense of *who* we are (becoming) happens in tandem with deci-phering and expressing *when* and *where* we are. This is not as simple as it may sound. It turns out that the process of deciphering and expressing this "who, when, and where" is an ongoing challenge of negotiating and navigating through multiple ambiguities and contradictions associated with the following:

- being an *individual* fashion subject in the context of a *global* economy, in which fashion flows through complex, transnational dynamics that are at once visual and material, virtual and tangible, local and global;
- embodying—simultaneously—gender, race, ethnicity, sexuality, class, na-tional identity, age/generation, place, and other "positions" that are them-selves shifting through complex power relations;
- desiring at once to fit in with one's social world and to express some de-gree of uniqueness within that world; and
- an ever-changing interplay between freedoms and constraints; this inter-play refers to an ongoing structure-agency debate in the social sciences and humanities.

Fashion is never finished, and it crosses all kinds of boundaries. It is ongoing and changes with each person's visual and material interpretations of who he or she is becoming and how this connects with others' interpretations.

Fashion is also about producing clothes and appearances, working through ideas, negotiating subject positions (e.g., gender, ethnicity, class), and navi-gating through power relations. It involves mixing, borrowing, belonging, and changing. But it is also about matching, creating, differentiating, and con-tinuing. It is a complex process that entangles multiple perspectives and ap-proaches. The study of fashion, as well, requires integrative and imaginative ways of knowing. Throughout this book, I draw on fashion studies and feminist cultural studies concepts, metaphors, and models that challenge simple oppositional (either/or), linear (straight), and essentialist (predetermined, fixed, bounded) ways of thinking about and *with* fashion.

Oppositional thinking, for example, oversimplifies differences and limits options for the analysis of connections and entanglements. Framing fashion in either/or terms also prevents understandings of what the feminist spatial theorist Doreen Massey (1993) calls "power geometry." That is, power is multidimensional, not just oppositional. Fashion helps us to contemplate power in ways that multiply, complicate, and intersect beyond oppositional thinking.

Studying fashion is a *both/and*, rather than an either/or, activity. Fashion thrives on contradiction (conflicting truth claims) and ambivalence (conflicting emotions): both/and ways of knowing and feeling. Combining fashion and (feminist) cultural studies perspectives encourages thinking that disrupts, blurs, and transcends binary (either/or) oppositions. One of the fundamental binary oppositions feminist theorists have critiqued is masculinity versus femininity, because this either/or way of thinking limits options for thinking about gender in a more expansive sense, perpetuates power-related hierarchies, and prioritizes masculinity as the dominant way of being in the world. In the realm of modern Western fashion, as we will see, this has meant that there has been a dominant myth that men are not supposed to care *too* much about how they look. Their power comes from being "unmarked" (Phelan 1993) as contrasted with women, who assume the "masque" of femininity (Tseëlon 1995) and hence become more "marked" as the "other," according to the mythical binary opposition.

Gender (considered in more depth in Chapter 6) is not the only problematic binary opposition or dualism that limits thinking with fashion, however. Indeed, modern Western thought is riddled with either/or thinking that has limited what and how we know fashion in the context of a transnational world:

- fashionable (i.e., modern) dress versus "fixed" (i.e., traditional) costume,
- Western dress versus "the rest,"
- the future versus the past,
- time versus space,
- agency versus structure,
- masculinity versus femininity,
- white versus black,
- straight versus gay,
- unmarked versus marked,
- dressing to belong versus dressing to differentiate,
- mainstream consumer fashion versus alternative street style,
- production versus consumption, and so on.

In each of these cases, the first term gets prioritized over the second, and herein lies the problem: power becomes constructed in simplistic terms. Obscured by these constructions are the overlapping realities, the contradictions, the third terms (e.g., bisexuality, Latino ethnicity, distribution) or other multiple possibilities that fall between the cracks and the subtle, subversive ways in which power operates in everyday life. We always need to be on the lookout for additional terms, beyond two. Most of the pairs of terms above would benefit from further terms, as we will see throughout this book. Some of the terms used above, such as *fixed* and *the rest* should probably be dispensed with altogether.

However, sometimes there are two terms that need to be looked at together in order to get a sense of a both/and whole. Among the binary oppositional terms listed above, four stand out in this way: time *and* space (considered in Chapter 8); and unmarked *and* marked or, better, processes of unmarking *and* marking; agency *and* structure; and dressing to belong *and* dressing to differentiate. There are some terms that cannot be easily disentangled as a pair because we experience them simultaneously (in both/and ways) through everyday embodied experience. How can we visualize "twos" as interdependent or convergent, rather than oppositional? The cultural theorist Noam Chomsky (1986) talks about convergence as a kind of mathematical mystery, using the metaphor of the Möbius strip (see Figure 1.1). The German mathematician Augustus Möbius (1790–1868) found that a strip or ribbon

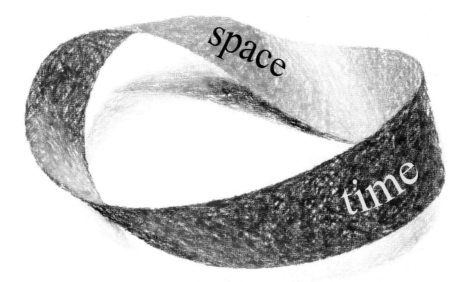

Figure 1.1 Möbius strip, illustrating convergence of time and space through the fashioned body. Developed with Ely Estoesta and Nan Turner.

that is two-sided can be experienced as one continuous surface. There is a kind of convergence that results when there is no inside, no outside, no beginning, and no end. When the ends of strip of fabric or ribbon are attached, and the resulting loop is slightly twisted, it becomes possible to move along a path without leaving a side or crossing an edge. Normally, fashion is all about crossings, intersections, and entanglements, but as the Möbius strip reminds us metaphorically, it is also about convergence. As individuals fashion their bodies (see Entwistle 2000), for example, they experience this process as a convergence of time and space. We cannot separate *when* we are from *where* we are in the course of everyday experience. This theme is addressed further in Chapter 8.

Fashion studies requires multiple metaphors or models to think *with* at once; part of the task of fashion studies is to mix metaphors in ways that enable critical and creative understandings of the pleasures and power relations associated with how we dress or style our appearances in everyday life (Kaiser 2008). We need multiple metaphors or models to think about the complex "hows" and "whys" of body fashionings. Throughout this book, a variety of metaphors are used alongside the Möbius strip (and its convergence of twos) in order to capture the complexity of flows, intersections, and entanglements among multiple concepts (identities, materials, practices). We need multiple metaphors or models to think about the complex "hows" and "whys" of body fashionings.

We need multiple metaphors or models, in part, because the process of fashioning bodies in everyday life is inclusive: it is more than just a white, Western, heterosexual, bourgeois female consumer affair. Indeed, fashion highlights the multiple intersections and entanglements among gender, race, ethnicity, national identity, social class, sexuality, and other facets of our identities. The field of fashion studies brings these intersections and entanglements to light and helps us interpret flows and convergences along the way.

At the same time, the field of cultural studies has much to offer to the field of fashion studies. Both fashion studies and cultural studies remind us that we have to move beyond either/or, binary oppositions in order to make sense of everyday life. Why and how? Let's pursue an example using a key idea in cultural studies: articulation.

Articulation is both a concept and a method in cultural studies. The word articulate has at least two meanings: to connect or to join (as in a joint in the body) and to express. Articulation is an embodied concept. Think about all of the parts of the body that have to work together to allow articulation through speech: the tongue, the lips, the jaw, and other speech organs. It is only through their everyday articulations that we are able to speak—as just one form of connection and expression—through a complex blending of physiological and symbolic processes. In many ways, this kind of spoken articulation becomes a metaphor for having a voice or a sense of agency through everyday looks or fashionings of the body. Individuals mix and match different elements to formulate temporary expressions about who they are or, more accurately, are becoming. Articulations are especially noticeable when something is slightly out of context, as shown in Figure 1.2. The man in this photograph has just arrived at a wedding reception in Washington State in the United States. He is part of the wedding party that has just taken place in another setting and is still wearing his (temporary, rented) tuxedo but has added an additional accessory: an indie rock record company cap. His articulation between the formality (and conformity) of the tuxedo and his own musical preferences let us know a little more about him; his cap softens and personalizes—as it articulates with—his rented tux.

Figure 1.2 In the moment: articulation as temporary closure. By adding his indie rock record cap, this member of the wedding party reveals more of himself at the reception afterward. He expresses that he is *both* a member of the wedding party *and* a lover of indie rock music. Washington State, USA, 2010. Photo by author.

Articulation provides a sense of temporary closure. Like the temporariness of the tux, the look (or appearance style) itself in Figure 1.2 is ephemeral. It works for now, in this particular context with family and friends (and second and third degrees of family and friends) who have the opportunity to make sense of his "this and that" articulation for the time, place, and situation. His tux represents dominant U.S. cultural norms for weddings, but his cap, too, has a cultural dimension—albeit more alternative. With his cap, he represents his identification with the local indie rock community. Interpreting his tux and cap together (along with his facial hair and other appearance cues) helps the guests at the wedding to learn a little more about him and his *subjectivity* (how he thinks, what he likes, and how he is able to mix, meld, and express). He differentiates himself at the same time he communicates shared cultural and community ties. His articulation combines items that were not necessarily intended by designers or retailers to go together but that together make a new, somewhat ironic *both/and* statement.

In cultural studies, articulation is also a method that can be used to analyze culture. It is a method based on the recognition that people articulate—combining this and that to make all kinds of visual statements through style and other everyday practices. Analytically, the method of articulation involves breaking down wholes that appear "natural" or harmonious, and identifying differences, contradictions, or fractures in the whole. The method of articulation is not just a process of negative critique. It goes further by rearticulating into other wholes, by considering new possibilities and formations (Grossberg 2010: 22) or by envisioning and building up new frameworks for interpretation. Grossberg uses the metaphor of a Lego set, among others, to demonstrate how this works. But we can see how the metaphor of a body that is continually fashioned and refashioned—through articulations and rearticulations—is an especially vivid, compelling, and revealing metaphor.

ARTICULATION: STYLE-FASHION-DRESS

Fashion theorist Carol Tulloch (2010) articulates *style-fashion-dress* as a system of concepts; she uses the hyphens between each term to propose whole-and-part relationships. She also uses each term on its own: "As long as the precision of their meanings are clear, they are always connected as part of the overall purpose of a subject of study" (Tulloch 2010: 274). Tulloch uses *style* as "agency—in the construction of self through the assemblage of garments, accessories, and beauty regimes that may, or may not, be 'in fashion' at the time of use." She further describes style as "part of the process of self-telling, that is, to expound an aspect of autobiography of oneself through the clothing choices an individual makes"—what she has come to call *style narratives* (Tulloch 2010: 276). The larger articulation of style-fashion-dress locates style in the context of *fashion:* a social process in which style narratives are collectively "in flux with time" (Riello and McNeil 2010: 1). Fashion as a social process encompasses more than clothing style. Its reach also spans food and furniture preferences, popular culture, language, technology, science, or any other dimensions of culture and change. However, there is something that is especially compelling about fashion in the context of the body's appearance because it is so "up close" and personal in everyday experience and perception. Fashion matters in everyday life; it becomes embodied.

Dress, like style and in conjunction with fashion, begins with the body. Style-fashion-dress theorist Joanne Eicher (2010: 3) defines dress as "body modifications and body supplements." The term *dress*—like style, appearance or appearance style, or look—has the advantage of being rather neutral and useful for historical- and cultural-comparative purposes. All of these terms, including fashion, can be used as verbs as well as nouns; they refer to processes and concepts, so there is a family resemblance among them (Barnard 2002).

Style-fashion-dress, as a system of concepts, is useful in analyzing Figure 1.2. Together with the use of articulation as a method in cultural studies, we can recognize the parts (the individual terms) and wholes (the system that connects them). It becomes possible to break down the system, while recognizing that new articulations will occur. We can consider the wedding party member's sense of agency and the narrative he has constructed with his style—especially as he donned his cap between the wedding ceremony and the reception, mixing and matching elements that are not usually combined. We can think about fashion as a social process that is part of what it means to be "in flux with time": the cut of the tuxedo, the width and color (hot pink) of the tie, the vest, his facial hair. The cap, too, and the music to which it refers, is not immune to fashion change. Dress, specifically, refers to the body modifications (his facial hair, for example) and body supplements (everything he is wearing, including his earring, his pocket handkerchief). Clearly, the terms overlap, but each sheds some light on a different practice or process. Together, style-fashion-dress is a complex system that recognizes the parts and wholes. Style-fashion-dress (a fashion studies concept) and articulation (a cultural studies concept and method) work well together; they cut both ways to enable understandings of context.

THE FIELDS OF FASHION STUDIES AND CULTURAL STUDIES

Both fashion and culture demand more than one discipline or field of study to capture their complexity. As interdisciplinary fields, both fashion studies and cultural studies require the perspectives of multiple fields, theories, methods, and practices in order to analyze fashion and culture adequately. Both fashion studies and cultural studies developed in the latter half of the twentieth century, although their roots, in some form or another, go back for centuries. They both blend various disciplines in the humanities (e.g., art, art history, design, the dramatic arts, history, literature), the social sciences (e.g., anthropology, geography, sociology), and related interdisciplinary fields (e.g., gender studies, ethnic studies), as well as the biological and physical sciences.

Fashion studies has roots in the centuries-old historical and cross-cultural interest in dress as a universal phenomenon. According to the British dress historian Lou Taylor (2004), over 200 collections of engravings, etchings, and woodcuttings were published in Germany, Italy, France, and Holland between 1520 and 1610. Europeans had an intense interest in understanding people in the "newly discovered remote corners of the world." Yet they did so in a way that created a binary opposition between self and other. Taylor indicates that these early publications are a major source of information on the visual representations of "European notions of the barbarous and exotic Other" (Taylor 2004: 5). Taylor goes on to discuss the distinct histories between museum collections focusing on ethnographic (e.g., folk, peasant) dress versus those highlighting "fashionable Euro-American dress" (Taylor 2004: 311). She also notes how the study of dress history has moved toward more interdisciplinary, critical, and inclusive approaches in recent decades, yet there is still much to be done to recover diverse dress histories around the world. Similarly, Christopher Breward (1995) has called for, and demonstrated the benefits of, blending art history, design history, and cultural studies to foster a "new cultural history" with "a more questioning framework which allows for explanations which are multi-layered and open-ended" (Breward 1995: 3–4).

Fashion studies as an interdisciplinary field also emerged from late nineteenth-century thinking about culture, social class, and modernity in the "Western" world—in fields as varied as anthropology, the arts and humanities, psychology, and sociology. A notable example includes the German sociologist Georg Simmel (1904), who was fascinated with the interplay between social-psychological impulses of imitation (to be like others) and differentiation (to distinguish oneself from others). This interplay, he argued, propels fashion change in modern societies. He, like the American economic sociologist Thorstein Veblen (1899) attributed much of this change to social mobility in an open society. Veblen highlighted the hypocrisy associated with the "conspicuous consumption" and "conspicuous leisure" of the bourgeois (upper-middle) classes (to be discussed further in Chapter 5). Unlike Simmel, Veblen did not take fashion seriously as a social process and cultural phenomenon; he seemed to think that fashion made no economic sense and was the source of society's ills.

In the 1980s, the British feminist fashion theorist Elizabeth Wilson (1985) critiqued Veblen by pointing out his masculine, utilitarian bias. She argued instead for a more complex approach using themes of ambivalence and contradiction. She noted that "we both love and hate fashion," just as we both "love and hate capitalism itself" (14). She argued further that there is a profound modern, Western (masculine-biased) sense of unease and ambiguity about the body and its relation to clothing. Somewhat similarly, the American sociologist Fred Davis (1992) attributed fashion change itself to "culturally-coded identities" regarding gender, social class, and other identity issues. Like Wilson (1985) and Davis (1992), colleagues and I interpreted fashion through concepts of ambivalence and (its cousin) ambiguity (Kaiser, Nagasawa, and Hutton 1990). Also drawing on symbolic interaction—a school of thought within sociology that has had strong ties with cultural studies since the 1980s—we highlighted the importance of negotiation as a social process in fashion change. We synthesized this theme from the works of Gregory Stone (1969) in his analysis of appearance and the self in relation to others; Herbert Blumer (1969) in his treatise on fashion as a process of "collective selection"; as well as from earlier essays by Fred Davis, which were revised and then integrated into his 1992 book.

There are multiple genealogies of fashion theory. Just a few are included here by way of introduction, but the works of other contributors are included to the extent possible throughout this book. Genealogies of fashion theory are complicated and cross-cutting; interdisciplinary routes are neither separate nor linear. In his book, *Fashion in Focus*, sociologist Tim Edwards (2011) contrasts ambivalence-based (symbolic interactionist) explanations of fashion with Elizabeth Wilson's contradiction-based analysis of modern Western fashion. Yet Wilson's (1985) *Adorned in Dream: Fashion and Modernity* (1985) revolves around themes of ambivalence (conflicting emotions), as well as contradiction (conflicting "truth" claims). These themes are integral to the work of Davis (1992) and Kaiser, Nagasawa, and Hutton (1990), as well. Ambivalence and contradiction both rely upon both/and ways of knowing.

Another, overlapping genealogy derives from social studies of textiles and clothing developed in the United States in home economics programs in the land-grant system (historically, an agricultural system) of higher public education. Initially, this system addressed issues of production and consumption in highly gendered ways: with production as a masculine process and consumption as a feminine activity. These programs have emphasized the quality of everyday life, in recognition of clothing as a basic human need (along with food and shelter). Beginning around the 1950s, textiles and clothing scholars have conducted research on issues of self-esteem, social meaning, and other social and psychological considerations (e.g., Damhorst 1985; Horn 1965;

Kaiser 1997; Miller-Spellman, Damhorst, and Michelman 2005; Rosencranz 1950, 1962, 1965; Ryan 1966); ethnographic and cross-cultural research (e.g., Eicher, Evenson, and Lutz 2008; Roach and Eicher 1965, 1973); historical studies (e.g., Farrell-Beck and Gau 2002; Paoletti 1985, 1987), and economic analyses of clothing consumption (Winakor 1969). Other fields in the interdisciplinary textiles and clothing programs have included fashion design and fashion merchandising. By the early 2000s, these areas had become dominant in many university programs throughout the United States, with the other areas (e.g., social psychology, cultural and historical studies, textile science) still playing important fundamental supporting roles. A perusal of *Clothing and Textiles Research Journal* over the last thirty years reveals changes in research publishing trends toward the fields of consumer behavior, fashion marketing, and merchandising.

Interdisciplinary, transnational, and critical studies of style-fashion-dress have burgeoned since the 1990s. Berg Publishers has produced the Dress, Body, Culture book series, along with the journal *Fashion Theory* (edited by Valerie Steele), launched in 1997. These works have circulated a wide range of interdisciplinary scholarship on historical and transnational cultural studies of style-fashion-dress. In 2010, Berg launched the journal *Fashion Practice* (edited by Sandy Black and Marilyn DeLong), and the publisher Intellect introduced the journal *Critical Studies in Fashion and Beauty* (edited by Efrat Tseëlon, Diana Crane, and Susan Kaiser). Also in 2010, Oxford University Press published the ten-volume *Encyclopedia of World Dress and Fashion* (edited by Joanne B. Eicher), which included entries from scholars around the world. In addition to the existing interdisciplinary academic programs, new fashion studies programs emerged in France, Italy, the United States (e.g., Parsons New School for Design), the United Kingdom, Sweden, and elsewhere.

Transnational fashion networks and conferences in Korea and China, as well as in Europe and North America, have fostered a lot of ferment in the field. One notable example is Carol Tulloch's organization of an African diaspora network and a special issue of *Fashion Theory* (2010) that summarizes the activities and collaborations related to this network. Increasingly in fashion studies, old assumptions about what constitutes "fashion," for example, have been shattered, and new questions have emerged in the context of critiques of globalization, garment labor, and Eurocentric stories of style-fashion-dress. Interactions with the field of cultural studies—directly and indirectly—have been pivotal in new articulations within fashion studies. (Throughout this book, I use the term *fashion studies* as a shorthand phrase to refer inclusively to the study of the whole system of concepts: style-fashion-dress.)

The field of cultural studies also developed in the second half of the twentieth century, at a moment "when culture becomes both visibly central and explicitly ambiguous" (Grossberg 2010: 173). The same could be said about style-fashion-dress. The late 1960s and early 1970s witnessed resistance against older stories of gender, "race," ethnicity, sexuality, national identity, and age/generation. In many ways, cultural studies sought to ask new questions about culture as it articulates with everyday life power relations associated with these older stories.

The feminist movement, the civil rights movement, the gay and lesbian rights movements, and other (e.g., anticolonial, environmental) social movements around the world contributed to the development of cultural studies as a field interested in understanding how cultural processes, including fashion, shape everyday life. These movements began to "unframe" some of the frameworks that had previously been taken for granted as "natural" or "the way it should be." These movements reacted to, or at least questioned, a number of assumptions associated with dominant (white, masculine or feminine, upper-middle class, heterosexual) culture.

The feminist movement of the late 1960s and early 1970s fought not only for crucial economic and reproductive rights but also raised questions about the extent to which fashion and beauty systems entrap women in traditional feminine roles. As Evans and Thornton (1989) note, some feminists rejected exclusive symbols or practices of femininity (e.g., makeup, bras, skirts, leg shaving). Fashion itself, they argue, is a process of experimentation, and feminists have taken on different projects to fight for change (for example, garment worker rights) as they have explored the complicated ways in which feminism is not only about gender relations but also about their interplay with other vectors of power (e.g., class, "race," ethnicity, sexuality).

The study of this interplay among power relations through social movements is key to cultural studies, which emerged in various sites around the world, attempting to make sense of culture and power through everyday issues. Most visible among these was the vibrant center of theory and practice at the University of Birmingham (the Center for Contemporary Cultural Studies) in the 1970s. Stuart Hall, a Jamaican-born black British sociologist, played an important role in the formation of the center and its mission, drawing on the class-based studies of Raymond Williams and E. P. Thompson. Hall and colleagues and students pursued studies of the interplay among class, "race," and opportunities for young people (especially working class males) to articulate their identities through style-fashion-dress as a visible system of representation. Feminist interventions in the center further complicated the studies by highlighting gender biases in understandings of "subcultures" (McRobbie 1989, 1991, 1994).

Key to a cultural studies approach is the idea that gender, race/ethnicity, sexuality, nationality, class, and age/generation and other subject positions organize identities, social relations, and the objects and images that culture produces (Newton, Kaiser, and Ono 1998). Cultural studies refuse "to reduce human life or power to one dimension, one axis, one explanatory framework" (Grossberg 2010: 16). It also works against a logic of *essentialism*: the belief that things are the way they are because that is "just the way they are." Essentialist thinking fosters stereotypes because it suggests that a subject position such as gender predetermines (biologically or otherwise) a set of traits that apply to "all women" (e.g., "women's drive to shop is in their genes") or "all men" (e.g., "men are not into fashion").

In other words, cultural studies rejects the idea that "everything is sewn up in advance" or that "identities are fixed" (Grossberg 2010: 22). In cultural studies terms, articulations and rearticulations continually challenge fixed ideas that gender (or any other subject position) is an essence or a thing that should be accepted as a "natural" or biological given (as discussed further in Chapter 6). Rather, as a feminist cultural studies perspective tells us, gender is embedded in social interactions, cultural understandings, and webs of power. It cannot be completely separated from ethnicity, social class, national identity, religion, and other power-related issues.

CONCEPTUALIZING CULTURE AND FASHION

A dialogue between cultural studies and fashion studies can be highly fruitful for thinking through concepts of culture and fashion: Both are good concepts "to think with." The definitions of the two words are interrelated and remarkably similar, although they have different connotations. The *Oxford English Dictionary* (2010) defines *culture* as "the distinctive ideas, customs, social behavior, products, or way of life of a particular society, people, or period." And *fashion* is defined as "a prevailing custom, a current usage; *esp.* one characteristic of a particular place or period of time" or, more specifically, "the mode of dress, etiquette, furniture, style of speech, etc., adopted in society for the time being." It seems that culture is a somewhat broader and more enduring concept than fashion, although both concepts include the idea of *custom*: "a habitual or usual practice; common way of acting; usage, fashion, habit (either of an individual or of a community)." Perhaps we can think of fashion as "custom for a time" and culture as "custom over time." Interestingly, the word custom is related to *costume* (a form of dress that often has rather exotic connotations, as we shall see in Chapter 3). Similarly, custom also closely relates to the cultural studies concept of *habitus*: the routine cultural practices embodied in everyday life (Bourdieu 1984), discussed further in Chapter 2 and later chapters.

Fashion, like culture, is both a social process and a material practice. Both fashion and culture simultaneously undergo continual change and continuity. These simultaneous processes are complex and even contradictory.

They remind us that everyday life and, indeed, global capitalism are full of contradictions. Either/or ways of thinking (i.e., change *or* continuity) are insufficient to understand how fashion and culture work. Instead, understanding fashion and culture requires both/and thinking (i.e., change *and* continuity). That being said, analyzing fashion and culture in tandem provides an opportunity to consider what these two concepts—and the fields of fashion studies and cultural studies that pursue them—have to offer one another. Given that both fashion and culture simultaneously undergo ongoing processes of change and continuity, perhaps fashion can best be understood as *change within continuity*, whereas culture reveals practices that emphasize *continuity within change*. Each concept, in its own way, offers a lens through which to make sense of simultaneity: how different ideas or process not only coexist but also interact dynamically.

Simultaneity, however, is not simply a combination of two items. Even both/and thinking, while necessary, is not sufficient to grasp the multiple complexities and contradictions associated with fashion and culture. Similarly, no single model or metaphor can sufficiently capture these complexities and contradictions. This book offers two models or metaphors that combine fashion studies and cultural studies, as alternatives to simple oppositional (either/or), linear (straight), and essentialist (predetermined, fixed, bounded) ways of thinking about and *with* everyday fashion in a transnational world: (a) the circuit of style-fashion-dress (introduced in this chapter and developed further in Chapter 2); and (b) intersectionalities, introduced in Chapter 2.

CIRCUIT OF STYLE-FASHION-DRESS MODEL

Figure 1.3 details the "circuit of style-fashion-dress" model, adapted from the cultural studies' "circuit of culture" (du Gay et al. 1997: 3). The original circuit of culture model contains the following elements: representation, identity, production, consumption, and regulation. The adapted "circuit of style-fashion-dress" model makes two revisions: distribution instead of representation, and subject formation instead of identity, as explained below. Overall, however, the rationale for the model remains the same: culture flows (and so does fashion).

The choice of a circuit in Figure 1.3, rather than a binary opposition (e.g., production *versus* consumption) or a line (e.g., a production pipeline or value chain), in cultural studies and fashion studies, is deliberate. A circuit connotes the idea of multiple sites, connected by routes with potential detours. The routes are not linear, and movements flow in multiple directions. Circuits of culture and circuits of style-fashion-dress recognize that time and space intertwine through cultural practices that are themselves interconnected. (Time

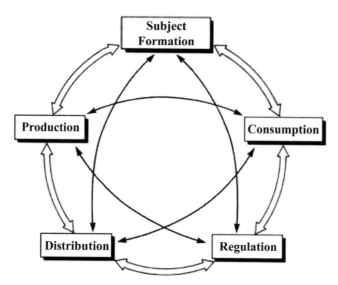

Figure 1.3   Circuit of style-fashion-dress. Adapted from the cultural studies "circuit of culture" (du Gay et al. 1997: 3) with Kelly Sullivan.

and space will be pursued further in Chapter 8.) Moreover, there are multiple circuits, overlapping in complex ways through diverse cultural histories and practices. Each concept in the circuit is itself a process. Let's consider each of them, beginning with production.

PRODUCTION

One of fashion's "early relatives" is the Latin root word *facere*, which means to make or to do (Barnard 2002). The French word *faire* (also derived from the Latin word *facere*) has similar meanings. Hence, one important idea underlying the concept of fashion—in some European cultural histories, at least—is the idea of twin processes of making and doing: engaging in a cultural practice. Produced by this practice is a garment, a look, or even social differences among groups of people.

Like the body itself, fashion is material. The circuit of style-fashion-dress helps to materialize culture's circuits. Fashion's materials (e.g., fibers, fabrics, garments) flow, and they are produced by and for bodies. Let's consider production across time and space. For more than 20,000 years, human beings around the world have fashioned their bodies with textiles and other materials (e.g., paints, beads). Archaeologist Elizabeth Barber's (1994) research on cloth/clothing in what is now Europe and parts of Russia led her to identify what she calls the "string revolution": the discovery of the ability to twist or "spin" fibers from local, native plants (e.g., flax, hemp) into yarns. Women did most of this work; they were the producers. And there is considerable evidence that only women wore the string skirts that they fashioned from plants into garments. They were therefore the consumers or users of their own products. Eventually, in multiple locations around the world, more complex textile materials emerged. There are strong family roots between the words "text" and "textile," both derived from the Latin word *texere*, which means "to weave" (*Oxford English Dictionary* 2010). Indeed, long before the advent of written languages, textiles told cultural stories around the world. Textiles (and other materials and media) record and represent culture. Hmong (or Miao, as known in China) textiles, traditionally made by women from hill tribes in Southeast Asia, offer a vivid example: reverse appliquéd—a complex technique that involves cutting and stitching through layers of fabric—and embroidered fabrics tell cultural stories that have been passed down from generation to generation. This was a way of recording history through material culture, rather than written language. With the migration since the 1970s of an estimated 180,000 Hmong people to the United States, Australia, and other nations, the traditional mode of storytelling has been challenged by the forces of globalization, as well as some loss of culture-making techniques over time (Wronska-Friend 2010).

Another compelling example of the cultural production of textiles is sericulture: the Chinese art and technology of silk production. Pictorial representations of silkworms, mulberry leaves (that silkworms eat), and silk have convinced scholars that sericulture was a widespread cultural practice in China during the second millennium B.C.E. Sericulture as a cultural production practice remained a guarded Chinese secret until the fourth century C.E. (Vollmer 2010: 20). Figure 1.4 shows how sericulture is practiced in contemporary China.

The Silk Road is more than 2,000 years old; this ancient network of trails extends more than 5,350 miles westward across deserts and mountains, through Central Asia and the Middle East to the Mediterranean. This route was used as a major east–west artery to bring silks, furs, gold, spices, and gems to the Roman and Byzantine empires, keeping the Chinese in contact with other regions of the world. This route was a critical part of international history at least until the sixteenth century, when maritime trade had become more fully developed. It was also a site of conflict, as the Romans, Mongols, and others tried to dominate the route in order to control the traffic and the profits. In addition to a vigorous trading tradition, there was a history of complex ethnic interactions as a result of the Silk Road (Appiah and Gates 1997: 600; Kennett 1995: 112).

Textile production was also an ancient art in India, with some of the most intricate woolen fabrics emerging from the mountains of Kashmir. Various

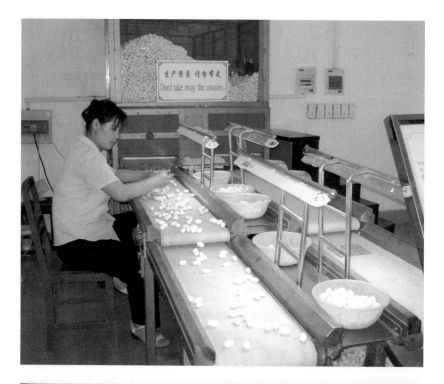

Figure 1.4   In the image above, a Chinese worker sorts silkworm cocoons by quality. Below, another Chinese worker sets up the loom to weave silk yarn into a textile fabric. Photos by author.

weaving techniques came to Europe by way of India, through Assyria and Egypt and then from Phoenicia to Egypt. Many of the English names of fabrics relate to their origins: calico from Calicut or Calcutta; cotton muslin from Mosul; chintz from the Hindu *chint* or *chete*; satin from Zaytoun in China; and damask from Damascus, Syria (Kennett 1995). So in many ways, textile material culture has been global for centuries, long before Columbus discovered the Americas when he was looking for a western route to India.

Highly complex and intricate textiles were part of the reason Columbus and other explorers wanted to find new routes to the Orient. Cotton had been domesticated and was being grown in the Indus Valley civilization as early as 4000 B.C.E. Cotton seeds have been found at a Neolithic site near Mehrgarh in Northern Baluchistan, and the remains of dyed cotton cloth have been excavated at Mohenjo-dara, dated around 2000 B.C.E. Dyeing cotton with natural dyes is no simple technical matter; it requires mordants (colorless metallic oxides) to help the dye to bind to the cotton fiber. The use of red (madder) and black dyes was most common. These technologies were disseminated by means of interactions with nomadic Indo-European tribes around 2000 B.C.E., contacts with the Chinese, and invasions by Islamic peoples between 7000 and 1200 C.E. (Lynton 1995: 8–9). Moreover, since the time of the Roman Empire, at least, Southern Indian merchants had been trading with the Portuguese and the French (Lynton 1995: 121).

The production of cloth became an industrialized process with the mechanization of spinning and weaving in the eighteenth and nineteenth centuries. The invention of the sewing machine in the nineteenth century made the production of clothing an easier and faster process. However, clothing production is extremely labor intensive; garment construction (sewing) technology has not changed significantly since the invention of the sewing machine. In the early twentieth century, the public became aware of labor abuses in garment sweatshops in New York City; and at the end of the century, the public became aware of sweatshop conditions in various sites around the world, from Los Angeles to Central America's "Free Trade Zones" to China. (Chapter 5 delves further into garment labor through the discussion of class.) By the 1990s, the "race to the bottom" by manufacturers to seek the lowest labor costs in the world had fostered an increasing disconnect between production and consumption. In particular, there was (and is) a huge gap between (a) consumers wearing heavily branded and marketed "fast fashion," and (b) the workers around the world who would be unlikely to afford to buy the very garments they have made.

College students organizing against sweatshops, together with the Worker Rights Consortium (WRC) in Los Angeles, have resulted in some successes in monitoring the production of licensed apparel (e.g., T-shirts and sweats) sold in university bookstores. One success story is the Alta Gracia factory and label in the Dominican Republic:

> Every Alta Gracia product carries a tag from the WRC confirming that the product was sewn at a factory that respects workers' rights. The WRC only allows us to use this tag as long as we are in compliance with our labor standards. So when you see the WRC tag on an Alta Gracia t-shirt or sweatshirt, you can be sure it was sewn by workers who are paid a living wage, have a union to represent them, and are treated fairly when they come to work. (altagraciaapparel.com)

The complexity of monitoring even the fairly limited (although meaningful) market of university-licensed apparel in a global economy reveals how complex the disconnect between production and consumption can be. On the other hand, some clothing companies such as Patagonia have voluntarily found ways of making their production footprints and practices transparent. In many ways, the goals of sustainable production pertain not only to the environment but also to labor conditions. Yet as fashion cycles become faster, the flood of materials and garments produced to satisfy consumer demand profitably intensifies. Many companies have developed elaborate systems of contractors and subcontractors to do the actual sewing of the garments, to the extent that it is extremely difficult to foster a system of accountability and transparency. Meanwhile, consumers can buy "fast fashion" cheaply and frequently.

CONSUMPTION

Before the production of fibers, textiles, and apparel became industrialized, it was intimately connected with the consumption (use, wear) of these materials. Only wealthy people could afford to have many garments, which were often prized possessions. Industrialization changed the dynamic between production (making) and consumption (using, wearing). A binary way of thinking emerged between production—conceptualized as an "orderly, mechanized, and rational process of making good for the purpose of profit"—and consumption, framed as "the opposite of productivity" or as "using ('up') products or goods" (Kaiser 2008). Cultural studies scholar Raymond Williams (1980) discussed how the metaphor of the human stomach and digestive system shaped thinking about consumption as eating. In this way of thinking, applied much more broadly to consumer products beyond food, consumers became perceived as channels "along which the product flows and disappears" (43). In this framework, consumers become "the market, which the system of industrial production has organized" (Williams 1980: 43).

Everyone consumes clothing, but far fewer people actually produce garments in an industrial or postindustrial context. And, resources permitting, many consumers buy far more products than they actually need. Williams (1980) claimed that one important reason for this is the "magical system" created by advertising and related cultural practices that turn consumption into a process of human desires for promise, pleasure, and power:

> You do not only buy an object; you buy social respect, discrimination, health, beauty, success, power to control your environment. The magic obscures its real sources of general satisfaction because their discovery would involve radical change in the whole common way of life. (Williams 1980: 47)

DISTRIBUTION

Located strategically between production and consumption, the process of distribution has multiple meanings: the physical movement, as well as the marketing, of goods. In theory, distribution is the bridge, or part of the solution to the "disconnect" between production and consumption. In practice, however, distribution can also be seen as the site of rupture between the two material processes, when image making (e.g., advertising, branding) overrides material practice. Distribution is an inherently ambivalent or contradictory concept; it includes both dividing and dispersing (*Oxford English Dictionary* 2010). Synonyms for "distribute" include divide, dispense, dole, deal, and the like; yet "distribute" implies more strategic planning and segmentation than "dispersion" ("scattering in all directions") or "diffusion" ("wide distribution"). Because diffusion, in particular, is an important part of fashion as a process of social influence, and because material movement (e.g., from the factory to the local mall) is fundamental to fashion, the circuit of style-fashion-dress model adapts the cultural studies circuit of culture model by using distribution in place of representation. Distribution has connotations of *both* material *and* representational elements. Further, conceptualized as a link rather than a rupture, distribution ties together economy and culture through a kind of (distributive) network. The network metaphor used by science studies scholar Bruno Latour (2005) helps to map how humans (e.g., workers, managers, consumers) and nonhumans (e.g., fabrics, sewing machines, computers) must be considered together, through a "material-semiotic" network. In short, materials matter.

And so does *representation*. As cultural studies scholar Stuart Hall (1997) describes the concept, representation is a process that does not merely represent an idea or reality that already exists. Rather it *constitutes* (composes or establishes) our understandings of the world. Through cultural media such as advertising (a form of distribution), we experience images, stories, and sound bites that frame our understandings of what is authentic or natural, what we desire, and so on. Fashion branding, for example, strives to add a kind of symbolic value to "real clothes" by fostering or fulfilling fantasies (Hancock 2010). What kinds of fantasies might be represented to sell clothes?

Sexuality, glamour, success, coolness, and happiness are among the concepts in the cultural imagery that turn pretty ordinary items of clothing into objects of desire.

Fashion studies scholar Joanne Entwistle (2009) refers to the important role of "cultural intermediaries" (i.e., individuals in the business of distribution and representation). Cultural intermediaries such as retail buyers, photographers, journalists, and fashion models constitute the aesthetic markets that "operate through the careful balancing of 'cultural' and 'economic' calculations" (Entwistle 2009: 167). Part of this balancing act involves the strategic flow of materials as well as images through the spaces in between production and consumption.

Representation, then, is part of distribution (the space between production and consumption). But the use of distribution—the more general term—in the circuit of style-fashion-dress reminds us that materials, as well as images, flow in the spaces "in between." In many ways, however, representation represses the materiality of fashion production because we focus our attention on the image rather than product quality, garment labor, or environmental impacts. We begin to imagine who we can become through the goods that we buy.

SUBJECT FORMATION

Being and becoming are ongoing processes of subject formation. I use the terms subject and subject formation in the circuit model, rather than identity—the term used in the original "circuit of culture" model (du Gay et al. 1997), for a few different reasons. Although identity is an important concept in everyday life, cultural politics, and academic writing alike, I agree with fashion theorist Efrat Tseëlon (2010) that it has become a bit "shopworn" in its daily usage and has lost some of its critical, analytical edge. The term *subject*—especially with formation—allows both for more precision and more of a process orientation than identity. As a commonly used term, *identity* (for some) has a connotation of being "who I am," as though it is an essence. That is, it can become locked into particular identity politics without considering the complex intersections among identities. Cultural theorist Judith Halberstam (2005) has noted how and why identity politics are critical for organizing and community building around themes of sexuality, as well as gender, race, and so on. However, if identity politics become fixed or fossilized, the critical edginess and currency are undermined.

Secondly, subject formation is a process that prioritizes "becoming" over merely "being" as a priority and thus seems especially compatible with processes of style-fashion-dress, as well as the other components (processes) of the circuit model. Third, the term *subject* is the root word of both subjection and subjectivity; it deals with part–whole relationships. Subject is the root word of both *subjection* (which implies being subjected to something—such as a subject position—structured by others) and *subjectivity* (which implies having the agency to assert or articulate one's own ways of being and becoming)—each with its own connotations (Mama 1995).

Subjection refers to the process of power relations being imposed in some way. An individual is subjected to circumstances beyond his or her control. Indeed, one is not only born into his or her body but also into a complex network of power relations. These power relations are embedded in *cultural discourses*: ongoing, systematic cultural "conversations" that are not necessarily on a level playing field (discussed further in Chapter 2 and later chapters). Michel Foucault (1972) theorized how, historically and institutionally, cultural discourses have imposed and shaped certain understandings of subject positions (i.e., family background, gender, nation, race, ethnicity, sexuality). As individuals take up their subject positions, they become subjected to the regulatory power of cultural discourses (Barker 2002: 33). Much fashion imagery of women, for example, perpetuates a cultural discourse of thinness. The standardization of female fashion models' bodies as thin, coupled with digital technologies, functions as a cultural discourse that structures thinking about ideal fashionable bodies. A single fashion ad featuring a skinny model—further airbrushed and photoshopped—is a representation that shapes understandings of beauty and fashion. Yet this single representation is part of a larger cultural discourse on thinness that has become institutionalized historically through visual imagery, as well as other media conversations (e.g., blogs, talk shows, articles in magazines) regarding weight loss, "ethical fashion," eating disorders, and other related issues. How does such a cultural discourse influence one's subject position(s)? It is likely to structure perceptions of gender as a subject position: what it means to have a fashionably beautiful body. Other subject positions such as age, ethnicity, class, and sexuality are likely to be influenced, as well.

Subjection through cultural discourses is part of subject formation, especially in the context of fashion, because discourses themselves change. Yet subject formation is even more dynamic, because individuals generally have some degree of *agency*: the freedom or ability to exert one's voice and to resist power relations in some way (discussed further in Chapter 2 and later chapters). As Tulloch (2010) suggests through her concept of "style narratives," fashioning the body is one of the ways individuals can represent their momentary sense of who they are becoming. These representations through style allow individuals to combine, or move across, their subject positions with a sense of self-awareness and self-expression: processes of subjectivity—the ongoing, changing sense of exploring "who I am" and "who I am becoming."

The metaphor of a Möbius strip, introduced in Figure 1.1, helps to visualize the ways in which multiple subject positions (structure) and subjectivity (agency) become inseparable in the overall process of subject formation through style-fashion-dress. Similarly, processes of imitating others (belonging) and differentiating from others (demarcating) become inseparable; we do both at once. Self–other relations undergird and propel fashion change. As introduced earlier in this chapter, sociologist Georg Simmel (1904) described the dynamic interplay between identifying with and differentiating from others as the very engine of fashion:

> Thus fashion represents nothing more than one of the many forms of life by the aid of which we seek to combine in uniform spheres of activity the tendency towards social equalization with the desire for individual differentiation and change . . . Union and segregation are the two fundamental functions which are here inseparably united . . . [I]n addition to the element of imitation the element of demarcation constitutes an important factor of fashion . . . Two social tendencies are essential to the establishment of fashion, namely, the need of union on the one hand and the need of isolation on the other. Should one of these be absent, fashion will not be formed—its sway will abruptly end. (Simmel 1904)

Simmel (1904) argues that so long as imitation (the need of union or similarity) and demarcation (the need for differentiation) both occur, the game of fashion "goes merrily on." So, subjects, like fashion, are continually in the process of formation and change in relation to other subjects. Fashion theory highlights the interplay between these processes, beginning with both/and thinking and moving further toward more complex, multidimensional models such as intersectionality, to be discussed in Chapter 2. It spotlights, in cultural studies terms, the idea of articulation, which as we have seen involves making connections between, bridging, and joining different ideas, as well as expressing new concepts, in the process of doing so. In particular, consumer thinking about "who I am in my appearance style" is often more difficult to put into words than is "who I am not" or "who I don't want to look like" (Freitas et al. 1997).

Similarly, in his book *Fashion as Communication*, Malcolm Barnard (2002) analyzed the roots of the word *fashion* and found it relates back to the Latin word *factio* (*factionem*), which means more than making and doing, as we have seen. *Factio* is also related to the word "faction," which has political implications and suggests how fashion becomes a process of differentiating groups of individuals from one another. By the early seventeenth century, "faction" implied the use of "selfish or mischievous ends or scrupulous methods," and "fashion had taken on a connotation of contrivance or management" (*Oxford English Dictionary* 2010).

Fashion, it seems, plays a role in the ongoing creation, revision, and blurring of "borderlines" between self and other. But it also challenges these borderlines. Whereas Simmel's (1904) analysis primarily focused on how fashion continually challenges borderlines between social classes, it also does so through other subject positions (e.g., gender, race, ethnicity, sexuality, age).

The borderlines that shape subjectivities require ongoing construction and maintenance (Freitas et al. 1997). Borderlines, it turns out, are tenuous, fragile, and elastic; they require ongoing negotiation. The work of subject formation reflects this ongoing negotiation, within cultural discourses that supply limits to personal agency.

REGULATION

Subject formation is not without its limits. It does not go unchecked. As we have seen, subject positioning, one component of subject formation, includes historical and cultural discourses that may prescribe options for fashion subjectivity (i.e., expression through style). Yet it is often the case that social or legal processes regulate the course of subject formation, as well. The regulation of subject formation may be formal (e.g., labor laws, dress codes, uniforms) or informal (e.g., social pressures, cultural discourses, self-regulating tendencies, and the integration of all of these), but in either case, they can be personally devastating, socially contested, or culturally revealing.

Regulation, whether formal or informal, entails the concept of bringing the production, distribution, and consumption of clothing "under control" and reducing these processes to "adjustments" according to "some principle, standard, or norm" (*Oxford English Dictionary* 2010). Principles, standards, and norms are themselves embedded in cultural discourses.

Regulation related to production includes protections for and rights of garment workers, legal agreements regarding world trade, policies that protect the environment and consumer safety, and labeling issues that need to be stitched into the clothes themselves (for example, fiber content, care instructions, the country of origin). Regulations in terms of consumption may involve restrictions (proscriptions: what *not* to wear), prescriptions (what one *has* to wear, such as a uniform), or ambiguous norms about what to wear or what not to wear.

Individuals often find themselves regulated by multiple cultural discourses that might contradict one another. In recent years, there have been conflicts, for example, between religious discourse and sports discourse regarding appropriate dress. Muslim female athletes wearing *hijab* (i.e., covering their hair with a headscarf) have been prevented from participating in international soccer competitions, for example. The governing body, FIFA (the international football association) prevented the Iranian women's team from competing in a

2011 qualifying round for the 2012 Olympics, because they wore hijab. Since the Iranian Revolution in the 1970s, Iranian women have been required by law to cover their hair, necks, arms, and legs according to the Iranian nation-state's conservative interpretation of Shiite Islamic tenets of modest dress (Erdbrink 2011). (Not all Muslims interpret "modest dress" in this way. Interpretations vary by nation, community, and individual.) The Iranian female athletes were literally subjected to two different cultural discourses (i.e., Iranian national dress codes and international soccer dress codes), with little space for negotiation. The women's gender and national (and associated religious) subject positions conflicted with the sports-related regulations that also discipline bodies, but in different ways. In July 2012, FIFA overturned its decision about hijab, but it was too late for the Iranian team to compete. Certainly the Iranian soccer women have a sense of agency, but in the context of this confrontation, they had little opportunity to exercise it and were shut down from the prospect of competing at the 2012 Olympics in London (Reuters 2012).

In the United States, a similar conflict between religious and sports-regulatory standards of dress emerged in the case of Kulsoom Abdullah, a thirty-five-year-old Muslim female weightlifter with a PhD in electrical computer engineering from Georgia Tech. While cross-training for taekwondo (the Korean martial art), in which she acquired a black belt, Abdullah became enamored with general power weightlifting. After she finished graduate school, she began to train at a gym that taught Olympic weightlifting (not just for Olympic competitors but a sport with its own system of competition). She qualified for a USA national competition, the American Open, in 2010. However, the USA Weightlifting Federation would not allow her to compete unless she wore the standard uniform (a tight-fitting singlet); she was not allowed to cover her arms, legs, or head. She communicated with them in hopes of competing at the next U.S. competition in Iowa in July 2011, but they again refused, indicating that they followed the regulations of the International Weightlifting Federation (IWF). The IWF expressed concern that the judges would not be able to see if her elbows and knees were "properly locked" if they were covered with clothing. Abdullah received a great deal of support in her cause online and from the Council for American-Islam Relations, which issued a press release regarding her dilemma and also contacted the U.S. Olympic Committee, whose international relations director also had ties to the IWF. The IWF agreed to consider modifying its uniform requirements.

Abdullah developed a highly technical PowerPoint presentation, in which she documented how elbows and knees could be covered and yet still allow IWF judges to determine if they were properly locked according to the sports rules for competition. She proposed a modification of the regulations to enable the wearing of a unitard under a looser-fitting singlet, along with a headscarf. As a result of her compelling argument and evidence, the IWF agreed to modify its regulations to accommodate Abdullah's proposed standards.

The IWF announced its ruling just two weeks before the USA Nationals in Iowa in July 2011. Elise Beisecker, a PhD student at Georgia Tech, creatively and quickly fashioned a singlet for Abdullah to wear. She wore the singlet over a unitard that covered her arms and legs, along with her headscarf. Following that competition, Abdullah continued to work on the development of her competitive wardrobe, which can be analyzed via the circuit of style-fashion-dress presented in Figure 1.3. She characterized this process as "a combination of random purchases" in an e-mail to me (February 11, 2012). Let's explore the mixing and matching—the articulation—required to put a "uniform" together in greater depth through the circuit of style-fashion-dress. However, before doing so, let's consider her subjectivity—her agency, which cuts across subject positions and intersects them in meaningful ways through the looks she puts together to navigate, negotiate, and interpellate their interplay with the circuit of style-fashion-dress. In particular, she challenges regulations in the circuit that do not mesh with her subject formation, which can be conceptualized as a Möbius strip of subjectivity and subject positions. Figure 1.5 articulates Abdullah's subject formation through her athletic achievement, her faith, and her style-fashion-dress.

Abdullah negotiates her various subject positions and articulates her subjectivity through her website, which allows her to express her subjectivity in words, as well as through images. As she says on her website, "I am an American who happens to also be Muslim and female . . . I want to be able to compete and follow my faith at the same time" (Abdullah 2011). She wants both/and opportunities; this is her subjectivity, which moves across diverse cultural discourses and subject positions. These subject positions include not only gender and her role as an athlete, but also nation (American), ethnicity (Pakistani American), religion (Muslim), education (doctoral degree in computer engineering), and age (thirty-five years). Through her research on uniform solutions, she navigates between her interpretation of her faith's standards of female modesty, her sport, and other subject positions and cultural discourses.

Referring back to the circuit of style-fashion-dress in Figure 1.3, we can move through the various processes in the circuit and analyze their interplay. Abdullah successfully challenges the regulation of her weightlifting attire through her subject formation: the ongoing interplay between her overlapping subject positions (e.g., gender, religion, ethnicity) and her subjectivity as a weightlifter, engineer, blogger, and activist who seeks to expand athletic opportunities for Muslim women. In a speech she delivered at the U.S. State Department, for example, Abdullah talks about "the power of people—individuals—to bring about change" (state.gov/secretary/rm/2011/09/171860.htm). She expresses her agency and ability to negotiate conflicting cultural discourses through her style-fashion-dress.

Other processes in the circuit of style-fashion-dress include the production, distribution, and consumption of Abdullah's clothing. She shares much of this

Figure 1.5   Kulsoom Abdullah wears attire that meets the modified clothing regulations for Olympic weightlifting: a custom-made green singlet fashioned by designer Stephanie Aylworth, worn over a long-sleeved unitard purchased from Capezio, a dancewear brand; together with striped socks from American Apparel and a headscarf. Courtesy of Kulsoom Abdullah. Photographed by Irfan Butt of the Pakistan Weightlifting Federation at the 2011 World Weightlifting Championships at Disneyland Paris.

information on her blog. After the IWF amended the uniform regulations, Stephanie Aylworth, a clothing designer in Georgia, began to custom-make singlets with short sleeves, reaching to Abdullah's knees. Abdullah is also a consumer of long-sleeved unitards from Capezio (a dancewear brand available online) and striped socks from American Apparel (also distributed online as well as through stores). Abdullah wears her headscarf, her custom-made singlet over a unitard, and striped socks, as shown in Figure 1.5.

In the American Open competition in 2011, Abdullah wore a full-body unitard and singlet (in black, maroon, and a dull gold) redesigned by Aylworth. In these scenarios, processes of production, distribution, and consumption are clearly intertwined, with direct input and distribution between producer (Aylworth) and consumer (Abdullah).

For the Worldwide Weightlifting Championships at Disneyland Paris in 2011, Abdullah sports a full-body unitard and singlet in green because she is representing Pakistan; Aylworth sews a patch with flag insignia onto the singlet.

Another supplier of clothing to Abdullah is friniggi Sportswear (friniggi.com), based in Botswana. Friniggi produces sportswear for Muslim women. Their website indicates the following:

> We're not just about covering your body. We are well past that. Just like you are. We are about sports and your athletic experience. Just like you.

Abdullah consumes warm up suits and headscarves from friniggi, which distributes active sportswear to Muslim female athletes throughout Africa and the rest of the world. Their distribution system involves online marketing and mail delivery. As the fashion anthropologist Emma Tarlo (2010) notes in her book, *Visibly Muslim*, the production, distribution, and consumption of clothing for Muslim women is a transnational business and community that involves a great deal of communication: blog and e-mail interactions, as well as marketing.

As we can see, the relationship among all of the processes in Figure 1.3 is circuitous. The interaction between regulation and subject formation comes to light in Abdullah's successful articulation of an alternative form of style-fashion-dress, which now meets her sport's regulations and initiates new relations among production, distribution, and consumption. Keeping the context of the circuit of style-fashion-dress in mind, Chapter 2 delves more deeply into the process of subject formation by pursuing the concept of intersectionality as the interplay among subject positions.

–2–

Intersectional, Transnational Fashion Subjects

The genie is out of the bottle. We can no longer pretend that there is a single way of fashioning appearances in the world. There is not merely one model for fashion subjectivity. Rather, there are multiple subjectivities, shaped in part by the interplay among diverse subject positions (e.g., nationality, race, ethnicity, class, gender, sexuality). These subject positions are embedded in cultural discourses over which individuals may have little control. These cultural discourses are historical and have preceded individual experiences; they range from the legacy of scientific discourses on race in the nineteenth century to dominant beauty myths; to the stories, symbols (e.g., flag pins, clothes, colors), or anthems that shape the histories, debates, and sentiments associated with nations.

Like the cultural discourses in which they are embedded, subject positions cannot be totally separated from one another; they intersect in complex ways. Consider the subject positions in Figure 2.1, featuring the famous Bollywood film star Priyanka Chopra. Although Chopra is Indian, she is very much a transnational, as well as intersectional, figure: a former Miss World, an actress whose films are distributed around the world, and a young woman who lived in the United States with her parents (both doctors) during her high school years (imdb.com). Moving through time and space, Chopra's body represents an articulation of multiple cultural discourses. Chopra's gender, national, ethnic, class, and other subject positions intersect to shape her subject formation across time and space. Manish Malhotra, the renowned costume and fashion designer, captures Chopra's complex subject formation in his styling of her ensemble, shown in Figure 2.1. Known for his fresh and contemporary interpretation of Indian aesthetics, Malhotra uses bright colors, textures, embroidery, and sequins in his gowns and separates (manishmalhotra.in). In Figure 2.1, Chopra wears a fur-hooded denim jacket (that can be seen as a symbol of globalization) over an Indian-inspired red and gold skirt with a short gold top. Articulating between national and transnational discourses, the ensemble seems fitting for a former Miss India and Miss World, and for a Bollywood actor whose films circulate globally, especially among Indian communities in nations such as South Africa, the United Kingdom, and the United States. At the same time Chopra's popularity serves to distribute Indian fashion in a

Figure 2.1 Bollywood actress Priyanka Chopra wears an outfit designed by designer Manish Malhotra for an upcoming film promotion. Consider how Chopra's style articulates multiple discourses and represents the ways in which she is an intersectional, transnational subject. Photo by Yogen Shah/India Today Group/Getty Images.

transnational circuit of style-fashion-dress, her own look represents the intersectionalities in her own subject formation.

This chapter is organized around six assumptions pertaining to subject formation through style-fashion-dress. These six assumptions articulate between cultural studies and fashion studies, revolving around the theme of intersectionality (see Figure 2.2) in a transnational context, as bodies move through time and space. Part of this movement involves fashion subjects' interactions with and influence on one another. In the process of moving through the six assumptions, we revisit and build on the circuit of style-fashion-dress model with the use of key concepts from fashion studies and cultural studies.

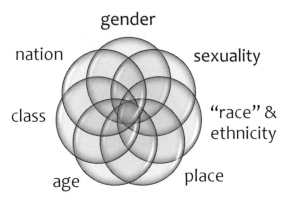

Figure 2.2 Intersectionalities among subject positions.

ASSUMPTION 1: INEVITABLY, PEOPLE APPEAR

This is not an option; it happens. The Danish philosopher Ossi Naukkarinen (1998) refers to appearance as "the aesthetics of the unavoidable." We cannot avoid becoming part of the visual world, and hence part of fashion discourse. As it was introduced in Chapter 1, *cultural discourse* entails ongoing, systematic cultural "conversations" that are not necessarily on a level playing field. Everyone participates, inevitably, in these "conversations" through style-fashion-dress. In the process, individuals explore—in an ongoing, changing way—"who I am" and "who I am becoming"; this exploration, as noted in Chapter 1, is the process of *subjectivity.* Because individuals do not accomplish this exploration completely by themselves—because they think about others as they get dressed, and because they rely on feedback from others—style-fashion-dress is a social process. Subjects interact with other subjects. Individual processes of subjectivity become collective processes of *intersubjectivity* when individuals engage, influence, and perceive one another.

Styling, dressing, adorning, or fashioning the body is a fundamental part of subject formation (shaping, sustaining, and shifting): an ongoing sense of self and identity in a changing world. In all cultures ever studied—historically and contemporarily—people have played a hand in modifying how their bodies look. If we can say that anything is "human nature," this tendency toward dressing, fashioning, or styling the body must surely qualify. Of course, *how* this occurs varies dramatically across time and space. One thing is clear: There is no single, "natural" way of appearing.

The desire, at least, to modify appearance (because these modifications may be regulated through cultural, religious, or legal discourses) can be linked to subjectivity and, more specifically, to the cultural studies concept of *agency,* defined in Chapter 1 as the freedom or ability to exert one's "voice" and to resist power relations in some way. The case of Kulsoom Abdullah, presented in Chapter 1 (see Figure 1.5), illustrated a successful example of how a fashion subject can exercise agency and resist regulations in the form of uniform dress codes. (Not everyone has this degree of agency, however.) To be a subject in the world is also to be an agent of creativity, control, or change, but it also means experiencing regulation, as we saw in Chapter 1. The degree of agency that individuals have depends upon the cultural (and political, religious, class) context and various social circumstances. There is an ongoing debate in the social sciences—and in cultural studies especially—about the extent to which individuals have the agency to choose their courses of action (including how they dress) versus the extent to which "social structures" limit choices and opportunities for individuals. Generally, cultural studies strikes a middle ground in this debate, and so does fashion studies. That is, style-fashion-dress as a system of concepts conveys a sense that people create their own "fashion statements" but are ultimately constrained by what is available in the marketplace, by dress codes and social conventions, by political regimes, and the like.

Part of dressing or fashioning the body is a kind of ritual experience or personal conditioning that occurs in everyday life. The sociologist Pierre Bourdieu (1984) referred to this ritual/conditioning as *habitus* (defined in Chapter 1 as the routine cultural practices embodied in everyday life). Everyday life—a critical concept in cultural studies and fashion studies alike—can be described as "uncatalogued, habitual, and often routinized" (Grossberg 2010: 278). Examples of habitus include showering, shaving, styling one's hair, applying makeup, donning layers of clothing and accessories, and so on. Habitus is a highly embodied experience that helps to explain the link between the individual and the social: how the fact that we live in our own bodies is structured in part by our social positions (e.g., social class, gender) in the world (Entwistle 2000: 36).

The concept of habitus reminds us that it is not just what one wears that matters, but also *how* one styles, fashions, or dresses the body that tells us about everyday processes of subject formation as the interplay between subjectivity and the subject positions people inhabit. As Entwistle (2000) has pointed out, habitus is one of the ways in which people navigate issues of agency and structure in everyday life, through situated bodily practices that are culturally ingrained but that also have their own personal spin. The case study presented in Chapter 1 (Figure 1.4) reveals how a Muslim female weightlifter navigates agency and structure. Her headscarf—along with covering her arms and legs—is part of her habitus: what she is accustomed to, and conditioned by, wearing on a daily basis.

In earlier work (Kaiser 2001), I introduced the concept of *minding appearances* to bring together situated bodily practices with streams of consciousness that are themselves embodied. The mind, after all, is in the body, so the mind and body cannot be separated, as feminist philosophy tells us. I asked the following kinds of questions: "How can I *know* when I am focused on how I *look*?" Are these processes, in fact, contradictory? I argue that they are not. "To what extent does my appearance style represent or create truth(s) about who I am?" I argue that we do create everyday "truths" (with a lower-case *t*) or meanings as we work through our ideas about who we are becoming, in the moment. And, of course, the fashion industry is pleased to comply with this process of discovery—hence the need for critical, reflexive awareness of what we are doing and why. The process of minding appearance acknowledges that self-truths are contingent or provisional, as well as embodied.

Minding appearances poses challenges that become especially apparent in the context of a global economy, in which the Western mind/body "disconnect" becomes situated in "a larger disconnect between the efforts of production and the pleasures of consumption" (Kaiser 2001: 80). Yet, as we shall see in the following section, the idea of a "global" (or better, transnational) perspective is not new. The problem is actually the binary thinking (e.g., West versus "the rest," mind versus body, production versus consumption) that has limited imaginative approaches to the possibility that fashion is transnational. Bodies, materials, and images flow through time and space.

ASSUMPTION 2: FASHION IS TRANSNATIONAL—NOT MERELY WESTERN OR "EUROMODERN"

In other words, there is more than one "fashion system" (Craik 1994)—more than one way in which appearance styles change and why they do through the "circuit of style-fashion-dress" (Figure 1.3 in Chapter 1). "Modern" history itself is often framed exclusively as *euromodern*—a term that includes Europe, especially Western Europe, North America, Australia, and New Zealand (Grossberg 2010). Grossberg argues that euromodernity is just one of multiple possibilities for imagining modern histories. Just as history itself suffers from a "Western" bias, fashion history has had its own limited story/stories. Much of it has revolved around the dominant story of the birth of fashion in the Italian Renaissance and in the French courts of the fourteenth and fifteenth centuries, respectively (e.g., Steele 1988; Davis 1992; Lipovetsky 1994). Historian Sarah-Grace Heller (2010) complicates the idea of identifying a particular time and place for fashion's beginning. She argues that historians tend to discover a "birth of fashion in whatever period" (and place) they study. Fashionability, she concludes, is "in the eye of the beholder" (Heller 2010: 34). Rather than attempting to look for the origin of fashion, she argues that it is more fruitful to explore "when the cultural value placed on novelty becomes prominent, and when the desire for innovation and the capacity for the production of innovation" become part of an ongoing system of change (Heller 2010: 25). And she argues that in Europe, there was some kind of fashion system operating in the growing towns and courts of France since at least the twelfth century; by the thirteenth century, "full-blown fashionable values were in evidence" (Heller 2010: 34).

If we broaden our conceptualization of fashion (and, indeed, culture more generally) to include Africa, Asia, and the Southern hemisphere of the globe, then we can begin to consider how social and cultural change happens in a variety of ways, with different paces and within different spaces. Eicher (2001) makes this point in her introduction to the National Geographic Society book, *Fashion*:

> Fashion is, after all, about change, and change happens in every culture because human beings are creative and flexible. However, when we encounter people in other cultures who appear not to be part of our modern world (maybe they don't dress the way we do) and whose past does not include written history, paintings, or drawings, we often categorize them as coming from static worlds. (17)

Eicher (2010) proposes the term "world fashion" to break out of the binary opposition of style-fashion-dress as "west versus 'the rest.'" She uses it in a way that is very similar to the way anthropologist Aihwa Ong (1999) employs *transnationality* to refer to "the condition of cultural interconnectedness and mobility across space—which has been intensified under late capitalism" (4). This term suggests that there are some new relationships between nations and capitalism (economic systems based on a profit motivation), but the prefix *trans* also implies crossings of various sorts: through space or across boundaries (more on this in Chapter 8). And it indicates some ways in which new arrangements or possibilities are imagined: translations, transactions, transversals, and even transgressions (Ong 1999: 4).

Like Ong (1999), I use the term "transnational" to describe larger cultural contexts that transcend nations. I use globalization and global more narrowly—to refer to those transnational arrangements that involve "new corporate strategies" (4). Since the 1980s, especially, and the restructuring and spread of capitalism worldwide, transnationality has become part of everyday life in the circuit of style-fashion-dress. As feminist theorist Gayatri Spivak (1999) puts it, we "wear globalization on our bodies." The circuit of style-fashion-dress, discussed in Chapter 1, articulates the complex interplay of subject formation with in the production, distribution, consumption, and regulation of textiles, clothes, images, and ideas that circulate globally.

Fashion historians Giorgio Riello and Peter McNeil (2010: 4) discuss two challenges associated with transnational histories of style-fashion-dress. The first challenge is to redefine fashion to include "consumers, producers and mediators well beyond the geographical boundaries of Western Europe, North America and perhaps those outposts frequently forgotten in the northern hemisphere, of South Africa, Australia, and parts of South America." They go on to note the compelling issues associated with "the emerging economies of India and China"—nations that have rich and fascinating textile and style-fashion-dress histories, as well.

The second challenge is to refrain from thinking that a transnational understanding of fashion has only recently become possible because of "the result of globalization and the growth of new middle classes":

> Recent innovative research underlines how places as disparate as Ming China, Tokugawa and Meiji Japan, Moghul India or Colonial Latin America and Australia, engaged and produced their own fashions both in conjunction, competition, collaboration and independently from Europe. The fact that these historical traditions of fashion are not as well known or advertised as the European one should not diminish their value. Braudel [the historian] famously wrote that "Europe invented historians and then made good use of them." (Riello and McNeil 2010: 4)

Fashion is more than a white, bourgeois (upper middle class), heterosexual female affair. Yet the stories that get told and retold reinforce the myth that fashion is only Western or white or female. The cultural studies concept of *hegemony* helps to explain how and why this works. This concept seeks to understand how certain ways of knowing the world dominate and persevere, even when these ways are not in the best personal interests of those who seem to buy into them. Why do people, this concept demands, accept and even endorse stories or myths that do not pursue their own self-interests? How does this happen?

The Italian political activist and theorist Antonio Gramsci (1971) contemplated the above questions when he was in prison in the 1930s, reflecting upon how Mussolini and the Fascist political movement had been so effective, and how his own political counterefforts had not succeeded. As a result of this self-reflection and time for contemplation, Gramsci articulated a theory of hegemony: how power works not only through guns and warfare (although these too obviously influence power relations), but also through clever arguments, compelling language, and visually embodied imagery, such as the black shirts associated with Mussolini and his followers (Falasca-Zamponi 2002).

Through processes of hegemony, people become compelled to submit or buy into ideas that may be counter to their own everyday life interests. Examples of hegemony abound in the contemporary global economy: beauty norms that privilege white Western appearances, including the production, distribution, and consumption of "good hair" (discussed further in Chapter 4 on how this relates to "race"); what gets chosen to represent "national dress" in the context of multiple ethnicities (discussed further in Chapter 3); and the dominance of the European-derived male business suit as a relatively enduring kind of world fashion (see Chapter 6).

These and other hegemonies are not distinct from one another. Rather, they are distributed across subject positions. Scattered hegemonies (Grewal and Kaplan 1994) intersect, crosscut one another, and in the process become harder to trace. For hegemony is not only about politics or social class; it also pertains to other subject positions such as gender, "race," ethnicity, national identity, sexuality, and the like. Some of the question of what gets included under the umbrella of hegemony is the larger question of power itself. Power is complex, multilayered, and nuanced. Through cultural discourses, it tends to operate less like a hammer and more like a process of entanglement.

ASSUMPTION 3: SUBJECT FORMATION THROUGH STYLE-FASHION-DRESS IS A PERSONAL PROCESS OF NAVIGATING INTERSECTIONALITIES

Subject positions are not isolated. Instead, they are multiple, and they intersect. They defy singular, *essentialist* ways of being. As discussed in Chapter 1, an essentialist perspective involves focusing exclusively on one subject position at the expense of others: Gender, "race," sexuality, or other subject positions "rule" over other ways of knowing. It is as though one of these subject positions is the essence (existence) of being, and the other subject positions do not exist. And this is not the case: they coexist and overlap. This simultaneity of subject positions is probably nowhere more evident than through styled-fashioned-dressed bodies.

The concept of intersectionality, or the idea of using an intersectional approach, derives from feminist theory and has become an important framework in feminist and gender studies. Initially, an intersectional approach to research was applied to issues of race, class, and gender, in recognition of the fact that these subject positions are not completely separate issues for individuals in dominant and subordinate groups alike. It spread to cultural studies and to other fields in the social sciences, the humanities, and beyond. The term "intersectionality" is attributed to the law professor and critical race theorist Kimberlé Crenshaw. She came to the concept while trying to make sense of what she was experiencing as an antiracist activist in college; she found that the antiracist social movement was not sufficiently addressing gendered power relations. At the same time, she was engaged with women's studies and feminist issues and was frustrated by a lack of attention at that time to race. As she was conducting research on domestic violence in Los Angeles, she became acutely aware of how diverse systems of oppression (i.e., race, class, and gender) overlapped and interlocked with one another (Guidroz and Berger 2009). The use of the concept has since broadened to explore how intersectional analyses apply to ethnicity, nation, age, sexuality, physical ability, and other subject positions as well as race, class, and gender.

The Venn diagram in Figure 2.2 reveals how subject positions intersect. This model provides a framework for the six subject positions that organize the rest of this book: nationality (Chapter 3), ethnicity and race (Chapter 4), social class (Chapter 5), gender (Chapter 6), sexuality (Chapter 7), and time/age and space/place (Chapter 8). None of the subject positions in Figure 2.2 are distinct from one another; instead, they intersect with each other and, indeed, with other subject positions that cannot be covered in greater depth due to space limitations. Although each of the subject positions in the Venn diagram becomes the highlighted focus of discussions in the later chapters, they are always considered as inseparable from other subject positions.

As you can see from the shading on the circles in Figure 2.2, they are not flat; rather, they are three-dimensional. Imagine them as transparent globes—rather like balloons, except with permeable boundaries that enable each subject position to intersect with every other subject position. Additional globes can always be added; there is no limit (except for page limitations). In fact, we could continue to multiply subject positions in this model: what is relevant and to whom in the process of establishing a sense of identity (who I am, who I am not, where I'm going with my life, and how these processes connect with those of others in the world). We could continue to add globes infinitum; religion, sports, art, music, and other potential globes abound as potential additions. And inevitably, any additions pertain to style-dress-fashion. Indeed, additional globes intersect in complicated and, at times, contradictory ways to the subject positions that comprise the focal points in the remaining chapters.

Let's examine the globes in Figure 2.2 a bit more closely, however. They are not static; nor are they fixed. Rather, they are in motion. They rotate but not only in one direction. Somewhat erratically and jerkily, they can move in multiple directions. At times and in certain contexts, they may spin more quickly and perhaps even light up, commanding our attention and becoming especially salient in terms of self-awareness and a sense of subjectivity. And yet even when some globes "fade" from our awareness, they are still there, intersecting. How and why might some globes be more apparent to us than others? Issues of power and privilege come into play. Many of us take our national subject positions for granted, for example, until we travel outside our nations and/or interact with individuals from other nations. Similarly, masculinity (a gendered subject position) is most likely to become salient when one is the only male in the room. Similarly, many individuals take whiteness or heterosexuality for granted as "assumed norms," unless or until they are challenged to consider alternative ways of experiencing everyday life.

Style-fashion-dress affords opportunities to connect the dots across a variety of subject positions and, indeed, to explore ways of being and becoming as subjects in the world in ways that may be otherwise difficult to articulate (as in words). And yet, we carry on. We have to style our appearances on an everyday basis; we connect with others through processes of fashion/ change; and we dress our bodies in a variety of ways as we bathe, groom, shave, apply makeup, put on clothing and various accessories, and do a final check in the mirror (or not) before facing the world "outside."

The interplay among everyday subject positions is the key idea in intersectionality as a concept. Especially compelling are the overlapping or "in between" spaces, through which fashion subjects exercise agency and articulate more than one subject position simultaneously. Navigating and negotiating these spaces is key to the articulations represented by style-fashion-dress.

As referenced in Assumption 2 (discussed previously), hegemonies are scattered (Grewal and Kaplan 1994), and they intersect in unpredictable ways (as the globes variously spin, light up, or call themselves in a variety of ways into our perceptual fields), based on social circumstances.

The spaces in between subject positions can be conceptualized as sites of ambiguity and open-ended possibility, as well as articulation. Let's consider Figure 2.3 as an example of intersectionality and the spaces in between subject positions. In this photograph, the gay activist Harry Hay (1912–2002) speaks at a gay pride parade in New York, on the twenty-fifth anniversary of the 1969 Stonewall Riots in New York. These riots have been credited historically with igniting the lesbian, gay, bisexual, and transgender (LGBT) liberation movement. However, Hay's activism predated the Stonewall Riots by nearly two decades; he was one of the earliest gay activists in the United States. With his lover Rudi Gernreich in the early 1950s, he founded the Mattachine Society in Los Angeles: the first sustained activist group to fight for LGBT rights. Gernreich later went on to become a famous fashion designer; in 1963, he designed the women's topless bathing suit (seen on only a few beaches but making a big splash in terms of publicity).

Hay's ensemble in Figure 2.3 articulates volumes about his subject positions and his politics. He had a long-standing fascination with and immersion in "two-spirit" (blending masculinity and femininity) Native American culture. His founding of the Radical Faeries social movement in 1970 drew upon Native American culture and two-spirit spirituality. In Figure 2.3, his necklace reflects this spirituality and appropriation. His skirt, too, involves a critical appropriation of camouflage into a complex articulation that juxtaposes masculinity (the camouflage fabric and military belt) and femininity (in the form of the petticoat-like skirt). The camouflage itself has multiple meanings: the military,

Figure 2.3 Gay activist Harry Hay speaking at the New York Gay Pride Parade, at the 25th anniversary of the Stonewall Riots. Photo courtesy of Joan E. Birren (JEB).

as well as peaceful blending with nature associated with Radical Faerie spirituality. Through his style-fashion-dress, Hay represents the intersectionalities among his gender and sexual subject positions and communicates his spiritual affinity with Native American culture. We might envision this affinity as a positive, meaningful entanglement with a spiritual and ethnic community that is different from his own ethnic (white, British) subject position.

ASSUMPTION 4: ENTANGLEMENTS: FROM IDENTITY *NOT* TO IDENTITY (K)NOTS

In everyday discourse, fashion subjects are generally able to articulate in words who they are *not*, but it is much more difficult to express verbally who they *are* (Freitas et al. 1997). In interviews, most fashion subjects are fairly emphatic about who they *are not* or *do not want to look like*. Undoubtedly, the scattered nature of hegemonies across subject positions contributes to this difficulty. Through style-fashion-dress, individuals have opportunities to articulate—visually and materially—what might be too challenging to express in words. Harry Hay's appearance, in Figure 2.3, represents not only the intersectionalities among his subject positions but also his entangled, spiritual connection with subjects who differ from himself in terms of ethnic subject positions. What would Hay be likely to have said about who he was *not*? Based on his biographies and his commitment to foster a separate gay minority culture, we can infer that he would have been likely to say that he did not identify with hegemonic (white, heterosexual) masculinity. Rather, he articulated a different form of masculinity: one intersecting with his sexuality and entangled with "other" concepts of femininity and Native American spirituality.

The metaphor of entanglement complicates strict binary oppositions between identity and identity *not*: female versus "not female," gay versus "not gay," etc. Such oppositions cannot capture how power works; they cannot explain complex interactions and influences through which people negotiate, regulate, and appropriate style-fashion-dress. Although *not* patterns are inevitably part of entangled (k)nots, opening our imagination beyond binary limits enables more complex ways of thinking about subjectivity and intersubjectivity (interactions between subjects).

If we begin to interpret difference not as something that is apart from our own identities, but rather as a kind of entanglement, we can begin to imagine more openness to difference and the discovery of unexpected commonalities. "Not" becomes embroiled in a more complex "(k)not" as entanglement replaces opposition as an organizing logic. New questions arise: What happens when nodes "pop" or stand out and hold disparate subject positions together? What connections might overlapping threads reveal? And what becomes concealed?

> The knot metaphor of fashion allows us to consider how some truths can be covered over temporarily, only to be revealed as a knot is loosened. Hence, truth is partial and contingent, according to issues of time, space, and power relations. The three-dimensional surface of a knot both reveals a temporary prominence and conceals portions of the threads underneath. In the process, self-other relations emerge as entangled, rather than binary. (Kaiser and McCullough 2010: 381)

Let's consider how a transnational fashion subject experiences entanglement across time and space. Cultural studies scholar Stuart Hall (1990) discussed circuitous (or entangled) routes that individuals from Africa have traveled. These routes are not just one-way trips from Africa to the United

Kingdom, for example; nor are these routes straight. Rather, they loop around, reverse on themselves, and change courses as individuals have had the agency to explore new possibilities for subjectivity, in the context of the African diaspora.

The Greek-derived word *diaspora* means dispersion; to disperse is to sow or scatter. The term diaspora was first used to refer to the dispersal of Jewish people around the world, due to persecution. It is also used to describe diasporas from Africa, whether they are based on slavery (as in the case of U.S., Caribbean, and Brazilian history between the seventeenth and nineteenth centuries) or on immigration (from Africa to Europe, for example) or some combination (e.g., from Africa to the Caribbean centuries ago due to slavery and then immigration from the Caribbean to England in the 1950s and 1960s: the route traveled by many individuals in the Black British community).

Fashion subjectivity in the African diaspora involves more than an either/or kind of style-fashion-dress. Instead, it represents and articulates all kinds of entanglements based on uneven power relations and the movements that result from these: the flight from religious persecution, slavery, the search for a better life beyond poverty, and so on (more on this in Chapter 4). Fashion studies scholar Leslie Rabine (2002) has shown how some African Americans in Los Angeles, for example, design and wear styles such as dashikis (loose pullover tunics) made from West African printed fabrics to express their transnational, ethnic identities. The influence is not only one way, however. Artisans in Dakar, Senegal (known as the "Paris of Africa"), adapt African American styles and prints. Entanglements abound with mutual aesthetic influences. Complex distribution networks link production with consumption across continents, as structures of feeling become part of the circuit of style-fashion-dress (see Figure 2.4 in the following section).

ASSUMPTION 5: STRUCTURES OF FEELING—EXPRESSED THROUGH SUBJECT FORMATION AND THE FASHION PROCESS ALIKE—ARTICULATE BETWEEN EVERYDAY LIFE AND CULTURE THROUGH THE CIRCUIT OF STYLE-FASHION-DRESS

As we have seen, articulations involve a complex web of power relations that regulate but generally do not completely squelch individual creativity and expression. Culture both "empowers and disempowers" in contradictory ways (Grossberg 2010: 8) through the interplay of subject positions and subjectivity. Perhaps nowhere is this more evident than in the realm of everyday appearances: structured but not stymied by the norms of dominant fashion; limited but also inspired in various ways by gender, "race," and other subject positions; regulated but resisted, at times subtly and at other times substantially.

Not surprisingly, given the multiple and often contradictory power dynamics involved in style-fashion-dress, a mixture of emotions and meanings emerge through this system. The cultural studies scholar Raymond Williams (1977) used the term "structures of feeling" to capture the idea that affect (the emotional realm) connects the personal with the cultural in everyday life. For example, as suggested in Figure 2.4, emotions such as ambivalence and anxiety are not only personal; they are also articulated through cultural discourses, in the process of "working through" ideas that cannot yet be pinned down. They are "under construction" and generate a sense of unease (in the case of cultural anxiety) or mixed emotions (in the case of cultural ambivalence).

By combining "structure" with "feeling," Raymond tapped the sense that many of us experience similar emotions that are in part derived from and articulated through cultural discourses. It is as though a cultural experiment is underway, and we do not yet know what the outcome will be or how the future will play out. Cultural anxiety, in particular, has this future-oriented quality, as we shall see. In the concept of "structure of feeling," Raymond Williams captured the ambiguity of "the social" that has not yet been fully articulated (Huehls 2010). It is this ambiguity somewhere between the old and the new that generates structures of feeling: What is the same? What is different? What will change in everyday life? This space "in between" finds expression

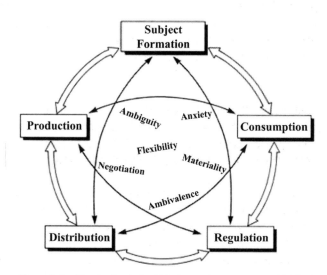

Figure 2.4 Circuit of style-fashion-dress with structures of feeling. Developed with Kelly Sullivan.

in style-fashion-dress and articulates in complicated ways with processes of production, consumption, distribution, subject formation, and regulation.

AMBIGUITY

As subjects fashion their everyday looks, negotiating diverse power relations in the process, *ambiguity* abounds. The concept of ambiguity has multiple meanings: (a) mixed metaphors or numerous layers of messages; (b) vague or fuzzy messages, such as those that cannot be put easily into words or that constitute a novel stimulus (e.g., a new style); and (c) inconsistent or contradictory messages that are unclear because they are somewhere in between different possibilities. The distinctions among these are themselves blurry; one kind of ambiguity can overlap with another. Ambiguity often occurs in the use of words, but the potential for ambiguity in visual communication such as fashion is rampant, whether it is intended by the wearer or imputed by the perceiver (or both).

Ambiguity can foster a sense of ironic play and can be deeply thought provoking as it brings contradictions to the surface; it can also create confusion. Consider again the image of Harry Hay in Figure 2.3, using ambiguity as a conceptual lens. One gets a sense of his ironic play with gender symbolism, his spiritual tribute to Native American culture, and other messages. He mixes metaphors as he articulates his subjectivity: what matters to him, the hegemonic gender norms he is challenging, and so on. Sociologist Gregory Stone (1969) argued that the richest meanings often emerge from ambiguous appearances, because such appearances require mindful interpretation on the part of perceivers. As perceivers, they weigh alternative meanings, work though the fuzziness, and navigate spaces of meaning in between competing possibilities. Ambiguity, in other words, may foster a kind of questioning or deliberation that may contribute to further interaction (e.g., verbal exchange) and new negotiations of meaning or understanding.

New styles—introduced on the runway or on the street—are often ambiguous, but they become even more so when subjects fashion them into their own looks—mixing and matching in ways that may not have ever been anticipated by designers. Fashion as a social process relies upon ambiguity to influence new looks and change interpretations of what is "in" (Kaiser, Nagasawa, and Hutton 1990).

Several factors contribute to ambiguity in appearance styles. First, clothing itself marks an ambiguous and even uneasy boundary between the biological body and the social world (Wilson 1985: 3). Second, fashion is a form of communication that functions somewhere in between art and language. Fred Davis (1992: 3) indicates that fashion " 'merely suggests' more than it can (or intends to) state precisely."

CULTURAL AMBIVALENCE

A third factor contributing to ambiguity (mixed meanings) in appearance styles is its relation to ambivalence (mixed emotions). Davis (1992) sees the confusion between these two words as instructive, because it reminds us how meanings and moods intertwine as subjects sort through diverse cultural experiences and ask themselves questions such as "Whom do I wish to please, and in so doing whom am I likely to offend? What are the consequences of appearing as this kind of person as against that kind? Does the image I think I convey of myself reflect my true innermost self or some specious version thereof? Do I wish to conceal or reveal? . . . and so forth" (Davis 1992: 24).

Fashion theorist Elizabeth Wilson (1985) indicates that fashion is ambivalent, because "when we dress we wear inscribed upon our bodies the often obscure relationship of art, personal psychology, and the social order." She goes on to say that fashion is endlessly troubling as we are "drawn to it, yet repelled by a fear of what we might find hidden within its purposes" (Wilson 1985: 246–47). Michael Garrison (1982), coming from a psychological perspective, suggests something similar when he describes how ambivalence not only "confuses, devours, and tortures" but also "defines and orders, transforming the unknown into a knowable opposite." Ambivalence, Garrison argues, has the potential when mediated to "constructively metaphor the world" in an imaginative or even therapeutic way (Garrison 1982: 229).

Davis notes how fashion's instabilities often stem from cultural discourses regarding identity ambivalences. Hence, ambivalences play or "constructively metaphor" (to use Garrison's phrase) both individual subject formation and collective fashion change:

> Among the more prominent ambivalences underlying . . . fashion-susceptible instabilities are the subjective tensions of youth versus age, masculinity versus femininity, androgyny versus singularity, inclusiveness versus exclusiveness, work versus play, domesticity versus worldliness, revelation versus concealment, license versus restraint, and conformity versus rebellion. (Davis 1992: 18)

Davis goes on to describe how fashion operates symbolically by encoding the tensions associated with the above identity ambivalences: "now highlighting this, muting that, juxtaposing what was previously disparate, inverting major to minor and vice versa" (Davis 1992: 18). Fashion articulates and represents the "collective tensions and moods abroad in the land" (Davis 1992: 18). It makes these collective tensions and moods visual and material, shedding light on potential meanings and opportunities for change.

The terms *ambiguity* and *ambivalence* both have connotations of "two" (in "bi"), and, as discussed in Chapter 1, binary oppositions can foster either/or thinking. Ambiguity and ambivalence, however, tend to emerge in the realm of both/and ways of knowing; they acknowledge the possibility of in-between spaces, blurry boundaries, contradiction, and irony. Further, they are not limited to two options, although modern Western thought has often framed options in binary terms (e.g., mind versus body, masculinity versus femininity, production versus consumption). As we have seen in the discussions on intersectionalities and entanglements, subject formation is a complicated affair. Ambivalence regarding masculinity and femininity, for example, cannot be completely separated from other "identity ambivalences." Few, if any, subject positions (including gender, as we shall see in Chapter 6) can be fully captured by binary oppositions.

CULTURAL ANXIETY

A fourth reason contributing to ambiguity in style-dress-fashion is related to cultural ambivalence but less delineated: cultural anxiety. The Danish philosopher Søren Kierkegaard (1980) described anxiety as the "ambiguity of subjectivity." Whereas cultural ambivalence involves some kind of crystallization into two or more conflicting emotions, cultural anxiety is a collective sense of free-floating uncertainty, coupled with emotions ranging from fear and dread to hope and anticipation. These emotions are much looser and harder to pinpoint in the case of cultural anxiety. They are up for grabs; they are not fixed with binary oppositions.

Although anxiety is often equated primarily with fear and dread, the German philosopher/writer Walter Benjamin (2004) said that for philosophers, "the most interesting thing about fashion is its extraordinary anticipations." Like art, fashion often "precedes the perceptible reality by years," and yet Benjamin argues that fashion has "much steadier, much more precise contact with the coming thing":

> Each season brings, in its newest creations, various secret signals of things to come. Whoever understands how to read these semaphores [visual signals] would know in advance not only about new currents in the arts but also about new legal codes, wars, and revolutions. (Benjamin 2004: 63–64)

Of course, depending on one's perspective, "new currents in the arts" and "new legal codes, wars, and revolutions" may indeed produce both a sense of excitement about what is coming and a sense of dis-ease (or even fear) with uncertainty. Dread and hope, in a sense, are two sides of the same coin (i.e., anxiety: a both/and phenomenon, in a loose sort of way). Fashion represents and articulates cultural anxiety as the ambiguity of subjectivity. Fashion suggests what is to come. It is a process of articulating abstract ideas and negotiating ambiguity.

ASSUMPTION 6: THE PROCESS OF NEGOTIATING AMBIGUITY IS NOT A LEVEL PLAYING FIELD, AND IT IS A MATERIAL PROCESS—ESPECIALLY IN A TRANSNATIONAL CONTEXT

Fashion, as a process, requires negotiation: give and take as individuals dress, perceive one another, articulate ambivalence and anxiety, work through ideas and possibilities, and modify appearances in an ongoing way. Sociologist Herbert Blumer (1969) used the phrase *collective selection* to capture how subject formation becomes a cultural process. As multiple subjects purvey available options in the marketplace (i.e., styles that have been produced and distributed, as shown in Figure 2.4), frequently there are some best sellers that seem to capture their collective attention. These are the styles that feel fresh or right; they seem to capture the moment and to articulate the tensions at play in cultural discourse.

Through the process of consumption (purchase and wear), individuals engage in subject formation (as they interact with one another in a cultural context). As shown in Figure 2.4, they negotiate various "structures of feeling." As subjects interact with subjects in the contexts of visual and material culture, subjectivities meld into intersubjectivities: shared ways of knowing and articulating structures of feeling.

The symbolic interactionist (SI) theory of fashion (Kaiser, Nagasawa, and Hutton 1990) pulls together many of the concepts and flows presented in Figure 2.4. The SI theory proposes that fashion change thrives on cultural tensions (e.g., cultural ambivalence and cultural anxiety) that contribute to individual articulations of appearance style that are at least initially ambiguous (new and fresh but hard to put into words).

The meanings of appearance styles are negotiated in everyday social life through interaction with others. These negotiations—involving both visual and verbal discourse—enable fashion subjects to grapple with ongoing cultural tensions in subtle but complex ways. Still, the underlying tensions themselves are not completely resolved, so the process of fashion change continues: the ambivalence and anxiety in cultural discourse, the symbolic ambiguity in fashion subjects' appearance styles, and the negotiation of meaning in social interactions (Kaiser, Nagasawa, and Hutton 1990).

Where and how does the negotiation of ambiguity occur? Hegemonic stories place fashion in modern, Western, urban contexts. These stories continue in global discourses about "world fashion cities," which Breward and Gilbert (2006) have challenged. As they observe, cities such as Paris, Milan, and New York "are routinely incorporated into the advertising of designer brands and retail outlets" (ix). Yet who gets to decide what constitutes a "world fashion city"? How do processes of production, distribution, and consumption articulate to create systems of representation? And how and why do power relations become a factor in fashion hegemony, from a transnational perspective?

This last question gets into issues of relations across national, ethnic, religious, and other subject positions. A bit of transnational, historical grounding will be helpful at this point—to have a context for understanding uneven processes of negotiation due to power relations.

By the second half of the nineteenth century, Europe had successfully cemented its position as the dominating force in the world. Paris had obtained a reputation as a major world fashion center (Steele 1988). By 1882 India was officially a part of the British Empire headed by Queen Victoria. At a Congress of Berlin in 1884, Africa was divided among the colonizing nation-states of Britain, France, Germany, Spain, and Portugal. People of European descent also governed Australia and New Zealand. People of European descent dominated the Americas and had displaced many Native Americans. Russia ruled a vast empire in Eastern Europe and was to become the world's first Communist state. The Chinese were already feeling the force of European culture and politics, and Japan was forced to open to the West by American naval pressure in the 1860s. Japan had already been dominating Korea by that time. And, the domination of the Islamic empire by the Turks ended when the Arabs and European allies created the "Middle East" (Appiah and Gates 1997: x).

Much of European colonizing can be connected with the discourse of modernity. With the spirit of modernizing came a desire to get out and use new technologies and opportunities for travel. There was interest in learning about the rest of the world; what is not often recorded as faithfully in the histories of European explorers is how and what they learned *from* the rest of the world. Sandra Harding (1999), a feminist philosopher, argues that colonization relied heavily on "discovered" peoples' ideas, technologies, and treasures (e.g., exotic textiles and spices). She argues that the colonizers rationalized their actions through representations of places outside of Europe as unchanging and timeless—as lacking cultural histories of their own. The European colonizing nations reasoned that they were more advanced and progressive than any other region of the world. To those involved in colonizing, colonialism offered the best of European civilization to Africans, Asians, and others: the opportunity to become modern.

In fact, Harding (1999) argues, Europeans "borrowed" heavily from the traditions of the cultures that European explorers encountered. These cultures had already created complex mathematical, theoretical, and technological traditions; and they also often had goods (exotic and luxurious fabrics, jewels, spices, and other objects) that European explorers wanted. For example, as the historian Beverly Lemire (2010) documents, printed Indian cotton textiles became wildly popular in the seventeenth and eighteenth centuries in England. Calico fabrics with floral prints captured the imagination of British consumers in a variety of social classes. In the early seventeenth century, Dutch and English traders made significant profits by selling these cotton textiles, produced in India, in Europe with high markups. Between 1664 and 1678, Lemire (2010) notes that the value of the English East India Company's textile imports represented 60 to 70 percent of their trade. The British textile industry reacted, and a discourse of cultural anxiety ensued:

> Oriental fabrics were imbued with alien and gendered characteristics. They were depicted as effeminate luxuries, corrupting in particular the female populace with their lightness and brightness, while impoverishing deserving artisans. The language of this debate was frequently couched in terms of gender antagonisms with women asserting their right to dress as they pleased and weavers claiming the right to work and constrain the choice of apparel for women, as necessary. (Lemire 2010: 201–2)

There seems to have been a kind of "disconnect" between British textile production and consumption. In 1721 most East Indian textiles were banned in England, and British textile manufacturers had the legal protection that gave them some leeway to work on developing new systems to "knock off" Indian cotton calico and chintz fabrics (Lemire 2010). Indian scholars have shown how India's highly developed cotton textile industry provided both technical and artistic ideas—especially related to dyeing and printing—which helped to advance the British textile industry. Britain needed to suppress or "de-industrialize" India's textile industry in order to enhance the development of its own industry in the late eighteenth and nineteenth centuries (Harding 1999: 32).

Harding (1999) argues that modern science is and has been multicultural, because it incorporated or *appropriated* the elements of a wide range of knowledge traditions into it. The same can certainly be said of fashion, which has been represented in Euro-American societies as modern and Western, as we have seen. Indeed, as the hegemonic story or discourse goes, fashion originated in Europe. What emerged as modern or Western fashion has spread to other parts of the world, along with processes of industrialization. In other words, wearing Western style-fashion-dress is part of the process of becoming modern. Ethnic dress, in contrast, is hence associated with traditional societies and is soon replaced with modern or Western dress when the benefits of modernizing are discovered. And the West, according to this story, has led the way in the industrial production of textiles and fashion, as in other scientific and technological advances.

Yet the story is actually more complex and more entangled. Historically and currently, many Western fashion trends derive from cultures not included in the hegemonic narrative of Western modernity. *Cultural appropriation* involves taking elements from another culture, often without giving credit to that culture or, worse still, at the expense of that culture (Ashley and Plesch 2002). Cultural appropriation becomes most problematic, from a cultural studies perspective, when there are power differences between the cultures, and when a more powerful "taking" culture has the motivation to dominate a less powerful culture (Ashley and Plesch 2002). When is cultural appropriation a somewhat innocent or even respectful process of aesthetic influence or inspiration, with the appropriate degree of credit or profit attributed to the other culture in question? When is it just a matter of cultural "borrowing"? (And when/how will the other culture be "paid back"?) Who profits? And how do people feel about having their culture taken?

Asian American studies scholar Sunaina Maira (2000) has studied cultural appropriation in the form of Indo-chic: the mainstream popularity of South Asian cultural markers and practices such as refashioned saris, styles worn in Bollywood Hindi films, *mehndi* (patterns painted on hands with henna), and *bindi* dots on the forehead. The young South Asian American women with whom Maira spoke were "deeply ambivalent about the implications of *mehndi*'s mainstreaming." She found that their feelings of anger regarding the appropriation of *mehndi* was "sometimes mixed with varying degrees of curiosity, pride, pleasure, guilt, and confusion." One woman, Shamita, had grown up in Calcutta, India:

> For us it [mehndi] goes back many years, it's part of our culture. . . . Sometimes I feel annoyed because we're so used to seeing it in the proper context . . . at home, you wear a sari, you have the proper jewelry, the proper makeup. . . . I also don't know where it's from, and the history, but we've just seen it around us, or we know the context, where it stands, but people not from South Asia wouldn't know where it stands. (Maira 2000: 350)

Maira goes to point out the contradictions or ambivalence in Shamita's comments: it is not that culture should be fossilized as static, but she does want to see her culture's symbols in a context that "fits" (and acknowledges that even she doesn't know everything she might know about her cultural symbols' histories).

Visual culture, including style-fashion-dress, is especially susceptible to appropriation, especially in the context of a global economy and digital technologies that make it possible to borrow an image and modify it slightly at the stroke of a computer key. Global capitalism, in fact, thrives on the principle of *flexibility* (Harvey 1990) in a variety of ways. Flexibility is a component of the circuit of style-fashion-dress model in Figure 2.4, and it propels the flow of materials and images in circuit. Since the 1980s, especially, textile and apparel production has thrived on processes known as flexible manufacturing with a flexible labor pool and an economic system of flexible accumulation. Distribution is also highly flexible, with Internet imagery and shopping, retail "pop-up" stores that are temporary events, and counterfeit goods sold on blankets that can be quickly folded up when law enforcers appear. Consumption, too, is flexible; with "fast fashion," clothes are more affordable (but don't last as long). Consumers can mix and match separates (tops, bottoms, and accessories), and those items to which they become attached often are those with *contextual flexibility*: the quality of "going" with a lot of other separates and providing a sense of continuity across changes in style-fashion-dress (Kaiser and Ketchum 2005).

As the circuit of style-fashion-dress model reminds us, the degree of flexibility in subject formation is limited by regulation, as well as subject positions. The limits to flexibility will be discussed in greater detail in Chapter 8. The following chapters (3 through 7) locate transnational, intersectional fashion subjects in the overlapping contexts of national, ethnic and racial, classed, gendered, and sexual subject positions. But first we will consider—to close this chapter—two examples of transnational, intersectional fashion subjects.

First, let us briefly explore the case of a (probably female) shopper at Anthropologie, a retailer headquartered in Philadelphia, Pennsylvania, in the United States, but with stores throughout the entire United States and expanding to Europe. Founded in 1992 by Richard Hayne—who had been an anthropology major in college—in Wayne (a suburb of Pennsylvania), Anthropologie (owned by the parent company of Urban Outfitters) is in many ways a store that capitalizes on transnational, intersectional female subjectivities. The store evokes feelings of romantic, whimsical, and cross-cultural happiness: an eclectic assortment of goods (roughly two-thirds clothes and one-third household accessories) in locally designed settings that exude global aesthetics tailored to euromodern tastes. Yet a group of Anthropologie staff spend over half of the year traveling through Europe, India, and the Far East, perusing and adapting (appropriating?) ideas derived from flea markets, estate sales, and antique stores (scene7.com/clients/anthropologie. asp). Female customers in the United States are encouraged to "shop like a Frenchwoman" at a global flea market. These customers tend to have the follow profile: 30 to 45 years old with a college or postgraduate education; a professional or ex-professional, in a committed family relationship with children; and with an annual household income of $150,000–$200,000. The president of Anthropologie describes their "model customer" as "well-read and well-traveled. She is very aware—she gets our references, whether it's to a town in Europe or to a book or a movie. She's urban minded. She's into cooking, gardening, and wine. She has a natural curiosity about the world. She's relatively fit" (LaBarre 2007). She is a privileged, transnational, and intersectional fashion subject.

Who produces/makes the clothes this fashion subject wears? A single store typically carries as many as 200 brands produced around the world: a mixture of exclusive contracts with clothing manufacturers and items with their own label (also contracted). In an interview, Hayne acknowledges that almost all of the apparel sold in Urban Outfitters (the parent company) is produced in Third World sewing shops; this is a pattern, he says, like nearly all of the apparel in the U.S. market. If the company were to rely on domestic union labor, he says, most customers would not be able to afford the price required to turn a profit. Still, he indicates that Urban Outfitters does not contract with factories that are overtly abusive to their workers (Valania 2003).

Let's take a second example: Forever 21. The clothes are much less expensive; in fact, some are knockoffs (appropriations) of Anthropologie clothing styles, as well as those of designers such as Diane von Furstenberg and Anna Sui. Due to the lack of legal protection for fashion products (e.g., stitching details, shapes, cuts), Forever 21 has typically settled out of court. Forever 21 was founded by the Changs, who immigrated from South Korea to California in 1981. As the company story goes, Do Won "Don" Chang was working at one of his three jobs, at a gas station in the Los Angeles area. He noticed that the customers with the best cars were fashion industry executives and made a mental note to pursue the fashion business.

Do Won and his wife Jin Sook opened their first store in a low-rent area near Pasadena, California. Jin Sook had been a hairdresser and had an eye for trendy looks. Together with their contacts within the Korean immigrant community (including managers of clothing factories) and their close affiliations with their church, they managed to foster a network of contractors and subcontractors to make the trendy ("fast fashion") clothes they sell in their stores. Their "journeyman designers" copy the latest styles on high fashion runways or at trade shows and, with the help of "flexible, eager manufacturers" in the Los Angeles area, they are often able to get their trendy styles on racks or shelves in their stores before the originals are available (Koyen 2008). The Changs—now in their 50s—began their journey as transnational, intersectional fashion producers/subjects with very poor origins. Their ethnicity and national origin, their social class, and their aspirations all intersected to shape their fashion subjectivities as producers. Now with hundreds of stores around the world and revenues over $1 billion per year, the Changs live in Beverly Hills but maintain their headquarters in the Los Angeles garment district. They are probably best known for another subject position, however:

their evangelical Christian religion. Each Forever 21 shopping bag bears the chapter and verse of a famous Bible verse, John 3:16 (Koyen 2008).

The critical theorist Karl Marx once said that capitalism thrives on contradictions. The Changs give their time and money generously to Christian missions around the world and support emerging Christian designers; yet they have been criticized and sued for design piracy and for unfair garment labor practices. In 2001, dozens of garment workers, through the Garment Worker Center in Los Angeles, filed suit against Forever 21 on the grounds that they had been denied wages they earned, and that they had been exposed to dangerous working conditions. The Garment Worker Center organized student groups (e.g., Students Against Sweatshops) and consumers to boycott Forever 21, which maintained that it was a retailer (distributor) and not an apparel manufacturer. In 2004, the garment workers—mostly Mexican American and themselves immigrant fashion subjects—settled with Forever 21, which admitted no wrongdoing but that made a commitment "to improve working conditions in L.A." (Earnest 2004).

Together, the case studies of Anthropologie and Forever 21 remind us that producers, distributors, and consumers alike are transnational fashion subjects with intersectional subject positions (social class, ethnicity, age, religion). We all become entangled in the circuit of style-fashion-dress and within the cultural discourses that shape not only what we wear but also how we feel.

–3–

Fashioning the National Subject

The world has not always been divided into the "patchwork quilt of differently colored countries" that is shown on today's maps and globes (Calhoun 1997: 13). Making maps of nations is a relatively modern process; it involves a neat delineation of borders and represents the world in a way that looks outward from one's own positioning. On a regular basis, new nations join the United Nations. Nations have "no clearly identifiable births, and their deaths, if they ever happen, are never natural" (Anderson 2006: 205). This description applies to fashion, as well, although nations present themselves as more stable, certain, serious, official, and political than fashion.

NATION ≠ ESSENCE

In cultural studies terms, a *nation* is not a thing or an essence that necessarily has a culture wholly distinct from other nations. Rather, a nation is a context and a site of articulation and ongoing formation: one that does not always neatly coincide with one's ethnic or other subject positions, or with the idea of being a transnational subject influenced by fashion produced, distributed, and consumed in a global economy. Given that, at the time of this writing, there are nearly 200 nations (not all of which officially belong to the United Nations), whose nationality assumes multiple forms as a subject position. In his development of a widely accepted definition of nation as an "imagined community," Benedict Anderson (2006: 6) argued that nations have to continually re-create themselves in order to foster a sense of belonging (a "we") on the part of their "members." Some imagination is required in this process because it is not possible for all of the subjects belonging to a nation to interact with each other on a face-to-face or daily basis.

Nations, like fashions, are made, not born. Fashion, like nation, requires imagination and fosters a sense of identification. Subject formation is inextricably linked to the processes of creating and re-creating both nation and fashion. And power relations are involved in the making of both subjects and nations.

Fashion theorist Efrat Tseëlon argues that in euromodernity, the concept of nation "was premised on the tendency of dominant cultures to appropriate the national narrative by claiming a coherence and uniformity that, on closer inspection, often provide to be more imagined than real" (Tseëlon 2010: 152). The identification and storytelling of national differences have more to do with *categorical thinking* (the drive to classify and compare in order to develop a sense of identity) than they do with distinguishable cultures or characters. Yet national stereotypes persist, and a critical evaluation of the concept of nation is especially important in the context of globalization and transnationality.

There was a long history of a global exchange of goods and ideas between the East and West well before Columbus discovered the New World while searching for India in 1492. (He named the people there "Indians" to "honor his confusion"; Calhoun 1997: 7.) In the other direction, looking east from Europe, the network of routes known as the Silk Road was developed before the birth of Christ; had its heyday during the Tang dynasty in China; and played a unique role in the foreign trade of silk and other goods, as well as in political relations and the spread of religion (Wild 2011).

Along with the desire for exotic goods and new ideas, the creation of modern nations in Europe contributed to the process of European expansion, also known as *imperialism* (the desire to expand one's nationalism into a broader empire) and *colonialism* (the desire to create settlements in other locations around the world). Modern European nations emerged, in part, to create a system for acquiring resources for—and extending—the production of goods, and to foster new consuming markets for goods. European nations were not pure in terms of ethnicity or religion. Essential national identities had to be created to make people feel that they were internally united and different from people in other nations (Calhoun 1997: 7). Imperialism and colonialism were belief systems that offered the incentive and need to create modern nations in Europe.

Another dimension of national representation is internal to the nation: its frequently nostalgic relationship to rural, peasant, ethnic attire. The dress historian Lou Taylor (2004) argues that rural peasant attire was never static but rather constantly shifting, although it became represented in modern Europe as "fixed" dress. In the context of nationalist turmoil in Europe (especially Central, Eastern, and Southern Europe), in the period between 1850 and 1914, museums collected such attire as a "precious carrier of local, regional and created 'national' identities," according to Taylor (2004: 201). Some of the heightened interest in rural attire could be attributed to cultural anxieties regarding a loss of authenticity in the context of industrialization and urbanization. Collecting European peasant and regional dress served "the political and ideological purposes of nationalists, artists, designers, utopian socialists, Fascists and Communists alike" to represent various forms of nationalism. Taylor argues that royal and aristocratic landowners fostered the preservation of their own peasantry's rural way of life, because they were

(a) very aware of the high degree of rural poverty; and (b) concerned about rural depopulation, as many rural peasants migrated to cities that were becoming industrialized (Taylor 2004: 200–201).

Today, in most nations of Western European descent, national identity has been represented by passports, anthems, flags, and the like, but seldom has there been an official notion of national dress. Such nations view and represent themselves as being too complex for such a concept. To be modern, after all, means continual change and progress. Still, unofficially, certain forms of ethnic and rural dress (the French beret, the Scottish kilt, German *lederhosen*) within nations serve to capture a sense of a nostalgic "imagined community" (Anderson 2006).

A number of ironies, ambiguities, and contradictions underlie the concepts of national dress and its more exotic-sounding cousin: national costume. Here, once again, Carol Tulloch's (2010) style-fashion-dress terminology helps to remind us of the importance of context, relationships of parts to wholes, and possibilities for both continuity and change. Just as a nation is not an essence but rather a context, essentialist notions of national dress limit opportunities for interpreting ironies, ambiguities, and contradictions, as well as intersectionalities among subject positions.

As a context rather than an essence, nation offers a way to study articulations that are both political and aesthetic and that bring intersectionalities to light. Style-fashion-dress is also a context through which aesthetic and political details can be represented and deciphered. The contradictions in cultural discourses have much to do with the entanglements between an individual's subjectivity (i.e., agency, ability to represent) and his or her "national fabric" (i.e., power, hegemony).

NATIONAL AND TRANSNATIONAL SUBJECT FORMATION

How does one represent the formation of national, as well as transnational, subjectivities? Let's consider a rather extreme example. Before being crowned as Miss Universe in 2010, Miss Mexico (Ximena Navarrete) explains the significance of her choice of a red gown for the evening gown competition: "I chose red to represent the 200th anniversary of Mexico." (The year 1810 marked the beginning of Mexico's war for independence from Spanish colonial rule.) For the Best National Costume competition, Miss Mexico wore an elaborate gown and headdress that celebrates the Kukulcán Pyramids of Yucután (see Figure 3.1). In these two garment choices, Navarrete not only consciously represents her national subject position; she also expresses her subjectivity through a link between her own body and the larger "body politic" (Parkins 2002). After she is crowned, she says in an interview that she

Figure 3.1 Miss Mexico 2010 with the gown she wore for the Best National Costume component of the competition. Ximena Navarrete, who eventually won the Miss Universe title, represented Mexico with this custom-made gown inspired by the Kukulcán Pyramids of Yucután in Mexico. Photo by Alejandro Godinez/Clasos.com/LatinContent/Getty Images.

wants "the whole world to know about my country and my people." She then poses for a picture in front of a Mexican flag with the last Miss Mexico (1991) to win the Miss Universe title. Soon thereafter, she posts the following message on Facebook: "We won, long live Mexico!" President Felipe Calderon tweets that her victory will help Mexico's image as a country: "Her triumph is a source of pride and satisfaction for all Mexicans, who see in her the fruits of perseverance."

As an introduction to the rest of the chapter, it might be helpful to use Figure 3.1 as a case study to introduce some of the themes woven throughout this chapter to explore the concept of nation through style-fashion-dress.

BELONGING AND PLACE

Part of having subjectivity or agency in the world means making sense not only of *who* we are becoming but also *where* we are going. Feminist scholar bell hooks (2009: 1) describes how "place, where we belong, is a constant subject for many of us. We want to know it is possible to live on the earth peacefully." Belonging to a place (knowing where we're *from*) grounds and fosters opportunities for becoming (somewhere) in the future. Places are not static. Whether one feels a sense of belonging to a neighborhood, a rural setting, a city, or a nation, visions of place shape processes of subject formation as place/spaces undergo their own changes (more on this in Chapter 8; for now, it is useful to think about a sense of belonging/place in the context of national subject positioning).

REPRESENTING NATIONALISM

Navarrete's need to explain the meanings of her clothing choices points to the fact that there is no single natural or authentic link between nations and style-fashion-dress. She explains her choice of red (from the Mexican flag) for the evening gown competition through its foundation in the Mexican Revolution, which led to independence from Spanish colonial rule. One cannot represent nationalism without understanding histories of colonialism, including the foundational stories and symbols of revolutionary fervor used to articulate a kind of authenticity.

NATIONAL DRESS, NATIONAL COSTUME

To understand the significance of Navarrete's reference to her clothing choice celebrating the Kukulcán Pyramids of Yucután for the national costume competition, it is helpful to consider the distinction between this costume and the modern, fashionable dress worn in the evening gown competition. We have to go back more than 500 years to understand how and why colonial inclinations shaped the creation of an opposition between national or ethnic (traditional or exotic—hence the word "costume") and "modern" or "fashionable" (Western or advanced) style-fashion-dress. We also have to consider the ambiguity associated with the choice of a national costume, when there is no single national model and when there are multiple ethnic groups and indigenous, precolonial cultures in Mexico. The Mayans built the miraculous pyramids, and then the Aztecs (who conquered them) inhabited the Yucután for centuries before the Spaniards colonized the land in the sixteenth century.

NATIONALITY *AND* TRANSNATIONALITY

When Miss Mexico becomes Miss Universe, she begins to publicly represent more than a national figure; she is now an international—or better—a transnational figure. Her representation crosses national boundaries; it is universal. The shift between national and transnational representations does not merely refer to belonging to place(s), however. Rather, it underscores the cross-cutting character of subject positions of gender, ethnicity, sexuality, and social class, as well as nationality. Gender, for example, is an obvious factor in the context of the Miss Mexico and Miss Universe pageants alike. It is often women's bodies that serve the purpose of representing the nation.

GLOBALIZATION

Economic and cultural strategies aimed at worldwide influence are not new ideas. The concept of globalization is often associated with the consequences of the restructuring of capital (financing systems) around the world in the 1980s, and certainly there were enormous changes that occurred during this period of deregulation and a blurring of national economic and cultural boundaries, made possible in part through digital technologies. Fashion historian Christopher Breward (1995: 229) describes contemporary global fashion—with its branding and worldwide distribution of clothing and advertising imagery—as "a kind of contemporary Esperanto [a universal language], immediately accessible across social and geographical boundaries." The Miss Universe pageant is but one of many contexts of globalization, with its beauty-product sponsorship and worldwide advertising. The following section delves into the issues associated with globalization in fashion studies and cultural studies.

GLOBALIZATION: FROM NATIONALITY TO TRANSNATIONALITY (AND BACK)

It isn't every day that people have the opportunity to represent their national subject positions and subjectivities so publicly (as does Miss Mexico, who becomes Miss Universe) to the world. Other contexts where this might occur include international diplomatic and business conferences, the United Nations, the Olympics, and the World Cup. Yet everyone's processes of subject formation are entangled in some ways with those of nation formation, transnational projects, and globalization.

Is globalization a remarkable opportunity for a cross-cultural exchange of ideas and understandings? Or, is it a nasty scramble for wealth and power? Does it foster an erosion of local cultures and traditions, or does it pose new ways of relating across cultural boundaries? Part of the complexity of the new corporate strategies is that they seem to suggest a lot of things at once. They include issues of political economy, such as the "race to the bottom" for the lowest labor costs for garment production to maximize corporate profits. Yet they may also include openings for innovative business models. Among the giant global "fast fashion" clothing companies (e.g., GAP of San Francisco in the United States, the British Topshop, Benetton of Italy, H&M of Sweden), Zara of Spain, owned by the company Inditex, initially flourished with a business model based on production that was closer to home (Spain, Portugal, India, Turkey, and Morocco; see Figure 3.2) but has eventually spanned to Vietnam, China, and other locations around the world. One of the secrets of Zara's appeal has been its garments' fashionability and feeling of quality. Its trend spotters constantly travel the world and surf the Internet to monitor trends at the same time Zara store managers send instant consumer feedback to Zara's in-house designers. Styles turn on a dime, with as little as a two-week lead time from feedback or inspiration to receipt of the garment in stores around the world, shipped from Zara's centralized distribution center (Tokatli 2008).

With production becoming increasingly transnational, is there a possibility of national fashion? Fashion theorist Simona Segre Reinach (2010) notes the national storytelling required to promote "made in Italy" fashion:

Figure 3.2 Moroccan garment workers in a factory owned by Nerminia, who manufactures primarily for Spanish clients such as Inditex (Zara). Photo by ABDELHAK SENNA/AFP/Getty Images.

During Pitti (men's fashion collection exhibition held in Florence, twice a year) in January 2009, men's socks were presented imprinted with the Italian national anthem, the story of Garibaldi and other cornerstones in the history of Italian national unity. The Lavazza Calendar for 2009 features episodes ranging from Roman history, with the Wolf and the Twins, Futurism, to La dolce vita (Fellini 1960), through the Renaissance, still the most quoted reference when the words "Italy," "creativity," and "fashion" are mentioned together. (Reinach 2010: 206)

Reinach goes on to indicate that the word "authentic" does not apply well to fashion, which "is always the result of many encounters and hybridization." Instead, she illustrates how contemporary communication strategy in Italy draws on history, which has "a peculiar role in fashion, especially when applied to matters of national identity" (Reinach 2010: 208). Ironically, she says, the "Renaissance artisan creativity associated with 'made in Italy' . . . is a considerable historical falsehood, since 'made in Italy' was born from abandoning artisan work for industrial fashion" in the 1980s with designers in Milan such as Armani, Ferré, Missoni, and Krizia: the creators of "made in Italy" (Reinach 2010: 210). Further complicating the picture is the fact that many of Italy's global luxury brands are produced in China, whereas Italian fast fashion brands are more likely to actually be made in Italy (often by Chinese factories that have relocated to Italy).

Although much of what we know as a globalized fashion business can be linked to contemporary digital technologies, speed and flexibility in production and distribution, and ease of imitation through trend spotting, globalization can probably best be understood through larger histories of intercultural and transnational interactions. Cultural studies scholar Stuart Hall (1997) argues that there has been a major transition in the technical, economic, and cultural forces connected with globalization. He suggests that there has been a shift from a British model of globalization, associated with the colonization around the world, to a U.S. model of globalization, characterized by a kind of transnational mass culture (Hall 1997). Both forms of globalization can be described as hegemonic because there are struggles over subjectivity and representation at play in each. Hall suggests that the British model was based on the construction of English identity as a kind of ethnicity, and it emerged over the last 300 years as a way of emphasizing the *difference* between England as a nation and other nations or cultures:

To be English is to know yourself in relation to the French, to the hot-blooded Mediterraneans, and to the passionate, traumatized Russian soul. You know that you are what everybody else on the globe is not. (Hall 1997: 174)

Although there are also certainly elements of "identity *not*" in the U.S. identity (e.g., not British in the 1770s when independence was being sought), the hegemonic U.S. way of developing its national identity has tended to revolve around the myth of a melting pot of ethnic diversity (discussed further in Chapter 4) and the idea of absorbing or appropriating difference. This model of globalization involves the quicker and more dramatic flow of money, images, brands, and goods across national boundaries; it is associated with global capitalism. It fosters an ethos of transnational hybridization, as national differences become blurred, absorbed, and appropriated (Canclini 2000). American companies such as Anthropologie, Forever 21, and Gap; the Spanish Zara; the Italian Benetton; the British Topshop; and the Swedish H&M represent hybridization as they absorb and appropriate cultural and national differences.

RETHINKING NATIONAL HISTORIES, MAPPING THE WORLD

The restructuring of global capital that occurred in the 1980s is one factor contributing to a major rethinking of the concept of nation. Well into the first half of the twentieth century, a nation had been imagined as a homogeneous community, framed by a shared history, language, culture, and economy. Globalization challenged this assumption, as geopolitical boundaries surrendered to the transnational flow of capital and commodities. At the same time, there was an increased awareness and understanding of ethnic diversity *within* nations, as well as ethnic belongings *across* nations, thanks to the development and expertise of ethnic studies and diaspora studies, discussed further in Chapter 4. The blurring of national boundaries does not mean, however, that national subject positions are erased. Rather, they intersect in complicated ways with other subject positions (i.e., ethnicity, gender, social class) within and beyond the nation.

Perhaps the cultural anxiety surrounding the rethinking of the meaning of nation in a transnational or global context has contributed to a renewed interest in nationalism. This interest is clearly evident in fashion studies, which is pursuing deeper understandings of style-fashion-dress in relation to place and space, as well as time and history.

There is a long history of thinking about nations as having distinct characters or cultures, and style-fashion-dress has been part of this thinking. Historian Eugenia Paulicelli (2010) conducted a close textual analysis of costume books (two editions of a book called *Habiti*) published by Cesare Vecellio, who had the goal of "mapping the world" through a kind of encyclopedic approach to national dress, first in 1590 and then in 1598. Paulicelli notes that Vecellio was extremely curious about other cultures and geographic spaces, but Vecellio inevitably depicted others as *different than* the European norm with which he was most familiar: Italy and Venice. Paulicelli sought to decipher "national character" using style-fashion-dress as a guide. In sixteenth-century Italy, there was already considerable anxiety about the blurring of many kinds of boundaries associated with gender, identity, moral codes, and appearance. This anxiety surfaced in the context of early modernity and a lessening hegemonic influence of the Catholic Church on moral codes, including appearance. Somehow the sorting of others in the world by national costumes (see Figure 3.3), perhaps, provided a sense of world order through classification, offering some assurance that nations, at least, could be organized to assuage anxieties about other kinds of blurred boundaries.

Vecellio used Rome and its history to represent a Eurocentric vision of the world where Christianity is a foundational context from which to imagine other nations and to represent their stories (Paulicelli 2010: 142). In part, this foundational choice was a strategy to ameliorate Italy's relative lack of power in Europe at the time of his writing. He characterized Italy, in general, as a site of tremendous diversity based on the fact that Italy has been "prey to foreigners and the site of fate; and for these reasons it should not be a

Figure 3.3 Cesare Vecellio's 1590s depiction of a Persian man in *Habiti*.

surprise if here one can see much more variety in clothing styles than in any other nations or regions" (Paulicelli 2010: 142). He worked with the artist Baldo Penna to represent the Italian in the book as a naked man, carrying a piece of wool cloth on his shoulder. No single form of dress could capture Italians, Penna explained; the naked "national character" himself could choose a tailor to cut his clothing according to his own taste and agency. The nation, as a whole, was too complex to be represented by one costume, he suggested. In contrast, other nations could be represented visually to offer some order to the chaos of a changing world. Vecellio illustrated Turkey, Africa, and America with exotic costumes. He drew a contrast between France and Spain and distinguished class and social status as they intersect with gender. Paulicelli notes that Vecellio seemed to be aware that his project could only be partial, "no matter how great his anxiety to map the entirety of the world through dress" (Paulicelli 2010: 156).

EUROPEAN EXPANSION: TEXTILE TRADE AND NATIONAL SYMBOLISM

Over the course of 400 years after Columbus's "discovery" of the New World in the Americas, while looking for India, Western Europe became dominant economically and politically. Colonies were established in Africa, the Americas, Asia, and the Pacific Islands (Appiah and Gates 1997: x). In the sixteenth century, indigenous cultures in the Americas were colonized by the Portuguese in Brazil and the Spanish in Central and South America; some native populations were almost entirely wiped out by warfare, disease, and genocide. Fabrics woven on narrow looms are described as "pre-Columbian," in contrast to those woven on wider looms, initially introduced by the Spanish in the sixteenth century (Kennett 1995: 26). African slaves were brought to the New World to produce goods in an economy built on free labor. They were virtually stripped of their identities (language, form of dress) and made to conform to the preferences of those who dominated them.

One of the luxury goods sought through world travels and trade was silk, as we have seen in the discussion of the Silk Road. Another good that was pursued was fur, which Europeans regarded as exotic. A lively fur trade developed between Britain and the New World. North America had become a source of wealth to Western Europe by the seventeenth century, as European traders began to dominate indigenous peoples' modes of gathering and hunting through such means as the Hudson Bay Company, established in 1670 (Emberley 1997: 67).

Julia Emberley argues that fur fashions became a symbolic, feminine "prop for the edifice of imperial trade and colonization in the 'New World' " (Emberley

1997: 17). Yet there were contradictions built into this symbolic dominati
While the British state was in full support of economic expansion, which the
fur trade represented and helped to accomplish, much of the spirit of British
nationalism was a discourse that had a strong need to protect the domestic
economy and its favored commodity: wool, the material and symbol of masculine tailoring (Emberley 1997: 63–64). Some historians have shown how
these feelings about wool could be equated with a kind of *masculine* British nationalism, associated with the business classes' need to establish an
identity that was differentiated from "feminine," foreign influences, such as
silks from France or China, and furs from the New World. During the seventeenth century, when trade with the New World was contributing to the growth
of the business classes, a British writer John Evelyn expressed concern that
mode (the French word for fashion) was the enemy of British national loyalty.
Instead, British masculinity needed to be "virile and comely" (i.e., manly, tailored, worthy of the business class):

> Doubtless, would the great Persons of England but owne their Nation, and assert
> themselves as they ought to do, by making choice of virile, and comely Fashion.
> (Evelyn quoted in Emberley 1997: 65)

Evelyn and others became anxious that Britain might lose its dominance if
it became too susceptible to the influence of the French, Oriental, and other
modes of consumption that they viewed as feminine and weakening. At the
same time, the economic benefits of trade with these other nations were a
vital part of Britain's successes, so there was some cultural ambivalence and
anxiety built into the discourse of nationalism. To help to deal with this ambivalence, it seems, there was a need to close off options perceived as un-
manly and un-British. British national identity was represented in such a way
that symbolized its difference from or identity *not* in relation to foreign others.

By the late eighteenth and early nineteenth centuries, modern nations had
emerged in Europe. Part of the process of creating modern nations was the
development of style-fashion-dress that represented modernity and nationalism alike. The hegemonic look epitomizing British national identity, for example, was the male business suit. It was not a coincidence that this suit
was also associated with white, Western, upper middle-class masculinity. Or,
perhaps more accurately, it was a style that was *not* associated with exotic or
colonized others, "Oriental" influences, the working classes, or women.

Meanwhile, the same British business classes were profiting from the
economic and political arrangements with the colonies. By the eighteenth
century, the British East India Company was preventing Indian peasants and
artisans from spinning and weaving their own cloth. The British, as other Europeans (e.g., the Portuguese) had been trading with India since the sixteenth

century. India had had a thriving textile export industry, but the British East India Company had a powerful economic influence and forced India, by the early nineteenth century, to export raw goods (e.g., cotton) to England in exchange for British manufactured products (e.g., printed fabrics). Indian peasants were hired locally to cultivate and dye cotton in a system that has been called "indigo slavery." The once flourishing agricultural and artisanal classes in India were decimated; thousands of skilled craftspeople were unemployed. The native industries were restructured around Britain's manufacturing and marketing needs; this restructuring was justified in terms of a "civilizing mission" (Sharpe 1993). The traditional hand weaving industries were hurt further when cotton mills were established in Bombay and Ahmedabad in the 1850s, as India developed its own industrialized textile business. The handloom industry might be gone altogether today if it were not for governmental programs to sustain India's craft heritage (Lynton 1995: 9). Nationalist movements within India helped it to declare its independence from colonial power. Handwoven cotton became a symbol of self-reliance through national independence from the British textile industry. Mohandas Karamchand Gandhi, the Indian leader, wore the traditional *dhoti* (cloth draped around the waist and legs and knotted at the waist) and shawl of handwoven cotton. India reappropriated the European concept of nation as an imagined community to establish an identity, using traditional Indian symbols.

NATION-STATE AND STYLE-FASHION-DRESS: WORKING THE HYPHEN

So far, we have been focusing on nation as an "imagined community," but when nations become recognized geographically and politically, internally and externally, they can be characterized as *nation-states.* Feminist theorist Judith Butler points out that the state is not always the nation-state, and the nation is not always the nation-state, but the two get "cobbled together through a hyphen" (Butler and Spivak 2007: 2). She asks: "[W]hat work does the hyphen do? Does the hyphen finesse the relation that needs to be explained? Does it mark a certain soldering that has taken place historically? Does it suggest a fallibility at the heart of the relation?" (Butler and Spivak 2007: 2).

Butler's questions about working the hyphen could apply, as well, to style-fashion-dress. Nation-state and style-fashion-dress are both terms that suggest, as Tulloch (2010) notes, critical questions about parts and wholes. The same is true of hyphenated national/ethnic identities, such as Asian-American and Mexican-American. Cultural anxieties that revolve around "working the hyphen" may account for some of the contradictions, ambiguities, and ambivalences surrounding each term. In the context of the nation-state, for example, it is instructive to examine the issue of the "right balance," or what is the "best articulation" between subject formation (and associated liberties or rights as citizens as individuals) and regulation by the state (presumably for the good of the whole nation)? When, for example, does the style-fashion-dress equation tilt toward uniformity in order to represent the nation, if not the nation-state? Let's consider two case studies to think through the importance of context (e.g., time, space, cultural and state politics) in cultural debates/discourses that bear some relation to the idea of a national uniform during the (a) French Revolution (the 1780s and 1790s) and (b) the Cultural Revolution in China (1966–1976).

FRENCH REVOLUTION

By the 1770s in France—during the reign of King Louis XVI—European Enlightenment philosophy and politics had contributed to a popular desire to replace old ways of thinking about being subjects of the "state" (the monarchy) with principles of individual liberty and expression. Dire economic conditions for much of the public, including poverty and starvation, fostered the sense of a disconnect between the lavish spending and decadent lifestyle associated with the royal court (epitomized during the reign of Louis XIV, the grandfather of Louis XVI), on the one hand, and the everyday life experiences of the courts' subjects.

The French Revolution sought to replace old ways, especially fashionable excess and hierarchy, with symbols of nationalism such as the red and blue *cockade* (a knot of ribbons usually attached to a hat) and *sans culottes* (i.e., long working class trousers, as opposed to aristocratic breeches; see Figure 3.4). Fashion was a deadly serious matter, as the French people could tell at a glance who supported the revolution as opposed to the monarchy.

Some European Enlightenment writers went so far as to argue for a *national uniform* as an alternative to the lure of fashion, excess, and status hierarchies (Möser [1775] 2004). During the French Revolution (1789 through the 1790s), based in part on Enlightenment thinking, some authors argued for a national uniform that made no major distinction between military and civilian attire. The *sans culottes* style—although not a uniform per se—came to represent the national subject. The underlying assumption was that citizenship was a masculine construct; men were to be on call 24/7 for military service as needed.

In *The Empire of Fashion: Dressing Modern Democracy*, Gilles Lipovetsky (1994) notes how the nation-state's marking of geopolitical boundaries through dress shifts a sense of responsibility from community as a whole, toward the individual as a "national subject." The Enlightenment thinkers who

Figure 3.4   "The Pretty Sans-Culotte under Arms with the Sans-Culotte of August 10th." Redrawn version (1842) of original drawing in 1792 by Émile Wattier in Augustin-Challamel, "Histoire-musée de la république Française, depuis l'assemblée des notables," Paris, Delloye, 1842. www.wikimediacommons.com.

argued against the idea of a national uniform reasoned that it would under-mine the idea of a national subject. A free nation, they submitted, required the ability for citizens to express themselves, whereas a national uniform would "suppress and stifle the taste of a people" (Witte [1791] 2004: 78). What was the appropriate way to articulate individual freedom, as compared to the larger, collective spirit of a new nation? If the nation-state was to re-quire everyone to wear a uniform, wouldn't this contradict the whole idea of democracy?

Not everyone was viewed equally as a national subject, however. The inter-sectionalities among national, gender, and class subject positions were key to the French Revolution. Although some women adopted symbols of the French

Revolution, they were not perceived as full citizens (Weber 2006). The new nationalism was gendered as masculine and also classed as working class. If, indeed, the project of the European Enlightenment was to make "men out of boys" (Butler and Spivak 2007: 116), then perhaps it is no accident that the American and French revolutionary movements of the 1770s and 1780s coincided with the so-called masculine renunciation of fashion (discussed further in Chapter 6).

The French Revolution was decidedly antiroyalist: against the monarchy associated with King Louis XVI and Queen Marie Antoinette. But it was Marie Antoinette who came to symbolize all that was wrong with the monarchy. Marie Antoinette, born in Austria and "traded" as a royal family member to France to marry Louis XVI, was trained as a young girl to become the future queen of France. Her roles in France were to represent the nation and to produce an heir for the future throne. In Austria, she had learned how to embody the French monarchy in a feminine fashion: how to carry herself and how to glide in the style of the French court. It turns out that this was necessary but not sufficient for the French public.

Marie Antoinette was already suspect because she was Austrian (and hence foreign), enjoyed luxury goods when there was rampant poverty in France (she earned the nickname Madame Deficit; see Figure 3.5), and was blamed for not readily producing a male heir to the crown. The media also questioned her sexuality because she spent so much time with female courtesans (and not enough time, according to critics, working on heterosexual reproduction—a charge that could not be fairly attributed only to her, but her foreign "otherness" carried over to other stigmatized subject positions). Marie Antoinette experienced gender trouble, as well as national, sexual, and class trouble. And much of this trouble played out through cultural anxieties about her style-fashion-dress:

> Upon first reaching the border between her mother's and her future husband's domains, she was stripped of her "Austrian" clothes, themselves expressly commissioned as reminders of her Frenchness, in order to obfuscate her true national origins. She recalled her great forebear Louis XIV by dressing and riding like a man, but disavowed her queenly stature by adopting styles accessible to women outside her own, rarefied sphere. At the Paris Opéra and the Petit Trianon, she gleefully checked her august identity at the door, only to reclaim it with a vengeance once her revolutionary foes demanded a more systematic and lasting suspension of royal authority. Even the white gown she wore for her execution simultaneously overwrote and underscored her status as the fallen monarchy's martyr. (Weber 2006: 291–92)

Aristocratic men in colorful attire and expensive materials were also the target of revolutionaries aiming for a more democratic nation. Many bourgeois

Figure 3.5 In June 1778 there was a clash between the French and the British navies; the French navy was supporting the United States against the British. The French ship, *La Belle Poule*, was victorious, and Marie Antoinette—in the spirit of nationalism—celebrated the victory with her hairstyle "pouf," topped with a replica of the victorious ship. Unfortunately, the hairstyle elicited a backlash by the French public, who was generally not impressed with the extravagance and was also not pleased with the huge sums of money France was spending on the American Revolution when there was widespread poverty and hunger within the French nation (Weber 2006: 123). Courtesy of Art Resource Inc. (artres.com).

and, especially, aristocratic men toned down their appearances to avoid looking like they thought they were above working class men. Accentuated cultural anxieties—indeed, fear and dread—contributed to innovative and ambiguous articulations through style-fashion-dress, such as the vest shown in Figure 3.6

Figure 3.6 Aristocratic man's vest during the French Revolution (1789–1794). Courtesy of the Los Angeles County Museum of Art (lacmaorg). Purchased with funds provided by Suzanne A. Saperstein and Michael and Ellen Michelson, with additional funding from the Costume Council, the Edgerton Foundation, Gail and Gerald Oppenheimer, Maureen H. Shapiro, Grace Tsao, and Lenore and Richard Wayne. Photo © 2012 Museum Associates/LACMA.

and displayed at the Los Angeles County Museum of Art (LACMA) in an exhibit called "Fashioning Fashion." This vest, although colorful (predominately red, blue, and white: the colors of the revolution) and decorative, apparently belonged to an aristocratic man who sought to display his support for the revolutionary cause. A caterpillar on the right lapel represents the French slang term *en chenille*, which meant being casually dressed (as well as caterpillar). Generally, aristocrats would "metamorphose into a colorful, flamboyant 'butterfly' through evening attire," but on the left lapel of the vest, the "airborne butterfly has its colorful wings clipped by an enormous pair of scissors." On the vest's pockets are well-known French sayings. The right pocket bears the phrase *"L'habit ne fait pas le moine"* ("The habit does not make the monk"), which roughly parallels the English expression, "Don't judge a book by its cover," and may also reference the revolutionary dismantling of the Catholic Church (associated with the monarchy). The other pocket contains the expression *"Honi soit qui mal y pense,"* which is medieval French for "Shame upon him who thinks evil of it" (an old English expression; English pastimes such as drinking tea had become very popular in France in the 1780s). The time and thought (and labor, undoubtedly not the wearer's) that went into this vest speak volumes about the importance of fashion in politics:

Flaunting the Revolutionary colors while protesting that clothes don't make the man, he wore his politics on his sleeve even as he distanced himself from them. The vest gives us a snapshot of a man—and a nation—undergoing a butterflylike transformation but, for the moment, still having it both ways. (Takeda and Spilker 2010: 155)

CHINESE CULTURAL REVOLUTION (AND BEYOND)

Cultural anxieties also became intensified during the Chinese "Great Prole-tarian" Cultural Revolution (1966–1976). This revolution did not involve the overthrow of an existing regime but rather an enforcement of the principles associated with the earlier (1949) communist revolution, which had resulted in the founding of the People's Republic of China. Mao Zedong was the Chi-nese leader between 1949 and 1976, and he attempted to destroy traditional culture, which had a rich history among the wealthy, at least, in terms of tex-tiles and fashion. He also wanted to resist Western bourgeois modernity; he and his Communist Party aimed for a different (anticapitalist) form of moder-nity. Their efforts had only been partially successful; coastal cities such as Shanghai, which had been semicolonized, still had a vibrant fashion scene that included Western business suits and leather shoes for men and the cheongsam and high heels for women. In other cities, some people still wore the traditional long robes and mandarin jackets associated with ancient China and the stratified system of ranking associated with Confucianist philosophy. Both Western modern fashion and Chinese traditional garb, as well as the be-lief systems that they represented, were rejected by Communists; Mao began to pursue an agenda of more radical change in China (Mei 2005).

Private companies in China merged with state-owned companies, so that the state would have more control over the economy. There was a shortage of materials, and in 1954 the state issued a coupon system for fabrics, food, and furniture (Tsui 2010: 15). During the Cultural Revolution (1966–1976), militarism became embedded in national subject positions as millions of young people moved from cities "up to the mountains and down to the coun-try" to engage in hard labor wearing the green military uniform (with a red badge on the sleeve) of the Red Guard, forcibly recruited from universities and high schools. This adaptation of the "liberation army uniform" became "the most revolutionary, pure and reliable symbol" of what it meant to be Chinese during this period (Mei 2005: 103). The uniform actually derived earlier from Sun Zhongshan (or Sun Yat-Sen in Cantonese), the "Father of Modern China." A tailor, Tian Jia-Dong, modified the style of the suit to make it more flattering for Chairman Mao, who was physically large. The suit became looser overall, the collar became wider, and the corner of the collar became squared (rather than rounded) (Tsui 2010: 16).

When a version of this military-inspired garb became the uniform for the Red Guard on young people's bodies, it came to represent the hegemonic nation-state's vision of the future. The concept of the military- and revolutionary-inspired suit spread throughout the nation with some variations. Christine Tsui (2010) asserts that "No country has ever been influenced so dramatically, across such a large geographic area and long period of time, over people's daily wear as has China" by the Cultural Revolution (17). Juanjuan Wu (2009) explains this conformity by the tense political environment, in which "the fear of being labeled reactionary led people to speak, act, and dress like other, since blending into the crowd was certainly safer than standing out" (2).

Yet Wu (2009) goes on to argue that despite a "rigid uniformity" in dress, the Cultural Revolution did not kill fashion (2). Instead, fashion just assumed a "different mask" of (a cover for a wider range of belief systems). In her nuanced analysis, Wu submits that there was a complex paradox or contradiction operating in the context of proletarian (working class) ideology of the Cultural Revolution. On the one hand, because fashion was associated with Western bourgeois cultures, Chinese people needed to avoid appearing concerned with "superficial, outward appearances." On the other hand, "any deviation from the rigid dress code could result in life-threatening consequences, and in this sense, ironically, one had to be fully aware of dress and appearance" to an unprecedented degree" (2). Hence, the minutest of details became very significant and assumed a deepened sense of importance, emotionally and politically.

To the Western eye, everyone in China looked alike (terms such as "blue ants" and "gray ants" were used to describe masses of Chinese people). However, there were a number of subtleties and differences that existed within the broader conformity. Colors included olive green (the Red Guard military garb) and white, in addition to blue and gray (Wu 2009: 3). And while there were not major differences between men's and women's styles overall, a number of details surfaced in the clothes that women often made for themselves to infuse a touch of femininity: Garments were sometimes decorated with floral patterns on inner or fake collars or scarves (Wu 2009: 4). Features such as these also helped to extend the use of materials, which were scarce. A common expression during the Cultural Revolution to describe the life of a new outfit or pair of shoes was "three years new, three years old, and another three years of mending and patching" (Yan 2009: 211).

After Mao's death in 1979, government economic reforms toward privatization changed consumption from a frivolous bourgeois pastime into part of the political agenda. This shift, too, generated cultural anxiety. For example, in 1980, the publication *China Youth* included an editorial written by 23-year-old Pan Xiao, who questioned the practice of "unselfishly serving the people" and suggested the value of pursuing individual interests. Xiao argued that "to act for oneself subjectively is to act for others objectively" (Wu 2009: 17). This sparked a national discourse; even the secretariat of the Communist Party's Central Committee, Hu Qiaomu, agreed with Xiao, but much of the Party was concerned with the idea of citizens speaking out so openly. Another editorial in *China Youth* in 1984 backed down from the idea of individual interests.

Wu (2009) notes how there was a great deal of ambiguity in what was considered appropriate during the beginning of the transitional post-Mao period. Part of this ambiguity came from the ambivalence of the Party itself, which was anxious both to promote reforms toward a market economy *and* to reinforce a confidence in Socialism. People were encouraged to dress "to reflect the spirit of socialism" and to emancipate their "minds to become more creative" (17). It wasn't exactly clear what this meant, and the ambiguity certainly played out in style-fashion-dress. Wu describes the "shocking sight of women in high heels, long hair, and jewelry and men with their long hair, sideburns, and mustaches, along with bell-bottom pants, flowery shirts, jeans, and sunglasses" in the late 1970s (2009: 1). Since then, post-Mao China witnessed the birth of the Chinese market economy, becoming the largest powerhouse of production in the world and a significant consumer market for international luxury goods (Wu 2009: xii). Chinese fashion itself was also reborn (Tsui 2010; Wu 2009).

Nationalist symbols prevailed in both the French and Chinese Cultural Revolutions—each with their own particular cultural/economic agendas, social norms, and power dynamics (e.g., a social movement "from below" to overthrow the government versus one imposed "from above" by the government). These symbols were neither fixed nor authentic, but rather they were part of fashion processes of articulation and negotiation as means of subject formation and nation formation.

INTERSECTIONALITIES AND ENTANGLEMENTS

Articulations and negotiations of what it means to be part of a nation are multidimensional, involving complex intersections and entanglements with gender, class, ethnicity, religion, and other subject positions. Often, for example, representations of nation are on the backs of women's bodies. This is one of the reasons why the global Mattel company marketed Barbie dolls dressed in saris in India; in contrast, Ken remained dressed in American clothes. And why was Barbie dressed in a sari, instead of one of the other many styles worn in the very ethnically diverse nation of India (Grewal and Kaplan 1994)? Who determines (and how is it determined) what gets the stamp of approval as national dress? In many ways, any kind of representation in terms of national dress can be seen as hegemonic. That is, power relations are operating, and these relations tend to be based, at least in part, on the ability to persuade. This does not happen accidentally. When there are multiple ethnic or tribal groups within geopolitical boundaries, what represents a nation, and how/why? Two specific examples help to open up this question further.

The sari often represents India as national dress. Yet within the vast diversity of Indian ethnicities, religions, and traditions, the sari is one of various competing styles. Representing Hindi style (and not other religions such as Islam), the sari became recognized as the emblem of the new Indian nation once independence was achieved after years of colonialism. Governmental posters, politicians, ambassadors, and even film stars from Bollywood enhanced the recognition of India's national identity (at least as it is represented by women). Indira Gandhi, representing India in the United States and other nations in the 1970s, was very aware of her role in the popular imagination—within and beyond the boundaries of India as a nation-state—according to Mukulika Banerjee and Daniel Miller (2003) in their book, *The Sari*. She became a trendsetter with her elaborate and impressive wardrobe of saris. Bollywood film stars have continued to foster an elaborate, transnational network within a rapidly changing Indian fashion system (including the sari and the Islamic-based *salwar kameez*) that circulates in geographic locations ranging from India to Indian diasporas in South Africa, England, North America, and beyond.

The case of Kenya offers a different dynamic. As Leslie Rabine puts it, Kenya has an "unfinished quest for a national outfit" (2002: 99). Although there is a strong desire on the part of some to develop national dress to represent Kenya (for example, at international business conferences, diplomatic and other transnational political functions, and global beauty pageants and model searches), the rupture between the wide array of tribal, precolonial histories, and a history of colonialism has been too great to overcome. There are more than forty ethnic groups in Kenya; who is to decide how to represent the nation? Despite numerous design competitions and, in 1971, an appointed committee from different tribes charged with developing a national dress style, the search to represent the nation as an imagined community continues. As Rabine points out, it has been extremely difficult to distinguish Kenyan national identity from West African fabrics and styles, in general. And the garments created to represent national dress have frequently ended up representing the very contradictions they set out to resolve. Authentic identity cannot easily be defined against the contexts of neocolonialism and tribal differences.

Still, the quest continues. In Kenya's fashion industry, designers are creating clothing styles that fuse various Kenyan ethnic elements with global fashion. Olivia Ambani, the design and marketing manager with the Kenyan fashion house KikoRomeo, thinks a national dress can be achieved with a bit of flexibility:

"I think it will take people being more open to cohesion and accepting that, if it is slightly more Maasai or more Kikuyu or more Luo or more coastal, it is okay because it still is part of the country and it will still represent us," she said. Kenya does have its distinctive fabrics, most notably the checkered or striped shukas worn by the Maasai, the lessos, or khangas, which originated on the coast, and the kikoy . . . KikoRomeo's designs draw upon cultures from all over Africa. Design and marketing manager Olivia Ambani said "For instance, one of the collections that we have is Afro-punk collection. There is a lot of imagery on it, embellishment that is taken from scarification, which is something that is quite big in the continent. We give it the punk style, which is obviously something that is very British and taken from that era." (Majtenyi 2010).

In addition to colonial entanglements, representations of nationhood have a strongly gendered dimension, and it is one that—once again—is contradictory. Both men and women represent the nation through their style-fashion-dress but in different ways. Whereas masculinity has become equated with modern cosmopolitan citizenship (through, most notably, the modern business suit), femininity—especially in developing nations—has become emblematic of traditional cultural imagery. Although the particulars vary by cultural context, the idea of a national costume is one that may represent the nation as an exotic entity and often, although not always, this entity is feminized. In contrast, the concept of national uniform is more likely to be masculinized, based on its connotations of (male-ordered) citizenship. The concept of national dress is probably the most gender neutral of these three terms. Yet entanglements prevail due to histories of colonialism, racism, ethnic diversity, and religious movements. The next chapter focuses on race and ethnicity as subject positions, as they intersect in complex ways with national, religious, gender, class, and other subject positions.

–4–

Ethnicities and "Racial" Rearticulations

Nation, race, ethnicity, and religion. As interconnected subject positions, they overlap and shift in meaning along with the cultural discourses in which they are embedded. None of them are things or essences; they are more like relationships (Tabili 2003). And thinking about them as subject positions allows us to think about possibilities for these positions to shift, as hierarchies and power relations change. All involve processes of self-labeling (i.e., agency, subjectivity) as well as subjection to labels and stereotypes supplied by others. All influence, and are influenced by, styling-fashioning-dressing the body. All need to be analyzed in terms of the cultural discourses that produce and change their meanings, and styled-fashioned-dressed bodies become a vital part of such an analysis.

As we saw in Chapter 3, nations are not pure or pristine. Cultural studies scholar Ien Ang (1996) notes that nations are dynamic and have multiple racial and ethnic groups. Hence, it is inappropriate to define national identity "in static, essentialist terms" with "authoritative checklists" that gloss over cultural struggles and power dynamics of what it means to be Chinese or Kenyan, for example. China has fifty-six state-recognized ethnic groups, with overlapping forms of style-fashion-dress influenced by geography, natural resources, religion, and other cultural factors. Kenya has more than forty state-recognized ethnic groups but closer to seventy distinct ethnic communities. Not surprisingly, it has been challenging to identify a single representative form of Kenyan national dress, as discussed in Chapter 3 (Rabine 2002).

The same problem with authoritative checklists occurs when contemplating how terms such as race and ethnicity—the primary topics of this chapter—get used and applied. Race and ethnicity become entangled in everyday styling-fashioning-dressing of the body. Further, race and ethnicity cannot be separated from nation (as we saw in Chapter 3) nor in some contexts from religion. They also intersect, of course, in complex ways with other subject positions such as gender, class, and so on.

In cultural studies terms, individuals continually navigate and negotiate between processes of belonging and differentiating. Styling-fashioning-dressing the body enables articulations of what cultural studies scholars call *belonging-in-difference* (Hall 1991; Scott 2005). Imagining and belonging to a community always involve some kind of differentiation *from* other communities. Most commonly in fashion studies, race is studied in the context of certain visible features of the body, such as skin color, hair texture, or facial features. Some of these features (e.g., hair) can be readily fashioned and refashioned on a daily basis, whereas others are not so easily manipulated and have historically become bases for discrimination. In contrast, ethnic dress has been studied as clothes worn by individuals to express their belonging to a community with a common heritage and to differentiate themselves from other communities (Eicher and Sumberg 1995).

ROOTS OF RACIAL AND ETHNIC CONCEPTS

As subject positions, the concepts of race and ethnicity share some common roots: Both have been constructed as mechanisms to classify human difference. The meanings of both have shifted over time and for various political, scientific, and economic purposes. Many centuries ago, they were often used in ways that were similar to the concepts of nation and religion. During the Middle Ages, religion "meant membership of a community much more than adherence to a set of principles or beliefs," and it was common to think of individuals as born Muslim, Jewish, or Christian, just as one was born English or Persian (Bartlett 2001: 41). Similarly, in the sixteenth century (and earlier) in Europe, race described a group of people who shared ancestors—also classified as a tribe or a nation or people of common stock (e.g., the British race or the Roman race; *Oxford English Dictionary* 2010).

In the eighteenth and nineteenth centuries, the connotation of race changed along with the emergence of modern nation-states and the biological sciences. Race came to mean visible genetic markers (e.g., skin color, hair texture, facial features) as the newly emerging biological sciences sought to classify and label differences within nature: humans, as well as plants and animals (Marks 2010). Scientific classifications and hierarchies of the human species were used to justify slavery, conquest, and colonization. Between the seventeenth and nineteenth centuries, for example, slave merchants sold an estimated 2.5 million African slaves, mostly to the Americas. An important factor in these sales was capitalism, which flourished through a trade in textiles, slaves, and sugar and spices (McClintock 1995: 113). In many ways, the modern nation-state was built on the backs of bodies classified as racially different. Still, the significance attached to visible markers varied dramatically from one society to another. For example, even the slave societies of Brazil and the Old South in the United States interpreted skin color very differently. Whereas the United States structured race in binary (black versus white) terms, the Brazilian racial system has included multiple categories of skin color.

As a concept, *ethnic* derived from the Greek word *hethnic*, which meant "heathen" or "pagan" in the fifteenth century. From a European perspective, ethnic meant "pertaining to nations not Christian or Jewish" (again, religion was a strong factor). In the nineteenth century, ethnic became known as "pertaining to race; peculiar to a race or nation; ethnological—common racial, cultural, religious, or linguistic characteristics." In the United States, ethnic came to assume the connotation of foreign or exotic (*Oxford English Dictionary* 2010). And yet, there was a contradictory discourse of the United States as a melting pot of ethnicities. This model of assimilation frequently assumed a white, Northern European (and generally Protestant) background: an assimilation or melting of individuals of British, German, and Swedish national backgrounds, for example.

The connotations of ethnicity changed in the 1960s, when the civil rights movements fostered the concept of *identity politics* and an increased awareness (and critique) of cultural representations of difference (including, but not limited to racial, ethnic, national, and religious difference). This awareness led to multicultural discourses to replace the older melting pot model of assimilation (Perry 2002: 8).

In the 1960s, *ethnic minority* came to mean "a group of people different from the rest of the community by racial origins or cultural background, and usually claiming or enjoying official recognition of their group identity" (*Oxford English Dictionary* 2010).

Cultural studies scholar Stuart Hall (1990) uses the concept of ethnicity to consider how identities related to space and cultural background are not only about the past, but also about the future. Ethnicities involve becoming, as well as being. They have histories, but at the same time, they undergo constant transformation:

> Far from being eternally fixed in some essentialized past, they are subject to the continuous "play" of history, culture and power. (Hall 1990: 225)

Similarly, Maxine Craig (2002), feminist scholar and author of *Ain't I a Beauty Queen? Black Women, Beauty, and the Politics of Race*, defines race as "a set of socially constructed boundaries, practices, and commonly held meanings mapped onto a population whose members themselves represent wide physical and social diversity" (Craig 2002: 9). She draws on the concept of *racial rearticulation* (Omi and Winant 1994) to show how the boundaries, practices, and meanings of race are continually revised *both* from the bottom up (through everyday shifts in self-fashioning) *and* the top down (from media and legal categories imposed through cultural discourse). The interplay between bottom up and top down processes of racial rearticulation parallels the ongoing dynamics of subject formation: a process of negotiating and navigating subjectivity within and across diverse subject positions (e.g., race, gender, class).

In the past fifteen years or so, scholars of race and ethnicity have begun to question the idea of a binary opposition between ethnic options (self-ascribed) and racial labels (imposed by others). They have argued that the concept of ethnicity tends to be overly romanticized, especially when applied to white populations (Kang and Lo 2004). Herein lies a striking contradiction: Ethnicity becomes constructed hegemonically both as a nostalgic version of whiteness (e.g., European peasant attire) and as "racial" (non-white) otherness/difference.

Indeed, the concepts of race and ethnicity are slippery, if not blurry, in everyday life (Kang and Lo 2004). As we saw in Chapter 3, the differences between national dress and ethnic dress are also slippery and frequently hegemonic (as when one of multiple forms of ethnic dress becomes hegemonic so as to represent the nation).

In their current usage, the concept of ethnicity seems to offer more opportunities than that of race for agency, articulation, and flexibility for self- and group expression through style-fashion-dress. Racialized discourses still have a tendency to fix race as biological or natural. Yet, as subject positions, both race and ethnicity are embedded in cultural discourses; both are socially constructed. As we have seen, the meanings of both race and ethnicity are fluid and have overlapped considerably at different times in history. What is at issue in this chapter is the extent to which individuals are *subjected* to oppressive, politically motivated and scientifically justified discourses based on physical attributes (i.e., how and why their bodies become racialized), and to what extent they are able to exercise agency and to articulate subjectivities of their own choosing (i.e., those that connect with community identities and cultural belongings).

Building on Stuart Hall's work on new ethnicities, cultural studies scholars have begun to explore the ways in which new ethnicities are as much about the future as they are the past. Opening up ethnicity as a subject position linked to the parts and wholes of style-fashion-dress (Tulloch 2010), rather than dress alone, offers critical and creative possibilities for imagining both subject positions and subjectivity, regulatory cultural discourses and personal agency, and past and future.

Questions such as the following become relevant when trying to make sense of processes through which bodies become classified and through which they are fashioned to connect with places, cultural spaces, and communities—past, present, and future: Where do I belong? With whom do I identify? Where are my cultural connections? What do I believe in? Do they coincide with the boundaries of the nation-state? How do they compare with the way I look? Where was I born? Where have I moved? Where am I going? How do style, fashion, and dress become strategies to establish and reinforce the idea of having a place to *be* and *become* in the world: to have a cultural history or perspective, to be from somewhere, and to face the future with a sense of connection, as well as agency?

RACIAL REARTICULATIONS

Beginning in the eighteenth century, race was represented through scientific discourse as a biological concept—tied to physical features such as skin color, hair texture, facial features, and other visible qualities of physical appearance. These qualities have been characterized as phenotypic—meaning that they are visible properties that can be traced in large part to genetics. Yet many scholars have noted how race is, in fact, a kind of fiction. For example, anthropologist and cultural studies scholar Roger Lancaster (2003: 77) indicates that race has been understood as a biological concept for so long "because a colonial history framed the way people, including scientists, perceived and thought about human bodies," not because it was a scientifically sound system for capturing phenotypic variation ("it was not").

As noted earlier, the concept of racial rearticulation (Omi and Winant 1994; Craig 2002) enables a way of rethinking, revising, and reclaiming race away from hegemonic representations. Because scientific and cultural representations have had so much do to with how race has been constructed and interpreted, the focus in cultural studies tends to shift from race as a thing to *racial formation* as a social process that categorizes people and creates social differences. The categories that emerged in the United States and elsewhere have often revolved first and foremost along the lines of color.

COLOR

In the United States, racial formation developed along an opposition between black and white, based on a history of slavery and the "one drop rule" that identified anyone with "one drop" of blackness as black (Russell, Wilson, and Hall 1992). This binary model has become more multicultural as the political agency of Native Americans, Chicana/os, and Asian Americans has made it apparent that there are many limitations to this binary, oppositional system of racialization. After 1965, for example, when many immigrants came to the United States from Central and Latin American countries, Spanish-speaking groups in the United States were all recategorized by language and called Hispanics. Immigrants from Southeast Asia (e.g., Vietnam, Cambodia, Laos) were classified by continental origin and called Asians—along with Americans descending from China, Japan, Korea, Indonesia, the Philippines and other areas of the Pacific. Individuals descending from India, Pakistan, and Sri Lanka became distinguished regionally, and so were called South Asians. (Individuals in Great Britain with the same backgrounds are called Asians; the categories vary by nation.)

A scholar of race and ethnicity, Herbert Gans (1999) has argued that there is a tendency in the United States to continue thinking of race as biological, scientific evidence to the contrary. Whereas most scientists agree that race is "not a useful biological concept," the lay public still sees visible differences in physical features and "treats them as racial differences caused by differences in 'blood.'" Although people do vary, of course, by skin color, the real issue is what gets noticed and judged:

> Some visible bodily features that distinguish people are noticed and judged; some are noticed but not judged one way or another; and yet others are not even noticed, seeming to be virtually invisible . . . [I]n general, the bodily features of the most prestigious peoples are usually adopted as ideals of physical perfection, while features found among the lower social classes are judged pejoratively . . . *A major ingredient of the social construction of race is the determination of which visible bodily features are noticed and used to delineate race and which remain unnoticed.* (Gans 1999: 382–83)

By going unnoticed or remaining unmarked and yet simultaneously representing the hegemonic norm, whiteness becomes a privileged visible bodily feature. This privilege manifests itself from class relations to beauty and fashion systems.

The civil right movements of the 1960s challenged these systems and heightened awareness of skin color with the self-accepting "black is beautiful" ideology, for example, that challenged, if not subverted, beauty standards. Activists (e.g., the Black Panthers) contributed to a process of racial rearticulation, enabling African American women "to see beauty where they had not seen it before" (Craik 2002: 108).

Asian American Studies scholar Susan Koshy (2001) demonstrates how whiteness itself has been rearticulated at different times in U.S. history; it is not a fixed racial category. The initial boundaries of whiteness expanded to include groups (e.g., Irish, Italian, Eastern European, Jews) that were initially seen as racially distinct. She also shows how, historically, the U.S. legal system has inconsistently classified Asian Americans—constructed through a "racial" category across a wide range of national, cultural, and linguistic boundaries—as white and not white. Some similarities of inconsistent racialization have applied to the experiences of Native Americans, Latina/o, or Hispanic Americans.

American Studies scholar Ruth Frankenberg (1997) has noted how whiteness often remains transparent, unmarked by history or practice, and hence continues to maintain superiority unless it is critically and self-reflexively examined. With such a perspective in mind, Pamela Perry (2002) conducted fieldwork in two high school settings to see how "shades of whiteness" are created and interpreted. She wanted to understand how students create boundaries between white and nonwhite and to examine the extent to which they use clothing, music, and other cultural forms to make sense of shades of whiteness. She found that most believed to be white "meant that you had no culture" (Perry 2002: 2). At one of the schools, the white students— influenced by media—wore hip hop clothing and listened to rap music with- out critique from other students (white, black, or other students of color). At the other, more diverse school, however, hip hop styles marked racial and ethnic boundaries that were more difficult to cross (Perry 2002: 21). Perry's research points to the ways in which style-fashion-dress, as well as visible physical features, is subject to racialized discourses. This is one of the places where the boundaries between race and ethnicity become blurry.

Also blurry is the binary opposition between black and white. U.S. President Barack Obama's biracial or multiethnic background (a Kenyan father and white mother from Kansas) represents the complexity of race and ethnicity—never simple but more highly visible in the twenty-first century. By the end of the twentieth century, fashion industry discourse had already appropriated and celebrated "in between" or hybrid racial spaces through "ethnic marketing" (note the shift from racial to ethnic terminology):

> [N]othing is actually black and white anymore. Neither the classic blue-eyed blonde nor the African queen [is] gracing the covers of fashion magazines. In- stead, the idealized beauty standard is somewhere in between, a mélange of off-white features and khaki tones in a two-way process in which the black-female ideal lightened up from the 1970s Afrocentric period at the same time that the archetypical white woman was darkening, if only slightly, to a more mestizo pre- sentation. Once black supermodels were on board, fashion magazines and cos- metic companies quickly began featuring Latina, Eurasian, and other mixed-race faces. (Halter 2000: 178)

Although probably overstated, the above quote from 2000, looking back from the present, is a helpful reminder that discourses regarding race and ethnicity shift, as ideologies become incorporated—albeit in a limited and toned down way—into dominant visual culture. As noted by Craig (2002), the boundar- ies of social meanings of race and beauty are fluid. They are not outside of the fashion process in terms of cultural representations, appropriations, and hegemonies.

Further, systems of racial formation vary culturally and nationally. In Nica- ragua, anthropologist Roger Lancaster (1992) has described how a complex system of "color signs" becomes negotiated in relation to the ambiguities as- sociated with *mestizo* (mixed) races:

People put color into discourse in a variety of ways. The ambiguity of Nicaraguan speech about color is perhaps its crucial feature. *Negro* refers to Atlantic coast natives of African heritage, but it may also refer to dark-skinned mestizos—the majority of Nicaragua's population . . . [I]n everyday usage and for most purposes, color terms are *relational* terms. The relativity of this sort of usage turns on the intention of the speaker, comparative assumptions, and shifting contexts. Not one but three different, perpetually sliding systems are in use . . . On one day, someone would be described to me as negro, on another as *Moreno* [brown hair, brown skin], and on yet another as *blanco* [white, light hair, blue eyes]. . . . Virgilio's skin was darker than that of many African Americans in the United States, although here his indigenous appearance would undoubtedly classify him as either Native American or Hispanic. But for Nicaraguan purposes, what was he? White, brown, or black? . . . The answer is, it all depends on the context. (Lancaster 1992: 216)

Lancaster (1992) goes on to discuss how there is ambiguity in the color system in Nicaragua, and yet whiteness still holds the most power and privilege.

HAIR

In addition to skin color, physical qualities such as hair texture have been used to mark race, along with facial features and other attributes. Hair can be altered: straightened, permed, dyed, cut, braided, teased, and so on. While there is a certain amount of agency in acts such as these, it is also important to locate them in the context of racial formation and systems of hierarchy. This section—recalling the roles of subject formation and regulation in the circuit of style-fashion-dress—focuses on the politics and aesthetics associated with black hair, to illustrate how subjects alternately, and even simultaneously, internalize and resist hegemonic norms.

In her study of African American beauty, Maxine Craig (2002) notes that historically, there have been no neutral words to describe varying textures of black hair. Prior to the 1960s, hair was classified as good or bad in everyday discourse. Good hair was straight, whereas bad hair was kinky or nappy. Ritual grooming practices for girls involved a hot comb with pomade, beginning around the age of seven or eight years. In the early twentieth century, Madam C. J. Walker (1867–1919) became a prominent social activist, philanthropist, and millionaire after she invented, produced, and marketed conditioning hair care products for African Americans. Born the daughter of former slaves and orphaned at age seven, Walker worked in cotton fields in the South and then as a launderer and cook before building her own factory and business from the ground up (Bundles 2001).

By the 1950s, most African Americans (especially women) had adopted grooming practices to straighten their hair. Craig notes how this changed with the civil rights activism of the 1960s and "black is beautiful" discourse and practice. Everyday habitus changed through a fashion cycle influenced by political activism:

> In 1952, a black woman proudly wearing "nappy" hair was unfashionable. In 1960, she was a curiosity, in 1965 a militant, and in 1968 stylish. In 1970, she might have been arrested for too closely resembling Angela Davis. By 1977, she was an anachronism. (Craig 2002: 78)

As the symbol of black pride disseminated as a fashion trend, it ran its course and lost the political edge associated with activists such as Angela Davis (see Figure 4.1).

In 1969 a fourteen-year-old African American girl named Gloria Andrews wrote a column, "It isn't enough just to wear an Afro," in *Seventeen* magazine. Andrews, who herself did not wear an Afro but was very active in the black movement, lamented that "about ninety percent of the kids I know are wearing Afros, yet practically none of them know anything about the black movement":

> I think kids should earn the right to wear an Afro. They can do this by working for their people. They can join in urging their schools to offer a black studies program. They can petition their cities to set up recreational centers for young people. They can involve themselves in urban renewal programs and do all kinds of volunteer

Figure 4.1   Angela Davis, American activist and philosophy professor, testifies at a meeting of the Soviet International Women's Seminar in Moscow, 1972. Courtesy of Getty Images.

work. And they should learn who their leaders are and what they stand for. They should learn to respect their own black values and not be satisfied with just looking the part. (Andrews 1969: 248)

By the mid to late 1970s, the Afro hairstyle had faded from fashion. Yet like many forms of style-fashion-dress, it has made a comeback. It fits critical theorist Walter Benjamin's (1968) concept of a "tiger's leap into the past"—wherein inspiration is derived from the past and comes back (never exactly in the same form) in a way that now feels fresh. In Figure 4.2, singer Solange Knowles, born in 1986, wears a hairstyle inspired by the Afro hairstyle popular forty years prior. Yet note how the cut, shape, and styling differ and have a fresh feel.

Freshness, in fact, is a key concept in African American cultural stylings, which have historically had an improvisational quality (Kaiser et al. 2004). The everyday process of minding appearances includes articulations

Figure 4.2 Singer Solange Knowles wearing an Afro-inspired hairstyle at a Victoria's Secret opening of "swimsuit season," March 2011. Courtesy of Getty Images.

and rearticulations that meld nostalgia with newness. The concept of *double consciousness* articulated by African American theorist W.E.B. DuBois ([1903] 1997) describes the experience of knowing two worlds at once: the dominant culture and the minority one. Similarly, black feminist scholar Patricia Hill Collins (1991) discusses the importance of both/and thinking in black feminist thought. Writing from perspectives that bridge fashion studies and cultural studies, bell hooks (1990) and Gwen O'Neal (1998) note how African American style is simultaneously political and aesthetic; it defies binary oppositions between political agency (which challenges hegemony) and "just fashion" or "just for looks." Yet as we have seen, the timing, the context, and the wearer's intent and motivation all contribute to the extent of the melding of politics and aesthetics.

The politics of hair did not end in the early 1970s. Hairstyle, like skin color, has been the focus of U.S. court cases revolving around potential racial discrimination. Issues such as these have been analyzed in the field of *critical race theory*—"a dynamic, eclectic, and growing movement in the law . . . challenging racial orthodoxy, shaking up the legal academy, questioning comfortable liberal premises, and leading the search for new ways of thinking about our nation's most intractable, and insoluble problem—race" (Delgado and Stefancic 2000: xvi).

One good example of a critical race theoretical analysis is legal scholar Paulette Caldwell's (2000) critique of a 1981 court case: *Rogers v. American Airlines*. The plaintiff in the case, Renee Rogers, was a black female flight attendant challenging American Airlines' policy that prohibited braided hairstyles. She argued that the policy discriminated against her on the basis of race (blackness) *and* gender (female). That is, the argument was one related to intersectionality: the airline regulation affected her especially because she was a black woman. The legal system, however, is not set up to deal with intersectionality, according to Caldwell (2000).

The court dismissed Rogers's claim and supplied three reasons. First, the court did not agree that there was any gender discrimination. It stressed that American Airlines' policy was "even-handed" and applicable to men, as well as women. Second, the court stressed that the airline's grooming policy "did not regulate or classify employees on the basis of an immutable gender characteristic." And third, the policy did not have any bearing on the "exercise of a fundamental right."

The court did analyze the racial discrimination claim separately but dismissed it on the same grounds as it did with gender discrimination, indicating that the anti-braid policy applied neutrally to "all races" and that there was no "impact of the policy on an immutable racial characteristic or of any effect on the exercise of a fundamental right" (Caldwell 2000: 281–82).

Caldwell goes on to argue, from a critical race theoretical perspective, that the court's treatment of race should be closely scrutinized. It did not seem to understand that phenotypic and cultural aspects of race are intertwined: First, it rejected the idea that there is any analogy between all-braided and Afro (natural) hairstyles. Let us pause for a minute to examine this assumption, as Caldwell recommends. Is there such a thing as "natural" in the way individuals style their hair as it grows out of their heads? Yes, there are many biological variations and many cultural possibilities, but there are so many in between or both/and options to fashion appearances. The Rogers's case is one that calls into specific relief the ways in which a binary opposition between biology and culture is neither helpful nor completely fair. Indeed, the *Rogers v. American Airlines* case reveals this very problem, as Caldwell comments:

> Stopping short of concluding that Afro hairstyles might be protected under all circumstances, the court held that "an all-braided hairstyle is a different matter. It is not the product of natural hair growth but of artifice." Second, in response to the plaintiff's argument that, like Afro hairstyles, the wearing of braids reflected her choice for ethnic and cultural identification, the court again distinguished between the immutable aspects of race and characteristics that are "socioculturally associated with a particular race or nationality." However, given the variability of so-called immutable racial characteristics such as skin color and hair textures, it is difficult to understand racism as other than a complex of historical, sociocultural associations with race. (Caldwell 2000: 282)

As Caldwell points out, the court strictly interpreted race as a biological concept. It held that "[n]atural hairstyles—or at least some of them, such as Afros—are permitted because hair texture is immutable, a matter over which individuals have no choice. Braids, however, are the products of artifice—a cultural practice—and are therefore mutable, i.e., the result of choice" (Caldwell 2000: 282).

Adding insult to injury, so to speak, the court asserted (in concert with American Airlines' argument) that Rogers adopted the prohibited hairstyle after it had been popularized' by Bo Derek, a white actress, in the 1979 film *10*. This film featured Derek as the perfect (white) female "10" body—with long blond hair braided in a cornrow style—while running in slow motion on the beach. The film popularized both Derek as a sex symbol and the cultural rating system of female attractiveness. The cornrow braid hairstyle worn by Derek also received a great deal of attention, but it was not new.

As Caldwell notes, black women have braided their hair in the United States and around the world for at least four centuries. In popular culture, the black actress Cicely Tyson wore a braided hairstyle in the early 1960s: "More importantly, Cicely Tyson's choice to popularize (i.e., to "go public" with) braids, like her choice of acting roles, was a political act made on her own behalf and on behalf of all black women" (Caldwell 2000: 282). Derek's use of the style is a classic case of cultural appropriation, and the court's use of the term "popularized" only amplifies the problematic power relations in the intersectionalities between race and gender. The court simultaneously reinforced white hegemonic beauty standards, trivialized the racial politics of hair, and failed to acknowledge that some black women may choose to wear braids for the sake of the long-term health of their hair (which can be permanently damaged by the use of chemical straighteners), as well as cultural identity.

This court case reveals some ongoing problems associated with *not* thinking critically and intersectionally about issues of race and gender. In 2009 comedian Chris Rock developed (with Nelson George) a documentary, *Good Hair*, to bring some of the social, political, economic, and aesthetic issues regarding black women's hair to a mainstream audience, in a way that was both ironic and informative (Rock 2009). The documentary and Rock's two appearances on Oprah Winfrey's show to discuss it generated considerable cultural discourse. Supporters of the documentary and Rock's approach praised the sincerity and humor with which he brought issues within the African American community to the general public's awareness. Some critics did not appreciate his telling tales (about African American women) "out of school"; some pointed to the need for more context or argued that hair is a topic of great concern to women of multiple races and ethnicities.

ETHNICITY: BELONGING-IN-DIFFERENCE

As we have seen, the concepts of race, racial formation, and ethnicity relate in complicated ways to other concepts such as national and transnational identities, religion, and cultural meaning systems. In research studies (surveys and interviews) over the past twenty years or so, graduate students and I have asked respondents about their ethnicities, using an open-ended format. Responses reveal the complexities associated with terminology, as well as sites of identification and differentiation. They range from Asian American to more specific national affiliations: Korean American, Japanese American, Filipina American, Chinese American, and so on. South Asian or Indian American or Pakistani American. Latina or Chicana or Mexican American. African American or Black. White or Caucasian or Norwegian American, etc.

In a 2008 national survey we conducted among 1,952 U.S. men, white men expressed the least interest in fashion and appearance, while African American men's responses indicated the highest level of interest. Latino and Asian American men expressed an "in between" level of interest. Interpretations of these results (discussed further in Chapter 6 on gender) need to account for the unmarked nature of whiteness, the history of racism in the

United States, the importance of style-fashion-dress in African American culture (Kaiser et al. 2004; O'Neal 1998), and other cultural factors influencing ethnic belonging-in-difference.

Individuals identify with, and differentiate from, one another on an ongoing basis. Part of the struggle for meaning within culture involves the *twin processes of identification and differentiation.* At times, due to historical and political circumstances, differences become glossed over; and yet at later points in time, they become extremely relevant, if not divisive. It is often difficult to sort out just which differences are racialized, which are ethnic, which are religious, and which are national or transnational in nature.

Ethnic studies scholar Lisa Lowe (2000) notes that it is difficult to completely disentangle race from ethnicity, because of the discourses that have historically linked them. She points to the importance of focusing on the cultural practices that produce identity, rather than focusing strictly on the identities themselves. The concept of "Asian American identities," for example, should not be seen as a fixed "given," but rather as a process of ongoing subject formation and "never complete" cultural formations. Lowe observes that discussions of ethnic culture and racial group formation vary widely among Asian Americans. There is tremendous heterogeneity in terms of national and class backgrounds, histories of immigrant exclusion laws, gender, and other factors influencing Asian American experiences in relation to hegemonic culture (Lowe 2000: 428).

As compared to race, however, ethnicity tends to be a more open or inclusive concept—allowing people to think through how (and with whom) they experience a sense of identity and belonging. Although hegemonic culture tends to regulate ethnicity (like race), and the meanings of both shift in an ongoing way, the concept of ethnicity tends to connote a higher degree of agency. The concept of *ethnicity* refers to the place or space from which people articulate their identities and communities. It also implies a kind of self-awareness or self-reflexivity about a group's own cultural uniqueness; it is a process of belonging-in-difference.

There is a great deal of fluidity in how people articulate ethnicity. Some articulations are grounded in nations or other kinds of "imagined communities": the Japanese kimono, the Chinese cheongsam, the Mexican sombrero, and the Scottish kilt, for example. Yet when we examine the cultural histories of any given form of ethnic dress, we frequently find complex appropriations and hegemonic processes, as well as invented (imagined?) traditions and complex intersectionalities.

The traditional dress for men of Highland Scotland, for example, is generally envisioned as a tartan kilt, knee-length wool socks, and other accessories. Yet in Malcolm Chapman's study of this look, he could find no evidence that it had ever been the popular dress of anyone, outside the Scottish Highland regiments of the British army and various "self-consciously folkloric circles" (e.g., dancing groups, choirs, Scottish festival goers). The kilt *is* reminiscent, however, of the plaid skirt popularly worn by Gaelic-speaking Highlanders in the eighteenth century. Although the kilt and the plaid skirt vary in many ways, neither is bifurcated into trousers: they are both skirts. Chapman argues that this "oppositional propriety" to cultural gender norms "excited the imagination of those who observed them; it continues to do so today" (Chapman 1995). One cannot analyze the kilt without considering the intersectionalities between gender, ethnicity, and nation.

Such intersectionalities, along with others (e.g., class) influenced the belonging-in-difference articulation of ethnicity by the famous Mexican painter Frida Kahlo (1907–1954). In an essay published in *The Latin American Fashion Reader*, Maria Claudia André (2005) describes how Kahlo articulated an ethnic nationalist Mexican identity, as well as complex gender and sexual subject positions through her style-fashion-dress. Born in a well-to-do family, just a few years before the beginning of the Mexican Revolution, Kahlo adapted indigenous Tehuana ethnic dress—from the Tehuantepec region of Mexico—to represent an anticolonialist and nationalist Mexican identity, as well as her own unique sense of style and representation. She articulated resistance to both Spanish colonial and local masculine domination through the aesthetics associated with a matriarchal society. She linked this articulation contextually with a nationalist project fueled by revolutionary activism. Representing herself in complex ways in her brightly colored dress and in her painted self-portraits, Kahlo has assumed the status of a cult figure since the mid-1980s. Her images—seen on everything from T-shirts to refrigerator magnets and wooden doorway beads—raise some interesting questions regarding representation: Was Kahlo aiming to articulate a "self-exoticizing" image? Or was she appropriating from indigenous ethnicities? Regardless of her intentions, global capitalism has benefited from her representations with commodities that continue to flow within and across multiple nations. And her imagery leaves ambiguous traces of intersectionalities that still capture the imagination and compel critical interpretations.

Capturing the imagination in euromodern cultural discourse has been the discourse of exoticism and anxiety surrounding "Gypsy" or "Roma" minority culture. The emerging field of Romani studies (similar in concept to ethnic studies programs in the United States) aims to (a) counter the strong, negative stereotypes that circulate in the media and among the European public about Romani people; and (b) to acknowledge the heterogeneity and complexity in Romani culture (Tremlett 2009). One of the debates in the field is whether Roma is an ethnicity in the sense of a group with a cultural heritage, when identity is continually made and remade in the present, through a variety of different cultural formations and social processes. Part of the debate concerns whether the Roma experience, especially in Hungary, is more akin to an underclass than an ethnicity. Using the cultural studies concepts of "new ethnicities" (Hall 1996) and hybridity enables a more expansive analysis of Roma experiences, thereby "de-essentializing" the debates on Roma, "without losing sight of ethnicity" (Tremlett 2009: 165).

In an ethnographic study of a Gábor (Gypsy) community in Romania, Saba Tesfay (2009) described the community's "customary dress" as follows: Men wore broad-brimmed hats around the age of ten. The hat is commonly called the "Jewish hat," because as one Gábor man told Tesfay: "We have a liking for the Jews and have adopted this hat from them" (Tesfay 2009: 14). (This liking is explained as representing "smartness and deftness in business and in trade," but it is also important to note that Romani, as well as Jewish, individuals were tragically subjected to Hitler's concentration camps during World War II.) Although Gábors admit that their appropriation of the hat comes from Jewish men, they claim it as their own, even in their self-definition: "hatted Gábor Gypsies." As one middle-aged man indicated, Gábor men used to wear velvet trousers: "We didn't care if it was dirty, but it has gone out of fashion" (Tesfay 2009: 14). Nevertheless, one older man indicated: "We haven't changed our dress, not at all . . . for the Gábors, this is ancient and has existed as long as the Gábors have" (Tesfay 2009: 7). Today, men wear loose-fitting black trousers (not velvet), a shirt, and a dark overcoat. They have distinctive mustaches and side whiskers; in the past they had long beards. Older men often wear a waistcoat with silver buttons. The waistcoat "used to be worn by the Hungarians, no one else but the Hungarians and the Gábors. When I die, I will leave it to Csabi [his son]" (Tesfay 2009: 14).

Gábor women have less agency than men in their choice of dress, according to women and men alike; the particular community Tesfay studied belonged to the Adventist Church, and Gábor Adventist women were not allowed to wear the large gold earrings that are so popular among non-Adventist Gábor women. They are also required to wear a colorful pleated skirt, a colorful patterned blouse, and a long pleated apron made of the same material as the skirt. Married women must wear a kerchief, tied in the front; both married and younger women wear a red ribbon in their hair (Tesfay 2009). Overall, it can be said that Gábor dress does change and is influenced by surrounding cultures, but Gábors very clearly articulate their ethnicity through their dress as well as their verbal discussions about issues of identity and community. Religion, too, becomes an important factor that inflects some Gábor subject positions.

RELIGIOUS REARTICULATIONS

Is religion a subject position that is distinct from ethnicity and race? Historically, as noted earlier, it has been difficult to distinguish completely between them. Ethnic identity and ethnic strife, for example, has often been identical to religious identity and strife (Bartlett 2001), as the history of Jewish people reveals. Yet in the above case of Gábor Adventists, it is their religion that distinguishes them (and the prohibition against gold earrings for women) from non-Adventist "Gypsies." If we were to picture a Venn diagram with two overlapping circles for ethnic and religious subject positions, in some groups the circles would completely overlap; whereas in others, there would be an intersection but also remaining space in the circles for different articulations of style-fashion-dress.

Style-fashion-dress scholar Linda Arthur (1999) describes conservative religious groups as exerting "control over their members' bodies." In other words, dress becomes a symbol of social control. This control applies to Gábor Adventist women, as we have seen. It also applied in an ethnographic study of orthodox Mennonite women, whose clothes (a shirtwaist dress and head covering) are supposed to display that one is on the "right and true path." As one woman noted, "I put on all of the Church's rules" about submission and modesty (Graybill and Arthur 1999).

However, religion may also offer a sense of freedom or a context in which to articulate ethnicity. Clothing scholar Gwen O'Neal (1999) notes how dress has functioned in "the black church" as a form of positive ethnic identification. In the black church, slaves articulated a blend of traditional African religions or belief systems with Christianity. The church came to serve as the social center of African American life, and church dress came to articulate the expression of African American culture. This tradition emerged from slavery, when a lot of effort went into "Sunday" clothes as a way to distinguish them from everyday work clothes and the oppression they represented. Sunday clothes, in contrast, became a means for expressing cultural agency (O'Neal 1999).

In a somewhat similar dynamic, religion occupies an important place in a sense of belonging-in-difference in South Asian communities in the United States. Since the end of the nineteenth century, the emerging indigenous elite in India and Pakistan promoted religion (i.e., Hindu and Islam) to garner support among the masses (Mohammad-Arif 2000). When people from South Asian countries migrated to other locations, religion became an effective vehicle to foster "community formation and identity re-composition" (Mohammad-Arif 2000: 67). It functioned to maintain a sense of ethnic identity to curb complete Americanization, or assimilation into U.S. society. The same principle applies to other ethnic minorities in the United States (e.g., Irish, Greeks, Jews). In the case of South Asian Muslims, there is a tendency toward a heightened religiosity in the United States, for two reasons: First, there is a relative space of religious freedom. And second, South Asian Muslim parents may find religion to be an effective mode of transmission of cultural heritage to their children (Mohammad-Arif 2000).

On the other hand, Muslims may also experience anti-Islamic prejudice (Islamophobia), perpetuated in popular media and punctuated by 9/11 and other terrorist events attributed to fundamentalist Muslims. Islamophobia (cultural anxiety about or fear of Muslims) as a concept has circulated in the United States, Europe, and around the world since 9/11, but its roots are older. Anthropologist Andrew Shryock (2010) asks: "Given the scant knowledge of Islam most Americans and Europeans bring to the creation of their anti-Muslim stereotypes, can we be sure that Islamophobia is ultimately about Islam at all?" (3). Shryock goes on to argue that Islamophobia may be a discourse that adapted from earlier Cold War polemics, or a residue from older battles between European and Ottoman power, or euromodern models of "race, empire, and human progress" (Shryock 2010: 3).

How do Muslims articulate their religious and ethnic subject positions in the context of contemporary cultural discourses about Islam? Anthropologist Emma Tarlo (2010) closes her fascinating book—*Visibly Muslim: Fashion, Politics, Faith*—with a discussion of young Muslim women who blog about a range of topics related to style-fashion-dress: from politics to shopping and how to wear *hijab* (a head scarf) in a variety of styles and with other clothes and accessories; reviews of fashion-related magazines and television shows; links to online *hijab* shopping sites; and different international Islamic fashion events in Britain, the United States, Canada, Turkey, Egypt, and Indonesia. In a transnational context, Tarlo argues, cultural discourse on blogs such as Hijab Style—as well as the styles worn in everyday life—represents the birth of modern Islamic fashion "in which *distinctions of ethnicity have become irrelevant*" (Tarlo 2010: 225, emphasis added).

Undoubtedly, Tarlo is using ethnicity here to refer to the diversity in the regional and cultural backgrounds of Muslims within national contexts: British, Pakistani, Indian, Bangladeshi, Arab, Albanian, Bosnian, Iranian, Nigerian, Egyptian, Iraqi, and Turkish; along with individuals of mixed backgrounds, including white British and European converts. Many of Tarlo's informants sought to distance themselves from the ethnic dress (or national dress?) of their parents' generation. Rather they sought to wear modern, Islamic style-fashion-dress. Tarlo's point about the diminishing importance of ethnicity and ethnic dress observation, however, raises a crucial question on the relationship between religion/faith and ethnicity, and a provocative possibility at the heart of subject formation through style-fashion-dress. For some individuals, religion can be interpreted as a cultural discourse to which they are subjected (i.e., a subject position). Yet many of the women Tarlo interviewed focused on their subjectivities and their relationship to *hijab* with a sense of agency and subjectivity.

Tarlo makes the persuasive case that new kinds of faith-based fashion subjectivity have arisen since 9/11. As one of her informants indicated:

September 11th was some kind of trigger. The media was portraying Muslim women as oppressed and making out that Afghan women were desperate to rip off their burqas, and that infuriated me. (Tarlo 2010: 24)

An entanglement of faith and politics permeated the discourse in Tarlo's interviews. Between this entanglement and the new media that put style-fashion-dress into transnational Islamic discourse, might we consider modern Islamic fashions as representing new modes of ethnicity? To the extent that culture creates ethnicity (Bartlett 2001), and ethnicity is as much about the future as it is the past, interactions through new media can be seen as new communities generating new visual and verbal discourses.

As described by cultural studies scholar Stuart Hall earlier in this chapter, ethnicities are continually in motion through the " 'play' of history, culture and power" (Hall 1990: 225). Transnational discourse opens up cultural spaces for new expressions of belonging and becoming. Perhaps these new (transnational) ethnicities offer avenues to explore the politics and aesthetics of style-fashion-dress through new sites of identification and differentiation.

At the same time, in the case of visibly Muslim style-fashion-dress, it is important to analyze it carefully through not only transnational subjectivities but also context-specific subject formation and cultural regulation: nation-by-nation policies, community-by-community practices, and subject-by-subject articulations.

One clothing style that articulates multiple, intersectional meanings of ethnicity, nation, and gender; along with religion, is the headscarf—banned in public schools in the nation-state of France, required in public spaces in the Iranian Islamic Republic, and the object of considerable transnational debate. When does a scarf become a significant religious symbol, whether its usage is prohibited or mandatory? What is at stake?

The practice of wearing a headscarf (*hijab*) to school by some French Muslim girls became a particular site of debate and contestation. In 2004 a law was passed that banned "significant religious symbols" in public schools. Examples of such symbols were Muslim girls' *hijab*, Jewish boys' *yarmulkes* (skull caps), Sikh boys' turbans, and necklaces with large Christian crosses or Jewish Stars of David (smaller symbols were okay). Because it was widely believed that the real target was *hijab*, the media have typically referred to the law as the "French headscarf ban."

Contradictions abound as one compares religious symbols in the context of nation, as one contemplates the role of religion in a transnational world, and as one considers the double standards between *haute couture* or high fashion (a turban on the runway) and religion (a headscarf worn to school).

What are the relationships among ethnicity, religion, nation, and gender? And how do gender and other subject positions intervene and become entangled in contexts of colonialism and other power relations? Textile head coverings may be, in part, a form of subjection for some, but the agency they may afford in expressing religion and ethnicity warrants attention.

Shifting gears (and decades), the two French women in the photograph in Figure 4.3, taken in 1944, are wearing headscarves. In this context, the scarves—fashioned into turbans—do not have a religious connotation. Their meanings are ambiguous. A bit of modern French fashion history is in order to interpret these styles, but the story of people wearing fabric on their heads actually goes back much earlier to Middle Eastern practices of veiling (with the fabric hanging down) and wearing turbans (with the fabric piled up on the head).

The practice of veiling among women is believed to have originated in Assyrian (now Iraqi), Persian (now Iranian), and Byzantine cultures, well before the birth of the Islamic religion in the seventh century c.e. The first known historical reference to veiling was an Assyrian legal text of the thirteenth century b.c.e. Urban upper class women wore the veil to mark their prestige and to represent their privilege to shield themselves from the "impure" gaze of commoners. It became illegal for lower-class women and sex workers to wear veils (Zahedi 2007).

Figure 4.3   Turbans fashioned from scarves in France in 1944. Photo by Fred Ramage/Hulton Archive/Getty Images.

The cultural practice of using fabric as a head covering became common to men (more commonly the turban) and women (more commonly the veil) throughout the Middle East and parts of Africa and South Asia. With the advent of Islam, this practice—widely varied in specific locations and contexts—came to have religious connotations (Zahedi 2007).

World trade, imperial conquests, and colonization helped to spread the practice of textile head coverings in various forms. In particular, Europeans became fascinated with what Edward Said (1978) called "Orientalism": biased and distorted "outsider" interpretations of the East—attitudes shaped by imperialist attitudes in the eighteenth and nineteenth centuries. The roots of Orientalism had been seen in a fascination with imagined national differences (recall the Cesare Vecellio's 1590s depiction of a Persian man in *Habiti* in Figure 3.3).

In the nineteenth century, Western fashion experimented with various forms of head coverings and the concept of bifurcated lower garments (i.e., trousers) for women. Inspired, for example, by Turkish styles, U.S. feminists such as Amelia Bloomer experimented with the appropriation of some aspects of Oriental (Turkish) styling into their everyday attire in the 1850s, as a dress reform alternative to corsets and hoopskirts. Although the bloomer style did not catch on and evoked substantial cultural ridicule, the style became incorporated into children's and women's bloomer or romper styles for active wear and young women's physical education uniforms (Warner 2006).

Yet it was probably the continuing influences of Orientalism that contributed most to Western masculine "harem fantasies." The Russian ballet set and costume designer Leon Bakst drew heavily on the European fantasies of Scheherezade—the heroine and storyteller (to the king) extraordinaire, depicted in exotic harem pants, turbans, and jewels—in *One Thousand and One Nights* (also known as *The Arabian Nights*). Bakst's extravagant and exotic set and costume designs in the Russian ballet adaptation of the story attracted the fascination of the French fashion designer Paul Poiret (1879–1944), who began to adapt the stage costumes for modern fashion. Poiret is famously known for his elaborate and exotic parties. In 1911 he and his wife, Denise, hosted "The Thousand and Second Night" party, requiring guests to wear style-fashion-dress inspired by *The Arabian Nights*—and coincidentally available through his own designs. Denise played the role of the Queen of the Harem and wore a turban with egret feathers and harem pants designed by Poiret. The turban epitomized the European perception of Persian dress. Guests were invited—indeed required—to wear similar Oriental styles such as harem pants and turbans, styles that Poiret himself had been designing (Takeda and Spilker 2010: 176–77).

Hollywood starlets wore turbans in the 1920s and 1930s on the silver screen, and turbans have continued to circulate now and then on fashion runways and in everyday life. In 2010 in New York, models wearing designer Jason Wu's spring collection wore black or cobalt turbans. Meanwhile in Milan, Giorgio Armani accessorized his monochromatic collection with North African-inspired turbans. Some of the models resembled Greta Garbo in the 1926 silent film *The Temptress*. How can one explain the fascination with head wraps? Harold Koda, curator of the Costume Institute at the Metropolitan Museum of Art in New York, does not believe it has anything to do with politics or world events: "It's not a part of a Kumbaya fashion movement. I think it's more of Poiret's view of Orientalism than women watching the news and referencing what's going on in Afghanistan. It's an exoticism, a sense of the other that is visually compelling" (Oliver 2010).

Issues of gender, nation, the appropriation of otherness, and other factors become entangled in what is considered the transnational flow of fabric head coverings. Whereas the turban becomes a fashion symbol now and again on runways in Europe and the United States, other forms of fabric head coverings generate cultural anxieties, based on their links to religion.

There is considerable debate about the issue of females covering their heads in public schools and in public settings in France and other countries in Europe. Since the French Revolution in 1789, the French nation-state has operated on a principle of *laïcité*, which roughly translates to secularism, or a separation between church and state. In 1905 a law was passed to prohibit the state from recognizing or funding any religion; the goal was to keep religion out of public education. Religion was to be a private, not a public, affair. The modern nation-state, according to this system of laïcité, "replaces religion as the privileged source of social and cultural integration" (Ortiz 2003: 432).

The dynamic shifts, however, in the context of globalization, in which the eighteenth-century ideas of nation, state, ethnicity, religion, and rights no longer apply so well to transnational political, economic, environmental, and other realities (Vesselinov 2010). Transnational religious communities, for example, propelled by diasporic immigrant communities and Internet access, cut across national boundaries. The French policy of laïcité becomes challenged in the transnational context, which is further complicated by France's former colonial histories in nations such as Algeria and Morocco.

In the context of discourses of globalization and multiculturalism, transnational target marketing to specific ethnicities and newly imagined communities flourishes. Some writers have referred to this new kind of consumer experience as portable ethnicity (Halter 2000: 9).

But does portable ethnicity always work so well? The politics of racism, classism, and other power relations remind us that there are always some hegemonic forces that make ethnic articulations a continual site of cultural struggle. And, ethnic articulations can easily be appropriated by capitalism at the same time that ethnic markets are represented in particular ways and for particular reasons. In the United States, for example, ethnic (especially Latina/o or Hispanic) consumers are frequently represented by marketers as "family-oriented, traditional, and brand-loyal, which, in marketing, serves largely as synonyms for conservative consumers" within a larger dominant culture that pays lip service to family values, brand loyalty, and religion; and that is cognizant of the growing demographics of the Latina/o or Hispanic communities in the United States (Davila 2001: 216–17).

Ethnic appropriations and racial and religious rearticulations cannot be separated completely from discourses of ethnic marketing, which situate style-fashion-dress subjects as consumers. This situating brings us to the subject position of class, considered in the next chapter.

Class Matters

Class is a tricky and unstable subject position: it is always *in relation* to the class subject positions of others. On the one hand, it can be viewed as a kind of bottom line in terms of one's economic circumstances. On the other hand, there is a certain kind of ambiguity and complexity surrounding class as a subject position. Some of this ambiguity and complexity revolves around class's relation to production, distribution, and consumption: processes in the circuit of style-fashion-dress discussed in Chapter 1. In the nineteenth century, critical theorists Karl Marx and Friedrich Engels (2002) defined class in terms of ownership and control over production, based upon—and critical of—the industrial model. Also in the nineteenth century, sociologist Max Weber (1974) made a distinction between class ("stratified according to their relations to the production and acquisition of goods") and *status groups* ("stratified according to the principles of their *consumption* of goods as represented by special 'styles of life' "). In other words, he argued, status is not just an issue of how much one has and can potentially consume, but rather *how* he or she consumes (Weber 1974: 52). Today, class is usually conceptualized in terms that include production, distribution, and consumption.

Consider the "what" and the "how" of consumption among the elementary school children in Figure 5.1. This class picture was taken in 1935, in the middle of the Great Depression in the United States, at Raphael Weill Elementary School in the working and middle class Western Addition district of San Francisco. There is always the bottom line of what one can afford, but there is also the issue of how one represents. Many of the children probably wear their Sunday best (sailor dresses, shirts and ties, dress shoes), and some (mostly girls) hold props (dolls, stuffed animals, folders) that further give us a sense of their subject formation and their consumption practices. When this photograph was taken, the United States and other industrialized nations had experienced more than fifty years of what has frequently been called the "democratization of fashion" (discussed later in this chapter), fostered by the invention of the sewing machine and the mass production of clothing. By the 1930s, the children's clothing industry was in full swing in the United States, but many homes also had sewing machines, and it was common for clothing to be made at home. Whether these children's clothes were produced in a factory or at home,

Figure 5.1   Students at Raphael Weill Elementary School in San Francisco, California, 1935. The school is located in a working and middle class, ethnically diverse area of the city known as the Western Addition. Courtesy of Shades of San Francisco, San Francisco Public Library.

they were made from fabric produced in a factory (and had been for more than 100 years, since the industrialization of the industry).

Figure 5.1 reminds us that class interacts and overlaps with social constructions of race, ethnicity, gender, and other subject positions. Class and other subject positions happen in changing economic and political circumstances, and issues of time and place. Known as "San Francisco's little United Nations" in the 1930s (Klein 2008), the Western Addition district (shown in Figure 5.1) was home to Japanese Americans, African Americans, Jewish Americans, Filipino/a Americans, and individuals of other ethnic backgrounds. The district's diversity was shaped partly by economic affordability and partly by processes of racial and ethnic exclusion from other areas of the city. Two events/policies highlight the interplay between class and ethnic politics. In 1942, seven years after the students posed for the photo in Figure 5.1, more than 120,000 people of Japanese descent—and about 5,000 from the Western Addition, including some of the children in Figure 5.1—were relocated from their homes to internment camps by the order of President Franklin Roosevelt, in response to anti-Japanese public sentiments after the Japanese bombing of Pearl Harbor in Hawai'i. Forced to leave their homes and close their businesses, the Japanese American families experienced personal hardship on top of the already challenging Great Depression.

Between 1940 and 1950 the African American population in the Western Addition increased from 2,144 to 14,888 (or 34% of the district's population), as migration occurred to pursue jobs in war-related industries. The Fillmore neighborhood within the Western Addition district became a hub ("Harlem of the West") for African American culture, with lively businesses such as jazz and blues clubs. After the war, the jobs moved out of the inner city to suburbs, and unemployment increased. Homes and businesses were in need of repair, but it was difficult for African Americans and some other minorities to get loans for renovation. In 1948, large sections of the Western Addition were declared urban blight, and the largest urban renewal project in the western United States began. Buildings were demolished, creating huge swaths of vacated land: 883 businesses were shuttered, and 4,729 households were forced out. It took forty years and $50 million to pursue urban renewal, but the African American community never recovered economically and culturally from the "renewal" that largely made the district unaffordable (Fulbright 2008).

Even knowing some of the context surrounding Figure 5.1, we cannot be completely sure about the class subject positions of the students in the photograph. Nor can we assume that their style-fashion-dress is democratic, especially in the context of the Great Depression. As the "democratization of fashion" argument goes, the industrialization of textile and clothing production made affordable clothing available to people of more classes. Historical research by sociologist Diana Crane (2000) indicates that this was partially true; that is, after the 1870s, working-class families in the United States, France, and England were able to acquire a limited number of clothes that would have previously been available to people of the middle or a higher class. These clothes were likely to have been reserved for Sundays or special occasions. People of the lowest classes, however, were still often unable to acquire fashionable dress at all.

We may know that class matters, but we cannot necessarily see it if we do not know the back stories of individuals' and families' circumstances. We cannot necessarily determine the extent to which people struggle or thrive economically simply by looking at their style-fashion-dress in a snapshot—not in the 1930s and especially not now—to a certain extent that we can keep up appearances, even with limited means. Further, as is the case with other subject positions, class is not fixed in meaning. Rather, it is unstable and shifts in relation to events, policies, and the shifting subject positions of others. Its potential for ambiguity generates cultural anxiety and cultural ambivalence.

In her book, *Where We Stand: Class Matters*, the feminist theorist bell hooks argues that class is "the uncool subject" that "makes us all tense, nervous, uncertain about where we stand" (hooks 2000: vii). She goes on to argue that race and gender politics are more visible and become "screens to deflect attention away from the harsh realities" exposed by class politics (hooks 2000: 7). One of these harsh realities is income inequality. For example, the top 1 percent of the U.S. population gains 25 percent of the nation's wealth and controls 40 percent of it, up from 12 percent and 33 percent, respectively, twenty-five years prior (Stiglitz 2011). Income inequality is not as high in Europe, but is higher in regions of the world such as the Middle East (spurring protests in the Arab Spring in 2011). Nations such as Brazil in Latin America have pursued policies to address income equality and have made some positive strides (Stiglitz 2011).

In many ways, fast fashion—fostered by the continual global search for the lowest garment labor costs—contributes to the screen deflecting attention away from income inequality. With globalization, sites of production and garment labor have become increasingly invisible. In the global circuit of style-fashion-dress, consumption is paradoxical when it comes to class. On the one hand, there is at least an *appearance of democratic fashion*, because fashionable clothes are simultaneously available at multiple price points. On the other hand, the quality of the materials and the lack of compensation for the labor that goes into the clothes' production are less visible, so class often gets a "pass" from critical scrutiny.

Still, the cultural anxieties about class are there, albeit beneath the surface. Those with the most wealth and power have the most to lose, and the fear (and reality) of job loss on the part of middle and working class individuals generates another kind of cultural anxiety. Class matters fuel thinking about labor issues, power relations, corporate branding, designer clothing, and consumer guilt and debt; these matters also generate cultural anxiety and spark political revolutions (as seen in Chapter 3). Because class matters so much, it often becomes stifled as a topic of verbal debate in cultural discourse. And yet it plays out in interesting and important ways in visual discourses of style-fashion-dress. Class matters foster ambiguity, as well as delineation, in everyday looks.

CONCEPTUALIZING CLASS

Class is more than what people do or earn for a living. It is a complex concept and subject position, typically located by combined demographic variables such as income, education level, occupation, and family background. Yet there is more to class in a cultural sense: the ambiguous issues of cultural "taste" and everyday habitus (Bourdieu 1984). Sociologist Pierre Bourdieu referred to these cultural aspects of class as *cultural capital*. Cultural capital includes tastes and attitudes, and ways of eating and grooming, as well as how individuals are taught to act and how they relate to the future: how they image and imagine themselves becoming. The resources people have, of course, affect their ability to buy clothes. However, social class is more than what people buy; it includes *how* they wear what they wear, how they carry themselves, and how they present themselves to others. Through cultural capital, class becomes embodied; it is part of an individual's habitus. Sociologist Joanne Entwistle (2000) describes habitus as "seemingly natural bodily demeanour we learn as members of a particular family/class" (135). One example of this would be the "royal carriage," or the way an aristocrat such as Marie Antoinette could glide so impressively through the Versailles palace in her debut from Austria to France (Weber 2006). This was a situation where class trumped nations, but they also intersected in important ways. As historian Caroline Weber (2006) notes in her engaging analysis of Marie Antoinette's fashion sense leading up to (and beyond) the French Revolution in 1789, issues of nationalism and other politics continued to plague Marie Antoinette; gender issues were no small factor.

Let's consider a different example of the intersectionalities among class, nation, and gender. When Prince William of Great Britain married Catherine (Kate) Middleton in 2011, the eyes of the world were upon her to see not only what she was wearing but also how she was wearing it: how she embodied the dress. There had been substantial media discourse about how Kate was a commoner from a family with new wealth. People around the world were rooting for her. Clearly, she exceeded all expectations with her beauty, grace, and taste, challenging the idea that it necessarily takes generations to cultivate cultural capital.

From the outset, the United States established itself in a way that differentiated itself from the European court system: the United States strongly rejected the idea of royal class lineage. Hence, a large part of the foundational myth of the nation is that "all men are created equal": a statement that initially applied only to white men of European backgrounds. The exclusion of women and people from non-European backgrounds from this founding principle was a significant part of the inequality in the United States. Yet the very idea of class—or lack thereof—itself needs to be interrogated. Even as early Americans espoused principles of equality, Brekke (2010) argues that they remained "uncomfortably mired in and dependent upon a system of style that upheld fundamentally hierarchical differences—of class, gender, race, ethnicity, age, and region" (263).

Still, there is a lot of shaky ground when it comes to class. Anxieties, ambiguities, and ambivalences abound regarding poverty, snobbery, striving for upward mobility, "fear of falling" (Ehrenreich 1989) or losing ground, children's well-being in the future, and dilemmas associated with looking respectable as well as fashionable. As a subject position, class is not *a* class, but rather a class "location-within-relations" (Wright 2005: 19). It is a *relative* concept that can only be understood in relation to other class subject positions. Hence, class dynamics and interactions become the key to understanding stability as well as mobility.

METAPHORS OF CLASS STRUCTURE

Various metaphors (or models) have been used across time and space to decipher class. These metaphors emerge from sociology, critical theory, and fashion studies. If we push these metaphors to their limits, it becomes possible to expose ironies and hypocrisies in class hierarchies.

First, the *pyramid* metaphor has characterized societies in which there have been very large peasant classes, slaves, or low-paid workers at the bottom or base of the society. At the very top is a small tip—the highest class (i.e., the nobility, the aristocracy, the upper upper class). In between the base and the tip of the pyramid is a small middle class; however, there is virtually no strategy for social mobility (e.g., no ladder). Further, the highest class at the tip of the pyramid may attempt to regulate how people below dress, so as to maintain its elite distinctiveness. Examples of this metaphor include the European and Asian feudal systems that historically regulated who could wear special furs or silks, as we will see later in this chapter.

A second metaphor is more binary in nature, and it describes the opposition between the haves and the have nots as a result of industrialization (e.g., factory production) and an increasing business class in the eighteenth and nineteenth centuries in Europe and the United States. Most famously, the critical theorist Karl Marx defined framed social class in binary terms relative to individuals' locations with respect to processes of production. Those who had control over these processes (e.g., the owners or capitalists) were classified as *bourgeois*, as compared to the workers (*proletariat*) who had little control or say and reaped little of the company's profits. He also noted how workers did not define their identities in terms of their work but rather in relation to whatever control they had over their lives and free time outside of work. At work, as Marx articulated, factory workers tended to experience alienation and a lack of agency. Between the 1830s and the 1860s, thousands of "mill girls" migrated from New England farms to work twelve- to thirteen-hour days in the textile factories of Lowell, Massachusetts: the first industrial city in the United States. Their diaries, letters, and essays reveal that although they felt a sense of agency and independence as wage earners, some felt like "living machines," as Ellen, a factory worker, indicates in 1841:

> As to the morality of the place . . . I have no fault to find. I object to the constant hurry of everything. We cannot have time to eat, drink or sleep; we have only thirty minutes, or at most three quarters of an hour, allowed us to go from our

work, partake of our food, and return to the bell—and out of the mill by the clang of the bell—into the mill, and at work, in obedience to that dingdong of a bell—just as though we were so many living machines. I will give my notice tomorrow: go, I will—I won't stay here and be a white slave. (Levinson 2007: 26)

In 1836 one of the first, large-scale labor strikes had occurred in Lowell, when the managers proposed an increase in room and board rates, which was equivalent to a 15 percent wage reduction. In the 1840s, the women fought for the ten-hour workday (Levinson 2007: 11). There is little evidence of alienation from the product (textile fabric) itself, however. They frequently wrote about their desire to purchase fabric for a new dress. The factory owners gradually replaced the original New England mill girls with immigrants willing to work for less.

A third metaphor, especially popular in the United States, is the idea of a *level playing field* (i.e., a classless society): everyone (or at least all men) are created equally. In a democratic society, as this cultural discourse articulates, class is not what defines us. We are free to make our own way with our own subjectivities. A sense of classlessness has been an almost invisible assumption that is counter to political economic facts, as we have seen.

Communist nations such as the USSR and China in the twentieth century also used a classless metaphor, but rather than highlighting the potential for individual subjectivities, the goal was a single, collective subjectivity. These conflicting ideologies between capitalist and communist nations—despite similar models of classlessness—were reflected in style-fashion-dress. Capitalist nations thrived on individualism and changing fashions, largely embracing the bourgeois class's penchant for status symbolism as a stimulus to the economy. In contrast, communist nations promoted an ethos of uniformity, with bourgeois values and appearances as a major threat and source of anxiety. The irony in both systems is the importance of the bourgeois class. How can nations simultaneously be classless and yet be so focused on a particular class—either as a threat or as a model for mobility? But how can one fall or climb in a classless society?

Yet a fourth metaphor—also very popular in the United States and contradictory to the classless metaphor—is that of the *social ladder*: the idea that it is possible to climb from rags to riches due to the social/upward mobility allowed in a free (capitalist) nation. (How can there be a level playing field and a ladder at the same time?) In the social ladder metaphor/model, there is a high degree of hope and aspiration; it is possible to transcend one's own economic station in life. In this scenario or cultural discourse, it behooves individuals to fashion their appearances in ways that look upward, toward the higher classes to which they aspire. The concept of upward mobility has been captured historically in terms of what has been branded as the "trickle down theory," developed to explain class dynamics around the beginning of the twentieth century. Attributed to Georg Simmel, although he never used the term itself, the trickle down theory relies on the social-psychological motivation to imitate the style-fashion-dress worn by higher classes, and that of the highest class to differentiate itself from lower classes by moving on to new looks. And hence, as Simmel put it, "the game goes merrily on" (Simmel 1904).

Fashion theory offers a fifth metaphor to the understanding of class dynamics: *percolation*. Emerging from social movements since the 1950s, the study of (primarily male, working class) subcultures in cultural studies (e.g., Hebdige 1979), percolation becomes a metaphor that points attention to bottom-up flows of fashion: for example, from street (e.g., working class subcultures such as teddy boys, mods, punks) to the runway. According to this metaphor or theory, most inspiration for new style-fashion-dress emerges from the innovative stylings of ethnic minority cultures (e.g., the African American community), the gay community, or working class youth subcultures. Fashion designers appropriate ideas from how people put their looks together and show them on the fashion runway, where they are much pricier. If we were to use Simmel's theory about imitation and differentiation, we would just flip it around and consider how the fashion industry imitates (appropriates) ideas from everyday street style; once these styles become commodified through capitalism, the individuals who initially created the looks differentiate themselves from these commodified styles and initiate new looks. Hence, the "game goes merrily on."

The social ladder metaphor can be described as a top-down (with upward climbing as a motivating force) model, whereas the percolation metaphor is bottom-up. A sixth and final metaphor has more of a *horizontal flow*. It assumes that each class has its own cultural system, and that influences happen *within* rather across classes. Marketing theorist Charles King (1963) proposed this trickle across model as a more democratic alternative to the top-down model of class influence. In 1969, sociologist Herbert Blumer published a paper entitled "Fashion: From Class Differentiation to Collective Selection." He critiqued the idea that the desire to look rich motivated people to adopt fashion. Rather, he indicated, what motivates individuals is the desire to be in tune with the times: to be *in* fashion. In other words, Blumer argued that being current or modern outweighed status concerns. Although Blumer argued against class as a factor in fashion change, one can interpret his work in a way that is somewhat similar to King: fashion is a process of influence among individuals sharing a cultural milieu (including, by extension, class cultures). This brings us to the theorist who most directly addressed class in a cultural context: Bourdieu, mentioned earlier as the individual credited with the idea of cultural capital. Bourdieu (1984) focused on how each class has its own culture of taste, socially reproduced from one generation to the next and yet susceptible to change through processes of fashion negotiation within classes.

Each of the above metaphors sheds some light on class dynamics related to style-fashion-dress. However, no single metaphor explains how there are multiple movements and flows occurring simultaneously: flowing down and percolating up, crossing and zigzagging, emulating and entangling. Moreover, the intersections between class and other subject positions (e.g., ethnicity, gender, national identity) complicate the extent to which any single metaphor (or model) discussed above can explain how and why people dress as they do according to class alone. The remainder of this chapter continues to grapple with different approaches to the interplay between fashion and class as a focal point among other subject positions. The following section considers historical shifts in class-related ambiguities and anxieties. Then, I consider the ways in which we might reconceptualize class in relation to contemporary, transnational style-fashion-dress.

HISTORICAL HEGEMONIES: RENEGOTIATING AND REGULATING CLASS BOUNDARIES

As we have seen, by definition, a person's class refers to his or her income and education level, as well as family background. One can enhance social class through higher levels of education and income, but in the case of the aristocracy or the upper upper class (i.e., old money), one must technically be born into it. This class theoretically would have little motivation to participate aggressively in fashion as a social process, because there is more of a vested interest in maintaining the status quo. Hence, classic (note the root word of class) styles such as cashmere sweaters, pearls, and woolen suits are considered to be typical styles worn by the British upper class. Simmel (1904) indicates that individuals in the highest class "dread every motion and change . . . No change can bring them additional power, and every change can give them something to fear, but nothing to hope for" (Simmel 2004: 305).

The French phrase *nouveau riche* refers somewhat derogatorily to people who have become newly rich or who have a lot of new money but who—as the stereotype goes—lack the cultural capital that the upper upper, or aristocratic, class has with its old money. The stereotype further extends to style-fashion-dress: the tendency to wear colorful, ostentatious status symbols, combining them in looks and outfits that are less refined than those of individuals whose families have had their money for generations, and have more cultural capital than individuals whose money may be newer (even if there is more of it). Wealthy bourgeois individuals pose a similar threat to the aristocratic class.

Hence, historically, around the world, the ruling classes have developed laws to prohibit imitation of the appearances they have wanted to maintain for themselves.

Almost always, such laws, known as *sumptuary laws*, have been unsuccessful in their attempts to preserve the status quo in the class structure by preventing people of the lower classes from purchasing and wearing luxury goods, such as fine fabrics. Sumptuary laws were intended to regulate consumption in order to preserve the existing class structure.

The historian Alan Hunt (2010) indicates that in Japan and China, as well as Europe, sumptuary laws represented attempts to reassert feudal hierarchies—associated with the pyramid metaphor of class—during periods of hierarchical decline. In China and Japan, sumptuary laws emerged when local feudalisms evolved into more centralized and bureaucratic class systems. This consolidation of power occurred in China in 220–250 c.e., and sumptuary laws were put into place in the T'an period, 618–906 c.e. In Japan, the centralized Tokugawa family clan dominated through a system of hereditary military dictatorship from 1603–1868 and instituted a rigid class structure. At the top of the classes managed by the Tokugawa system was the samurai warrior class, followed by farmers, artisans, and merchants. Justified by the Confucian belief system, merchants were at the bottom of the social class structure because they did not produce anything (Dunn 1969: 11). In Japan, as in China, the merchant class generated the most anxiety among the central leaders because they threatened traditional hierarchies. If they were successful, they could dress as well as or better than the higher classes. Hence, the key target of sumptuary laws was the merchant class, "whose irresistible rise was eating away at the very possibility of a stable system of social closure required by the bureaucratic regimes" (Hunt 2010: 43). In the seventeenth century, for example, a Japanese law prohibited commoners such as merchants from wearing finer silks and gold lacquer. In the eleventh century, a Chinese edict disallowed fine black sables and ermine for anyone except the nobility. Commoners could only wear sable sheep and moleskins. Similar sumptuary laws governing fur were enacted in late medieval England (Hunt 2010: 44).

In the Middle Ages in Europe, society was organized in a very hierarchical manner—again, in a pyramid-like feudal structure. The elite's wealth and power at the top resulted from their ownership of land. Below the elite was a class of merchants, clerics, and artisans. At the bottom of the class pyramid were peasants who comprised a large portion of the population and who often lived in poverty. In addition to the prohibitive cost of fabric and dyes, there was the issue of clothing and work. Because lower class individuals had to perform manual labor, it was difficult to keep their clothing clean. The color of clothing—dark colors to hide dirt versus lighter colors for those who did not need to worry about manual labor—also became a key indicator of social status.

Class was a subject position determined largely by birth; there was limited social mobility (i.e., no accessible social ladder), and people were expected to conform to the class-related nature of their life circumstances with respect to their dress, education, and personal choices in general. Historians Riello and McNeil (2010) indicate that there were supposed to be natural ways of dressing in accordance with social class: "[T]herefore a knight was supposed to wear precious fur to demonstrate his social rank, while the same material would have been seen as totally inappropriate for a merchant, and even more so for a peasant, even if they could afford it" (Riello and McNeil 2010: 20).

Clothes were expensive, but wealth is only part of the story. Typically a person would spend from 20 to 30 percent of their wealth on textiles and clothing. Fabrics themselves were the source of much of this cost because of the extensive hand labor that went into their making, and also into clothing production. However, between the twelfth and fourteenth centuries, the European economy developed urban and trading centers (e.g., Venice, Genoa, Amalfi); some merchants became wealthy and displayed their status through their own and their families' attire (Riello and McNeil 2010: 20).

Hence, prior to the industrialization of fabric production in the eighteenth and nineteenth centuries, the cost of materials prohibited most people from having very many clothes. Fabric was not widely affordable, and most people (at the bottom of the pyramid) had to spin their own yarns, weave or knit their own fabrics, and sew or drape their own clothing (in their spare time when not farming or working for other, wealthier individuals). Frequently, it was women who performed this textile labor. Homespun garments, as opposed to the more finely spun and woven fabrics and garments made by artisans or craft producers, were a mark of the lower classes. Clothes, when of fine quality, were prized obsessions that were bequeathed in wills. And yet, from time to time, people of the lower classes were able to secure relatively expensive fabrics or clothes (e.g., through hand-me-downs, second-hand markets, or production sites).

The historian Christopher Dyer (1989) argues that as early as the fourteenth century, peasant appearances challenged the natural categories of class style-fashion-dress. He found historical evidence that peasant clothes were not always made from the cheapest materials available. Some of the fabrics in wealthier peasants' tunics were not too different in cost from the cloth purchased by some people in the upper classes (Dyer 1989: 176).

Even with economic delimiters, then, there were sites of status ambiguity that made those with the most power nervous. Laws were passed to address this cultural anxiety and to maintain the existing social class order. Fashion historian Christopher Breward (1995) shows how the sumptuary law of 1365 in England was designed to limit lower-class individuals (e.g., servants, urban craftsmen) from wearing materials other than cheap woolen clothing, but the law did not really work. Among the higher classes, merchants who were worth 1,000 British pounds per year were not allowed to dress any better than "gentlemen" who received 200 British pounds per year in rent. Both groups could wear silks and some furs. In contrast, knights worth 1,000 British pounds could wear almost anything, except ermine. Although such laws were ineffective, their passage did indicate "a recognition within medieval society of the power of dress as a communicator of rank and a longing for that power" (Breward 1995: 27). Breward argues that such laws were based more on the desire to foster a system based on social positions than it was on wealth. (Otherwise, why would laws be necessary?)

By the end of the fifteenth century, some European artisans bequeathed fancy or ornate clothing in their wills. Breward (1995: 28) suggests that the "power of clothing to transform and transgress perceived social barriers was perhaps stronger than its supposed ability to define them." And by the end of the sixteenth century, aristocratic dress had become "fantastical" (Breward 1995: 44). Queen Elizabeth's reign was known for its dress and artifice (e.g., dark and deeply colored velvets and brocades, garments trimmed with fur, exaggerated colors or "ruffs") in the court, and status competition also played out on the streets of London (Breward 1995: 52), fostering anxieties about the "breakdown of the moral and economic status quo caused by over-zealous fashion consumption" (Breward 1995: 54) and imported luxury goods such as silks and dyes (Breward 1995: 56). A debate ensued in the late sixteenth century around men wearing velvet (imported, rich, wasteful) versus cloth (plain, simple, practical) breeches (Breward 1995: 58).

The industrialization of textile and apparel production in the eighteenth and nineteenth centuries, respectively, contributed further to class-related ambiguities, ambivalences, and anxieties. The writings of the Lowell mill girls, mentioned earlier in the chapter in relation to the bourgeois versus proletariat class model, reveal the extent to which they viewed themselves not only as active producers, but also thoughtful consumers, of textiles. Some writings refer specifically to the young women's desire for new clothes—as well as economic independence—as a motivating factor to move from their New England farms to work in the textile mills of the industrial city of Lowell, Massachusetts, which had tempting retail stores in the downtown area near the factory:

[E]ver since the visit of the Slater girls, with new silk dresses, and Navarino bonnets trimmed with flowers, and lace veils, and gauze handkerchiefs, her [Abby's] head had been filled with visions of fine clothes; and she thought if she could only go where she could dress like them, she should be completely happy . . . Yes, she would go to Lowell, and earn all that she possibly could, and spend those earnings in beautiful attire; she would have silk dresses,—one of grass green and another of cherry red, and another upon the colour of which she would decide when she purchased it; and she would have a new Navarino bonnet, far more beautiful than Judith Slater's. (Factory Girls of an American City 1844: 26–27)

Yet once Abby went to Lowell, she exercised considerable restraint—in keeping with the values of thrift in her family. Then her coworker Judith Slater encouraged her to buy a beautiful piece of silk or piece of beautiful muslin. Abby had wondered before going to Lowell how people lived there with so many stores, without spending everything they earned. Once in Lowell, she put most of her earnings in a savings bank. One Sunday, Judith did not want to go to church with Abby, because Abby's bonnet was too "dowdy," and "her gown must have been made in 'the year one.'" Abby made it through her one year (the promised length of stay she had promised her father) in Lowell without a single silk dress, but she did return home wearing a new straw bonnet with a light blue ribbon and a dark merino (wool) dress, and bringing gifts of "some little books for the children," a new calico dress for her mother, and a black silk handkerchief for her father to wear around his neck on Sundays. That night, she asked her father: "[M]ay I not sometime go back to Lowell? I should like to add a little to the sum in the bank, and I should be glad of *one* silk gown!" Her father agreed (Factory Girls of an American City 1844: 29–33).

Abby's story is similar to that of Mary Paul, of Barnard, Vermont. Mary Paul had worked for a short time as a domestic servant near her home but requested her father's permission to go to Lowell, with the following rationale: "I think it would be much better for me [in Lowell] than to stay about here . . . I am in need of clothes which I cannot get around here and for that reason I want to go to Lowell or some other place" (Dublin 1993: 20). Mary Paul worked in Lowell for four years. She expressed some guilt about not contributing to support her father. She worked as a seamstress in Brattleboro, Vermont, after working in Lowell.

Abby's and Mary Paul's stories reveal their ambivalent subjectivities: their love of style-fashion-dress, which sometimes competed with their family commitments and values.

By the 1870s, industrialization had reached the process of clothing production, with the invention of the sewing machine. Whether their clothes were made in the home or in the factory, some European and American working class families had a few, special occasional items of clothing typically considered to be middle class (e.g., a silk dress, a bourgeois-ish man's suit or hat), as noted earlier. A higher proportion of French working class family clothing budgets went to married men and children than to married women (Crane 2000).

Crane indicates, further, however, that single working class women (like the earlier Lowell mill girls) in France, England, and (especially) the United States had some flexibility to spend some of their discretionary income on the primary consumer good for working women: style-fashion-dress.

Breward (1999) provides a compelling example of status anxiety among bourgeois women in the 1870s. A letter in *The English Woman's Domestic Magazine* (February 1876) expressed some uneasiness that was presumably shared by many of the bourgeois readers who were noticing a blurring of the differences between how their servants dressed (with their growing access to dress patterns, fashion information, and needle and thread) and how they themselves dressed:

> My income is small, but I have to keep up a good appearance, and am therefore obliged to keep two servants, a cook and a housemaid. My cook I have had for nearly two years, and I have got on very well with her until the last few months. By degrees she has been getting gayer and gayer in her dress of late, and last Sunday when she started off for church, she wore a black silk made exactly like a new one I had had sent home in the beginning of winter, and a new bonnet which I am certain I saw in Madame Louise's window in Regent Street marked 25s. She looked as if she had stepped out of a fashion plate, all but her boots and gloves . . . I feel certain that if I remonstrate with her she will leave, do you not think I may well discharge her at once? (cited in Breward 1999a: 24)

"Getting gayer and gayer" had a different meaning, of course, in the 1870s than it would mean 100 years later. Part of what historical materials indicate about this meaning was the surprise that European visitors to the United States expressed about the appearances of single working class women. It seems like it was the brightness of the colors, the combinations of clothes, and the obtrusiveness of the accessories that drew the most attention. Color—one of the important factors—can be attributed in part to cost. In the 1830s aniline (synthetic) dyes had been developed, enabling a wide range of pastel colors (e.g., pink, lavender) that became a status symbol in middle class women's dresses (Crane 2000). By way of contrast, brighter textiles (e.g., red, purple) were less expensive and also easier to keep clean than lighter colors. Class and gender subject positions were also likely to intersect with ethnicity; by the second half of the century, many single working women immigrated from Eastern and Southern Europe, with a wide range of aesthetic dress traditions in color and color coordination.

Subtle or not-so-subtle differences between class and other aesthetics notwithstanding, it is evident that experimental challenges to traditional class boundaries generated cultural anxiety—uncertainty, to use bell hooks's phrase, regarding "where we stand" (hooks 2000). They also generated cultural discourse regarding democracy—drawing implicitly on the metaphor of the social ladder. In 1899, a little more than 100 years after the founding of the United States, the feminist sociologist Jane Addams (1860–1935) asked in an *Atlantic* magazine essay: "Have we worked out our democracy in regard to clothes farther than in regard to anything else?" She noted how visitors from Europe often remarked with surprise at American women's obsession with fashion. Of particular interest was the style-fashion-dress worn by working class young women. Addams explained this occurrence as follows:

> The girl who has a definite social standing, who has been to a fashionable school or to a college, whose family live in a house seen and known by all her friends and associates, can afford to be very simple or even shabby as to her clothes, if she likes. But the working girl, whose family lives in a tenement or moves from one small apartment to another, who has little social standing, and has to make her own place, knows full well how much habit and style of dress have to do with her position. *Her income goes into her clothing out of all proportion to that which she spends upon other things. But if social advancement is her aim, it is the most sensible thing which she can do. She is judged largely by her clothes . . .* Her clothes are her background, and from them she is largely judged. It is due to this fact that girls' clubs succeed best in the business part of a town, where "working girls" and "young ladies" meet upon an equal footing, and where the clothes superficially look very much alike. Bright and ambitious girls will come to these down-town clubs to eat lunch and rest at noon, to study all sorts of subjects and listen to lectures, when they might hesitate a long time about joining a club identified with their own neighborhood, where they would be judged not solely on their personal merits and the unconscious social standing afforded to good clothes, but by other surroundings which are not nearly up to these. (Addams 1899)

As Addams articulates, clothing had become especially important in the United States toward the end of the nineteenth century. Status competition in the nineteenth century seemed to intensify, and fashion figured prominently in this competition among women. Working class women (including garment workers) used style to make statements on city streets, such as in New York. To the upper and middle class eye, the colors they put together were startling, and their accessories were assembled in a way that created hybrid styles (Crane 2000: 60–61).

Class-related anxieties surrounded not only the young working class women's consumption, but also their production. Building upon the activist efforts of the earlier Lowell mill girls, young immigrant (Italian and Eastern European Jewish) working class women organized through labor unions to combat their poor working conditions as early as the end of the nineteenth century. In November 1909, in New York City, more than 20,000 shirtwaist

workers walked off the job in protest. These (mostly) working class, immigrant women were producing apparel separates such as blouses/tops,
known as shirtwaists (Esbenshade 2004: 9). In part, it was the mixing of
shirtwaists/tops with skirts and hats that fostered the hybrid styles of young
working class women. Rightly, garment (production) and retail (distribution)
workers played important roles in the circuit of style-fashion-dress, and they
viewed themselves as expert experimenters who embraced the idea that
their self-fashionings were an investment in their futures. However, as Nan
Enstad (1998) has argued, their ability to acquire "ready-made clothes in the
latest styles should not be heralded as the 'democratization' of fashion due
to industrialization" (754), because the clothes they could afford were often
of poor quality, especially in the way they were sewn. To counter this problem,
Lower East Side garment workers could purchase fabric remnants and sam-
ples from pushcarts and warehouses. Then, using their sewing skills, they
often produced their own shirtwaists and underwear and decorated dresses
and hats with lace, trims, feathers, and the like. They were able to inflect
"their consumer practices with an element of their own creative production"
(Enstad 1998: 755). Overall, Enstad concludes that the availability of fashionable dress shifted "but did not obliterate" the role of clothing in class
distinction (Enstad 1998: 754).

When middle class reformers joined the garment workers during strikes,
some of them, along with observers, were surprised to see how fashionable
the garment workers were:

"I had come to observe the Crisis of a Social Condition;" wrote one commenta-
tor for *Collier's* magazine, "but apparently this was a Festive Occasion. Lingerie waists were elaborate, [hair] puffs towered; there were picture turbans and
di'mont [fake diamond] pendants." Working women were well known for their
exuberant embrace of consumer culture products, particularly fashion, but elab-
orately-dressed female strikers did not meet middle-class expectations for the
proper demeanor of political participants, and the reporter for *Collier's* magazine
did not immediately recognize them as political subjects. The shirtwaist strike
is famous in labor history and women's history both because it was the largest female-dominated strike to that date and because it inaugurated a string
of large, "women's strikes" in the 1910s that dramatically asserted working
women's political participation and firmly established women's unionism. While
women's fashion does not play a large role in the established histories of the
strike, it did play a part in the unfolding events of the public strike debate. (Enstad 1998: 745)

A similar class- and fashion-related dynamic occurred in the 1930s when
Rose Pesotta ([1944] 1987) led strikes by the International Ladies Garment
Workers Union in Los Angeles:

[E]ach picket line was a lively parade. The girls came dressed in their best dresses, made by themselves, and reflecting the latest styles. Many of them were beauties, and marched on the sidewalks like models in a modiste's salon. (Pesotta [1944] 1987: 40–41)

The picketers were able to make their dresses despite the fact that 40 percent of them were being paid less than $5 a week: far lower than the federal minimum wage of $15 per week and the state minimum wage of $16 per week in the 1930s (Pesotta [1944] 1987: 40).

Without the sewing machine, it would have been much less feasible for working women to be able to produce clothes in factories and also have the time and energy to make their own clothes. Historian Nancy Page Fernandez (1999) argues that some of the anxieties surrounding class and clothing related to the sewing machine itself. It had two meanings, and they were contradictory. It represented "the exploitative conditions of the factory and homework" for working class women, but it was viewed as a form of leisure and "conspicuous consumption" for middle class women: "Anxieties about the impact of industrialization on American life shaped cultural constructions of the family sewing machine" (Fernandez 1999: 157). Advertisements sold the idea that a good middle class husband could relieve his wife of labor around the home, maintain family gender roles, and eventually eliminate the need for servants.

Fernandez describes a New Home Sewing Machine Company series of "trade cards": "The Sewing Must Be Done. A Home Drama in Four Acts." In the first act/card, a bourgeois couple with two children debate whether they should buy a New Home sewing machine or hire a "French sewing girl." In the second act/card, the decision has been made to hire the French sewing girl, who is shown arriving in the home. In the third act/card, the French sewing girl is in the home sewing by hand in the parlor, and the husband is kissing her free hand; the wife sees this through a slightly opened door. In the fourth and final act/card, the bourgeois family is intact again: all four family members are sitting around the sewing machine while the wife sews on her new machine. ("The French assistant did not give entire satisfaction. A New Home machine has been purchased. All's well that ends well.") The husband is faced away from the machine, reading the paper (Fernandez 1999: 163–65). According to this story as it unfolds, this newly configured, servantless middle class family has achieved freedom from the "dangers" of having a foreign, working class, nonfamily individual in the home, according to the narratives advertisements such as these articulated. Fernandez argues that the sewing machine became represented as a solution to middle class anxieties regarding new economic arrangements (e.g., industrialization) in American life (Fernandez 1999). By 1875 one-third of working families in Massachusetts owned sewing machines, and patterns were widely available (and less expensive than in France; Crane 2000: 75). Women could make their own (and their children's) clothing at a fraction of the cost of store-bought clothing of comparable quality.

Drawing on a general theme of ambiguity to consider the ways in which style-fashion-dress make and blur class and status boundaries, the following section draws on, and updates, Fred Davis's (1992) theory of identity ambivalences.

STATUS CLAIMS AND STATUS DEMURRALS

In my view, one of the most nuanced analysis of class/status subject formation is Fred Davis's (1992) chapter in his book *Fashion and Cultural Identity*. He framed his analysis in both/and, rather than either/or terms, or even linear terms such as one might ascertain in a trickle down approach. The title of this chapter, "Ambivalences of Status: Flaunts and Feints," points to the idea that class—as represented through status in style-fashion-dress—involves mixed emotions, contradictions, and reversals. Class-related subject positions entail entanglements.

Davis begins his chapter with a quote from fashion designer Coco Chanel's (1883–1971) admonition that "women should dress as plainly as their maids." Presumably, Chanel's use of "women" referred in fact to bourgeois or upper class women who could afford to have maids. Recall the anxious quote from a middle class woman from the 1870s, earlier in this chapter, about her maid dressing too fashionably or too "middle class" for their working class station. Chanel's use of plain jersey, typically used for underwear, and her design of plain black dresses (the "little black dress") in the 1920s, can be seen as flipping such anxiety around while blurring class boundaries in an appropriative sort of way. Plain black dresses, at the time, had associations with working class maid uniforms and became the ubiquitous dress of retail and office workers. But for a middle class woman, the newly appropriated little black dress became a fashionable, flexible, elegant, modern uniform that could be dressed up or down, and could move from daytime to evening cocktail wear. One way to address class anxiety (e.g., a "fear of falling"), it seems, is to face it head on and to appropriate symbols of the working class. As Davis (1992) notes, blue jeans represent a similar pattern of class appropriation—from its working class, Gold Rush roots in the mid-nineteenth century in California to premium denim jeans costing hundreds of dollars in the twenty-first century.

But what is the difference between cultural anxiety and cultural ambivalence? Whereas cultural anxiety (involving uncertain, queasy feelings of dread as well—potentially—as hope) is freely floating and hard to pin down, cultural ambivalence is clearly framed in both/and, oppositional terms, such as "status claims" and "status demurrals" in Davis's terms.

Claims to status through style-fashion-dress may involve flaunting what one has. Sociologist/economist Thorstein Veblen (1899) called this *conspicuous consumption* in his satirical analysis of the "leisure class": bourgeois and upper class individuals who derive prestige by revealing that not only do they have a lot of wealth, but they also need not engage in manual labor for a living (conspicuous leisure).

A number of fashion studies scholars have critiqued Veblen for being too utilitarian and hence missing the point of fashion (Wilson 1985), too focused on status differentiation (Davis 1992), too linear in his rank ordering of class (Crane 2000), and too dated and too dismissive of bourgeois women's agency (Entwistle 2000). Nevertheless, there is something compelling about Veblen's satirical tone and in his ability to point to hypocrisy, which makes his work still worthy of attention. Even if class boundaries have become less important than they were before the 1960s (Crane 2000), there is still a viable luxury goods market that seems to fluctuate with the stock market, even during times of economic recession (Clifford 2011):

> Nordstrom has a waiting list for a Chanel sequined tweed coat with a $9,010 price. Neiman Marcus has sold out in almost every size of Christian Louboutin "Bianca" platform pumps, at $775 a pair. Mercedes-Benz said it sold more cars last month in the United States than it had in any July in five years. (Clifford 2011)

The concept of luxury good fashion evolved from the Parisian *haute couture* (high fashion) system, attributed to the British textile merchant and fashion designer Charles Frederick Worth (1825–1895), who moved to Paris in 1845 and managed to obtain Empress Eugénie (wife of Emperor Napoleon III) as a fashion leader/customer, along with other wealthy clients. Worth, a creative designer with a deep knowledge of textiles, managed to move effectively in French aristocratic class circles; he also donned a beret to articulate a rather ironic national/class intersectionality. The century before, Rose Bertin (1747–1813) had been the dressmaker/designer/stylist for Marie Antoinette and had built a highly influential business in Paris. Historically, the luxury design fashion model appears to best fit the trickle down (upper to middle class) metaphor of fashion, discussed earlier in the chapter. However, this metaphor does not tell the whole story, and this is where Davis's idea of identity ambivalence becomes crucial to grapple with the complexities and nuances of class and status.

As it turns out, at least some of the individuals buying luxury goods in the 2010s are conscious of the need to avoid flaunting their status brazenly. As quoted in the *New York Times* article by Clifford (2011), a thirty-one-year-old entrepreneur indicates that she spends a lot on "class pieces," such as the Yves Saint Laurent tote she has in both black and chocolate brown. However, since the recession, she avoids conspicuously branded items, so as to be cautious about looking too "showy." Nevertheless, she also admits that she is quick to do her shopping at the beginning of each season, because she is concerned that the luxury goods will sell out. Hence, she simultaneously acknowledges her love of luxury goods and her desire to be somewhat subtle about her status claims. She demurs at the same time she claims status.

Davis (1992: 57) explained the interplay between status claims and status demurrals as "ever-shifting ambivalences regarding matters of wealth, worldly attainment, and social position." The ambiguity associated with identity ambivalences provides all kinds of opportunities for innovation, articulation, and the simultaneous endorsement of and resistance to class-related hegemonies—complicated as they are by inter and intraclass entanglements, as well as intersectionalities with other subject positions.

What Davis (1992: 72) describes as "the twists, inversions, contradictions, and paradoxes of status symbolism" can also be seen in Figure 5.2. Typically, female members of the British aristocracy (upper upper class) wear "classic" if not conservative suits but are allowed a little more room for expression in their hats. Consider the style-fashion-dress of the British Princess Beatrice in Figure 5.2 (on the right). Princess Beatrice wears a neutral coatdress (over a more cocktail-ish dress) with an interesting yoke pattern and high-heeled shoes and a matching clutch bag and gloves to the wedding of her cousin, Prince William, to Catherine Middleton. What stands out the most is her hat, which was ridiculed by the media and went viral on the Internet (Considine 2011). She sold the hat on the Internet and donated the proceeds to children's charities. For our purposes, it is helpful to interpret her wedding attire, along with the public and media response, via the circuit of style-fashion-dress, interlinked with the concepts of articulation, ambivalence, and ambiguity (discussed in Chapters 1 and 2). The production, distribution, and consumption of her Valentino dress and coat, and Philip Treacy "fascinator" can be analyzed within the *haute couture*/luxury good fashion system. We can analyze her subject formation through the interplay between her subject position(s) (aristocratic, royal class, twenty-two years old, British, white, female) and her subjectivity (for example, her feelings about articulating both "old money" and novel fashion: simultaneously claiming and demurring class and fashion alike). The regulation of her wedding attire through the lens of the circuit of style-fashion-dress plays out through the public/media response, which further interacts with her subjectivity.

Figure 5.2   British Princesses Eugenie (left) and Beatrice (right)—members of the British aristocracy and highest, or upper upper, social class—leave Westminster Abbey after the wedding of Prince William to Catherine Middleton. Vivienne Westwood designed Princess Eugenie's outfit, and Princess Beatrice wears a beige Valentino dress and coat. Both of their hats were designed by the renowned Irish designer Philip Treacy. Photo by permission of Getty Images.

FASHIONABLE HEGEMONY

The history of class and fashion in euromodernity reveals that status can depend more on unique taste and styling ability than on family background. The background of Ralph Lauren's Polo label is just one example of this. Although Lauren himself actually came from a modest Jewish background, he is known for creating functional, classy, and classic separates that seem to belong to "aristocrats, Ivy Leaguers, and adventurers" who ride horses on ranches, take safaris in Kenya, or yacht in Newport. As Lauren put it modestly, "I elevated the taste level of America." In the 1970s, he convinced Bloomingdale's that it would be effective to put all of his ties, suits, dress shirts, and raincoats together in their own special little boutique. He designed this space to feel like a gentlemen's club with wood paneling, brass fixtures, and elite accessories such as walking sticks and antique alligator luggage. His "rich man's look . . . stirred all kinds of longings in people, the dream that the upwardly mobile shared for prestige, wealth, and exotic adventure . . . Lauren's ersatz old-money look was more expensive than usual, but still within reach of those who lusted for a piece of the good life. And millions of Americans did."

He made new money look "old" (Davis 1992), in a hegemonic twist on status claims and status demurrals. Lauren's tweed jackets and polo knit shirts fit the old money lifestyle; he managed to appropriate elite "town-and-country style" and turn it into fashion (Agins 1999: 86–89; Manlow 2011). Ralph Lauren was not the first to appropriate and rearticulate aristocratic style. The modern, industrial and urban world in the late eighteenth and nineteenth centuries in England offered new opportunities for mobile subjectivities aimed at producing glamour and redefining taste. George Bryan (Beau) Brummell (1778–1840) was born into a middle class family but became known as England's "prime minister of taste" (Vainshtein 2010: 329). According to Elizabeth Wilson (2007), Beau Brummell made his mark as a figure of glamour who replaced the power of aristocrats and princes with his own personal charisma and uniquely, beautifully understated sense of style-fashion-dress.

Brummell was a British socialite known for his sharp dressing and wit. He was "not a self-made man in the bourgeois sense." Rather, he was a "self-produced modern individual" who was anti-bourgeois and aristocratic in his sensibility, but ironically had an enormous influence on bourgeois style-fashion-dress (Entwistle 2000: 125). Despite his modest background, Brummell was able to climb the social ladder by moving in aristocratic circles—including a friendship with the Prince of Wales (later, King George IV). Brummell was able not only to appropriate the style of the highest class but also to take it to a new level of elegance. Known for his subtly cut and impeccably fitted trouser suits and elaborate neckwear (especially the cravat), Brummell articulated through his style-fashion-dress the principle of "conspicuous inconspicuousness"—a principle that Olga Vainshtein (2010: 329) uses to describe the simultaneous ability to dress elegantly and yet unobtrusively. We might say that this principle fosters the combined ability to reveal how "clothes make the (high class) man" in a way that is "unmarked" (considered in greater depth in Chapter 6 on gender), or without visual overstatement or pretension. Brummel used clean lines and muted colors to modernize menswear. It was not just *what* he wore, but *how* he wore it that made his style so influential: it was the way he wore his hair, the way he tucked his fitted breeches into his boots, and the way he tied his cravat (scarf or tie).

Stories circulated that Brummell took as long as five hours to get dressed and that he recommended polishing boots "with champagne." The key to Brummel's successful fashion influence was in his ability to keep the labor that went into his style invisible. Enduring today is the principle that hegemonic masculinity should *not* look like it takes a lot of time and effort. Using his attention to detail and material quality in his style-fashion-dress, Brummell defined a way of blurring class distinctions not by mere imitation, but rather by erasing "the aristocratic pretensions to demonstrate wealth and noble origin through lavish clothes" and by privileging "deliberate self-fashioning and taste" above birth and wealth (Vainshtein 2010: 329).

Brummell was not a self-made middle class man; in fact, he barely worked except for a brief period in the military through an appointment by the Prince of Wales. He lived off the inheritance of 30,000 British pounds left by his father (the personal secretary to Lord North from 1770 to 1782); Beau received this inheritance in 1799 and proceeded to set up his bachelor quarters and his lavish lifestyle in London. In his style and ethos, he was "aristocratic and anti-bourgeois" (Entwistle 2000: 125). He epitomized the upper class principle of "conspicuous leisure" (Veblen 1899). Unfortunately, he did not have the funds to spend so profusely without working, and he went into tremendous debt. A few years after he fell out of favor with the Prince of Wales in 1812, he fled to France to escape his creditors and died penniless in 1840.

Wilson (2007) argues that cultural figures such as Brummell—known in fashion studies as a "dandy"—participate in a cultural discourse of glamour. Glamour, she submits, tends to parallel tragedy and related mixed emotions of desire, fear, anxiety, and loss. Perhaps part of what was lost through Brummell's popularity and fashion influence in the first decade of the nineteenth century was a faith in the idea that aristocrats are *the* trendsetters in society by function of their class of birth.

Ironically, although Brummell himself rejected bourgeois (upper middle class) style, ultimately his legacy was the novel unmarked masculinity that he articulated. His use of the trouser suit and neckwear "became the template for the nineteenth-century bourgeois businessman" (Wilson 2007:97). At the intersections of class and gender, Brummell's look of leisure paradoxically became the bourgeois masculine norm, discussed further in the following chapter highlighting gender. This chapter closes with the following quote by Fred Davis, on his theme of status claims and status demurrals:

> Not that anyone, or hardly anyone, wishes to be taken for Nobody, but conveying an impression with clothing that one is Somebody is neither as easy nor as obvious as it may at first seem. (Davis 1992: 58)

–6–

Gendering Fashion, Fashioning Gender: Beyond Binaries

From the moment of birth (or even earlier), gender becomes an everyday process of the body—navigating and negotiating through time and space. Becoming visibly gendered—binary oppositions notwithstanding—involves engagement with complicated, shifting coding systems of colors, fabrics, trims, forms, shapes, and patterns and other body fashionings. These systems are not natural; rather, they are arbitrary and vary by time and space, history and culture.

As seen in Sienna's various looks in Figure 6.1 (even without the benefit of color), female baby coding can be as nuanced as a trim on a collar or shirt sleeve, the cut of a sleeve, a headband, a flower, the type of fabric, or the fit of pants. Some of the clothes themselves articulate a mixture of gender symbols: for example, leggings that are striped or polka dotted in pink or lavender, a lavender fleece hoodie vest (upper right) in a floral pattern, or an orange polo shirt (bottom left) with pink trim inside the neckline. Or, it can be as gendered as a dress for a special occasion (e.g., as a flower girl for her aunt's wedding).

The contemporary U.S. baby clothing market is a far cry from that of the early 1900s. Boys and girls alike wore long white dresses, which became shorter as they began to crawl and walk. Gender "guessing games" were popular in women's magazines, because there were few, if any, cues that made it easy to distinguish baby boys from baby girls, according to clothing historian Jo Paoletti (2012). Gender ambiguity was tolerated, if not enjoyed. This began to change as the children's clothing industry developed in the first few decades of the twentieth century, and cultural discourse includes some debate regarding the gendered meanings of colors such as pink and blue. In 1918, a magazine advised parents that pink was the more robust and hence the more "masculine" color, like a boy with rosy cheeks who had been playing actively outdoors. Blue, on the other hand, was considered to be soft and demure, and hence more feminine (Paoletti and Kregloh 1989). This advice is mind boggling to consider today; it shatters a gendered social order or cultural logic that has become naturalized as some kind of essentialist law. (Upon hearing about this advice from 1918, students accustomed to the "pink is for girls" and "blue is for boys" maxim do a double take and frequently ask, "Wait; what?")

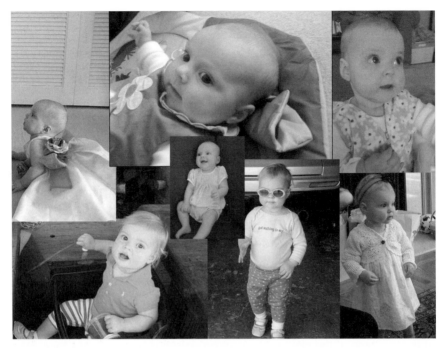

Figure 6.1   Sienna's style-fashion-dress. Note the range and, often, subtlety, of gender cues.

The gender coding system remained rather ambiguous into the 1930s and then began to settle down into the pink-is-for-girls and blue-is-for-boys maxim. Paoletti (2012) describes the baby boom generation (1946–1964) as the first U.S. cohort to be consistently color coded at birth. The pink-versus-blue system is so entrenched in the popular psyche that it is routinely accepted as natural well into the twenty-first century.

As is often the case with gender-coded appearance symbols, exceptions are made, but they often apply only in one direction. Girls can wear blue, but it is still largely considered to be anxiety producing for adults in the United States to see baby boys wearing pink, especially when they are very young (and not yet "fully formed"?). As we see in this chapter, this "identity *not*" (Freitas et al. 1997) principle—that masculinity is defined as *not* femininity—applies more generally to the fashioning of gender in euromodernity.

In 2011 Jenna Lyons, the president and creative director of J. Crew, was featured in an e-mail mailing with her five-year-old son, Beckett. The mailer said: "Saturday with Jenna. See how she and son Beckett go off duty in style." Jenna and Beckett are relaxed and smiling at each other. Beckett's toenails are bright (neon) pink; and the bottle of nail polish sits in the foreground. Soon after the mailing, conservative commentators began to criticize Lyons and J. Crew for abandoning "all trappings of gender identity" and for "blatant propaganda celebrating transgendered children" (Abraham 2011). Most bloggers and commentators, however, defended Lyons and J. Crew, pointing to the innocence of free play, creativity, and color choice.

This scenario shows how—even in the gender certainty associated with pinkness as a marker of a source of anxiety and identity *not* for baby boys—there is actually some room for play (in the minds of most, especially in the context of limited experimentation) with cultural gender codes through style-fashion-dress. Gender is always under construction, socially and culturally speaking. Yes, it is a subject position with all of the historical baggage regarding roles, ways of appearing, and expectations that one would expect from prescriptive cultural discourses that become embodied in everyday habitus. But it also interacts with other subject positions to become a form of subjectivity and—indeed agency—that requires ongoing articulation.

Gender is actually not just who we are; it is what we do or perform as we participate in an embodied way with cultural discourses. Feminist critical theorist Judith Butler (1990) refers to this gendered interplay between cultural discourse and everyday habitus as *performativity*. Style, fashion, and dress become critical components in this interplay, in everything from the use of mascara to shaving to pedicures to the colors, patterns, and materials that circulate in the gendered circuit of style-fashion-dress. By performing gender in an iterative way between our bodies and the social worlds we inhabit, we continually "map" both old and new ways of becoming. To the great extent that these mappings vary dramatically across time and space, we cannot think of gender merely as a biological essence but rather as a social construction that is embodied. From a performative perspective, gender can be described as a way of repeatedly styling the body; this styling is regulated by cultural discourse, but it becomes part of the ongoing experience of fashioning the gendered body on a personal and social level, as well.

Let's consider a few examples of gender as a social construction across time and space: The long white dresses worn by infant boys and girls alike in euromodern cultures of the eighteenth and nineteenth centuries would be considered too effeminate for infant boys of today. Contemporary Korean males may wear pink style-dress-fashion in traditional ceremonies; this would be unlikely in either a "Western" Korean wedding ceremony or in euromodern cultures, unless the color is restricted to the small spaces of a tie or pocket hanky. Sikh men wear wrapped turbans on their heads. In euromodern contexts, these turbans may be perceived as hats—and hence, for example, the inability of airport security systems to understand why they cannot be simply removed and put on a conveyor belt. But turbans are not hats, and they are not equivalent to euromodern feminine fashion statements. Turbans have religious and cultural significance for Sikh men, who carefully wrap and unwrap turbans in the processes of donning and doffing. This significance is undermined when they are reduced to a piece of fabric in an airport security system (Puar 2007). Meanings of gender vary historically and culturally, and so does the style-fashion-dress that represents and articulates gender.

Contributing to the complications or contradictions associated with gender is that it is part of a larger system of concepts (like style-fashion-dress): sex, gender, and sexuality. In euromodern terms, each of these concepts is framed in binary terms: male versus female, masculine versus feminine, and heterosexual versus homosexual. Since the 1970s or so, academic writers have strived to differentiate among sex, gender, and sexuality. Permeating these differentiations has been a fundamental debate between *biological determinism* and *social constructionism*: that is, the extent to which biology is destiny (the essence or truth regarding who we "really are"), and culture becomes constituted by creating social categories such as gender (through cultural discourse and everyday power relations). Most commonly, sex (male, female) has been contrasted with gender (masculinity, femininity), with sex referring to biology and gender referring to culture.

Unfortunately, as feminist biologist Fausto-Sterling (2003) points out, the sex-gender distinction easily becomes a binary opposition in its own right and oversimplifies or obfuscates some complexities: how "sex" too is immersed in cultural discourse, how the body meets culture through concepts such as *habitus*, or how different fields of study (e.g., the biological sciences, the social sciences, cultural studies) need to collaborate to bridge unhelpful boundaries. Sexuality (sexual preference, discussed further in Chapter 7) and transgender experiences (discussed later in this chapter) have also been debated in terms of biological determinism and social constructionism. At this point, it is helpful to understand that there is an ongoing debate that requires collaboration across fields of study to understand complexities within and across cultural contexts. Overall, the concepts and experiences of sex, gender, and sexuality—especially in conjunction with style-fashion-dress—include some kind of both/and or multiple, rather than strictly either/or combinations.

SOFT ASSEMBLAGES

As the feminist biological scientist Anne Fausto-Sterling (2003) notes, gender is not simply "hard wired"; rather, she points to the need to understand gender as "softly assembled" in a complex articulation of the body, time, psychology, and cultural space. There may be periods of tremendous instability in gendered subjectivities, followed by times of relative stability (Fausto-Sterling 2003: 128).

Viewing gender as a soft assemblage, rather than as a fixed essence, opens up the idea of plural ways of "doing" gender, especially when exploring transnational understandings and intersectional analyses of gender's interplay with sexuality, race, ethnicity, religion, social class, national identity, age/generation, and other subject positions. The material and symbolic interplay between the body and style-fashion-dress opens up all kinds of possibilities.

In the context of euromodernity, gender has been organized not only in binary terms but also through a cultural logic that visualizes fashion itself as feminine. And yet men, as well as women, wear clothes and modify their appearances. At the same time, there is a huge contradiction at play as we contrast this assumption that fashion equals femininity with the euromodern expression that "clothes make the man"—presumably applied most to signify hegemonic (bourgeois) masculinity (e.g., an understated but well-tailored business suit). Note that the expression is not "*fashion* makes the man," but one could well imagine the expression "fashion makes the *woman*." Feminist theorist Simone de Beauvoir (1947) wrote that "One is born a female, but becomes a woman," and style-fashion-dress are part of this process of becoming. The same is true, of course, for individuals who are born male or, more accurately, who are assigned the male gender. Yet in the case of males, it is a certain kind of clothing, rather than fashion as a social process, that is what makes him a man. "Fashion" seems to imply femininity as a process of frivolous change, colorful details and unnecessary flounces, and superficiality.

MARKING, UNMARKING, AND REMARKING GENDER

Fashion, like femininity, is marked as the context of the other. Masculinity (especially hegemonic masculinity), by way of contrast, is more serious, changes in slower and more subtle ways, and eschews elaborate ornamentation. Masculinity, in euromodern terms, is unmarked. But we can think of gender more generally as a process of marking, unmarking, and remarking as individuals articulate it—not only as a subject position but also as an ongoing process of subjectivity. To the extent that fashion as a mode of gender performativity has been imagined as feminine, the idea of "men's fashion" has been framed as a contradictory space (Edwards 1997: 135). Sociologist Tim Edwards (2006) argues that part of the problem lies in the lack of articulation among the literatures pertaining to fashion, performativity, and masculinity; he points to the need for more bridging, cross-fertilization across fields, and empirical research to understand how men do masculinity in their everyday style-fashion-dress. Indeed, in many of the interviews that my research team and I have conducted, many men often do not feel comfortable participating in a study on "men's fashion." At least initially, they often feel more interested in, or accepting of, the study when we use a more neutral term such as "menswear" (which is less marked).

The marked versus unmarked binary opposition reveals a number of over-simplifying binary oppositions that organize the process of gendering style-fashion-dress, with femininity as the first of each opposition.

- *Fashion/expression versus uniformity/standardization.* Indeed, the roots of the masculine bourgeois business suit can be found in the uniforms required to dress national militaries in standardized attire.
- *Elaborated codes versus restricted codes* (Davis 1992). Variety became the stuff of femininity, whereas masculinity became the epitome of understated elegance, with a much narrower range of options.
- *Disorder versus order.* Femininity was the messier, more complex sister to masculinity, which was streamlined of excess as it exuded euromodernity.

Euromodernity—framed by ideas, events, and social movements such as French Enlightenment philosophy (e.g., René Descartes, Jean-Jacques Rousseau), the United States and French Revolutions, and political discourses regarding national citizenship—fostered what some style-fashion-dress scholars have called the "masculine renunciation of fashion" (e.g., Flugel 1930). There are debates about when and how this happened, but most scholars agree that bourgeois men, at least, moved away from color; silk; pattern; ornamentation; wigs; knickers; and tights, in favor of darker, more somber, businesslike clothing.

What does unmarked mean in the context of gender relations through style-fashion-dress? We can think of it as a kind of euromodern project to rearticulate hegemonic masculinity. This project can be considered a flight from femininity, as well as fashion in terms of what it meant to appear visibly male. This hegemonic masculine discourse of differentiating gender and distancing from fashion and femininity was neither a sudden nor a decisive renunciation, according to fashion historian Christopher Breward (1999). Instead, it was a protracted process of emphasizing what were to become known as "manly" (heavier, darker, wool rather than silk) materials, cuts of clothing (gradually less shapely or form fitting and yet still streamlined), and subtlety in detailing (stitching, etc.): a whole sartorial (dress-related) discourse. (By way of contrast, nineteenth-century, euromodern bourgeois women tended to wear white, pastel, or brightly colored/patterned dresses that were fitted on the top but full and leg obscuring on the bottom.)

The protracted process of unmarking masculinity involved making style-fashion-dress more nuanced and less noticeable, still caring but not letting it show blatantly.

This demarcation from fashion and femininity was intersectional, in that it also involved a distancing from the upper or aristocratic class. You'll recall from Chapters 3 and 4 that male French revolutionaries in the 1780s rejected aristocratic masculine attire in favor of more influences from the working classes—such as trousers that were full in cut (*sans-culotte*, or "without knickers"), as opposed to the more aristocratic tapered pant style associated with upper class men. Similarly, middle class British men were already distancing themselves from anything they perceived to be feminine or "aristocratic" or "frivolous" or "French" (such as silk fabrics; Kuchta 2002). Fashion studies scholar Olga Vainshtein (2009) notes how the well-dressed euromodern "dandy" fashion of the nineteenth century—for example, Beau Brummell, discussed in Chapter 5—fostered an ethos of "conspicuous inconspicuousness." The idea was to be unmarked but with an eye for subtle detail; those "in the know" would be able to interpret the codes of fine dressing. This became the crux of being an unmarked man of style: modern and manly through a businesslike demeanor that thrived on tailored nuance rather than obvious fashion change. The business suit, in one form or a subtle another, has endured more than 200 years as a dominant symbol of hegemonic (bourgeois) masculinity. Not surprisingly, feminist studies, with its attention to deconstructing and reconstructing gendered power relations, has not only focused on women's issues but also on how hegemonic masculinity works.

SEX, GENDER, AND STYLE-FASHION-DRESS: FEMINIST DECONSTRUCTIONS

In the 1970s second-wave feminist theory made an important distinction between sex (as a biological construct: male versus female) and gender (as a social construct: masculinity versus femininity). In many ways, the body and its differentiating sexual characteristics (e.g., penis versus vagina) become a metaphor for sex, whereas clothing and its culturally coded meanings (e.g., pink versus blue in contemporary U.S. infant dress) become a metaphor for gender. Gender is socially constructed and culturally created and represented. Gender is something that people *do*. Applying makeup, shaving one's face or one's legs, and donning high heels or a face veil all fall within the realm of *doing* gender; these processes and practices vary across time and space (cultural discourse). It is important to remember, however, that gender is socially constructed in concert with other subject positions embedded in cultural discourses of race, ethnicity, national identity, class, sexuality, and religion, etc.

Cross-cultural studies indicate that in virtually every cultural context, male activities—whatever they may be—are considered to be more important than female ones (Rosaldo 1974). However, the *way* gender plays out varies across historical and cultural contexts. Cultural discourses frequently provide scripts that prescribe what men and women are expected to do (or not do), including how they are supposed to dress. A feminist perspective questions these scripts, especially to the extent that they prescribe essentialist ways of being and limit one's life choices. Feminists believe that men's and women's self-images, aspirations, and life chances should not be constrained by scripts (Ferrante 1995). Feminist theory aims to "complicate" gender: "to analyze gender relations: how gender relations are constructed and explained and how we think, or equally important, do not think about them" (Flax 1990: 40).

Notably, feminists have critiqued the binary opposition that organizes gender and other subject positions in euromodernity. Eschewing biological essentialism, a feminist perspective reminds us that gender is not a neutral concept; power relations are involved. The dichotomy between masculinity and femininity limits choices and life options; stereotypes what we are supposed to care about and how/why; and maintains a hierarchical order based in part on a gendered *system of looking*, in which "*men act and women appear*," according to the critical art theorist John Berger:

> *Men act and women appear.* Men look at women. Women watch themselves being looked at. This determines not only most relations between men and women but also the relation of women to themselves. (Berger 1977: 47)

Feminist film theorists (e.g., Mulvey 1975) have made similar arguments, built upon the hegemonic, gendered system of looking: The *gaze* involves an active, masculine positioning that has subjectivity (i.e., looking, gazing, knowing), whereas the observed (feminine) position—a fashion model, an actor on the silver screen or on the stage, a person on the street—lacks subjectivity in the simplest interpretation of feminist gaze theory; she is the passive object of the masculine gaze.

Jean Kilbourne's (2010) film *Killing Us Softly IV* (the first version of which appeared in 1979) details the ways in which advertising dehumanizes and demeans women—turning them into sexualized objects and proffering unattainable images of beauty. Kilbourne's lectures, films, and publications—and those of other feminist writers and activists—have contributed to a mainstream understanding of the problems associated with hegemonic female gender representation:

1. a narrow view of beauty (e.g., young, white, thin);
2. connections between the objectification of women and violence; and
3. self-esteem and body image issues (e.g., eating disorders) for the vast majority of women who cannot achieve the represented beauty ideal in fashion magazines. Indeed, even the models themselves cannot achieve looks that can only be created with airbrushing and Photoshopping.

Clearly, sex sells, and it is usually women's bodies that are represented and "consumed." Yet it is not only women's bodies, but more accurately it is most often young, thin, white women's bodies that are represented and consumed as objects of beauty in hegemonic cultural discourse. The third wave of feminism since the 1980s has sought to clarify the importance of intersectionalities and entanglements, so that we can understand how there are *multiple* ways of articulating masculinities and femininities.

Still, the gendered playing field is not level in terms of representation and subjectivity. And yet the situation is more complicated than a strict, essentialist framework that "fixes" the male (sex) body in the role of the gazing subject versus the female body in the role of sex object. In 1983, feminist film theorist E. Ann Kaplan (1983) questioned the strictly sexed dynamics of systems of looking. In her article, "Is the Gaze Male?" (Kaplan 2000), she cautions against "fixing" subject-object relations in terms of sexed bodies, arguing instead for a more flexible dynamic that acknowledges gendered power relations. This argument has been expanded in feminist theory since the 1980s to address intersectionalities between gender and race and ethnicity (e.g., black female spectatorship; hooks 1992); national and transnational identities (Tarlo 2010); gay, lesbian, and queer identities (Hanson 1999; Lewis 1997); and so on. Gender and other subject positions multiply when we take them into account jointly.

Even in the context of global hegemonic (young, white) fashion images, is it simply enough to "reverse the gendered binary" by switching from a focus on young, (mostly) white, feminine models to one on young, white, male models? What is to be gained? Turning young, (mostly) white, male (or any other) bodies into sex objects is not a feminist goal. Rather, the larger feminist goal is to deconstruct the subject-object binary or power hierarchy altogether: to break down either/or oppositions and to enable subjectivity on the part of all genders and other, intersecting subject positions. Here are just a few examples that may help to think beyond natural gender binary hierarchies, as represented in hegemonic cultural discourse:

- What should we make of the trend in euromodernity, since the 1980s (Thompson 2000), to represent young male models in shirtless, six-pack-ab(dominal) images on fashion websites, retail walls, and shopping bags? Since the 1980s, male models have been depicted in ways that show a lot of skin (at least on top); they too have become sex objects in some ways. But does just reversing the subject and object really circumvent power relations (gendered or otherwise)?
- To what extent is the binary, gendered "gaze" system biased in terms of sexuality? This question gets pursued in greater depth in Chapter 7, but for now it seems pertinent to question the degree to which the "masculine"

gazing subject and "feminine" (gazed at) sex object are hegemonically represented as heterosexual. What about other possibilities? What about same-sex or same-gender desires?

- Who gets to be in the "desiring" role and who is in the "desired" role? How do intersecting subject positions such as race, ethnicity, national identity, religion, class, age, and other subject positions intervene? Can a gendered binary framework really capture all of the possibilities?

- We can also complicate the idea of gendered objects (the "looked at" images/persons) of desire. The field of transgender studies, especially since the 1990s, has opened up a whole and wide range of options for considering who represents a desirable and desired image and how/why.

THEORIZING THE BODY AND STYLE-FASHION-DRESS

Just as *feminist theory* seeks to destabilize or to deconstruct gendered binary oppositions (e.g., male versus female; or more inclusively, masculinity versus femininity), *queer theory* (discussed further in Chapter 7) destabilizes or deconstructs sexualized binary oppositions such as heterosexuality versus homosexuality. Further, and even more deeply, *transgender theory* interrogates the whole binary opposition between sex and gender. Transgender theory grapples broadly with the relationship between the biological sex assigned at birth and an individual's own gender identity.

Sex, it turns out, is also socially constructed; it is a concept that is embedded in scientific and cultural discourses. Sex is generally "assigned" by a physician at birth (or several months earlier, with prenatal technologies). This process can be less straightforward that it may appear. Some individuals feel as though they were born in a birthday suit that does not match the gender identity they experienced early in life. Further, as many as two percent of infants are born with genitalia or other characteristics that vary from the medically defined ideal male or ideal female; yet they are labeled as either boys or girls. One or two out of 1,000 infants receive corrective surgery to reinforce the sex assigned by a physician. Most commonly in such instances, a penis is determined to be too small and is removed; hence the assigned sex is female. This decision, itself, points to values and assumptions regarding sex and gender (Blackless et al. 2000).

Human biology is more than genitalia; it includes a wide range of traits (e.g., height, build, voice), genes, chromosomes, hormones, and needs to be understood as a continuum of sex/gender development. Fausto-Sterling (2003) asserts that "bodies are not static slaves to their biology" (31), and that the biological aspects of the body need to be understood as they articulate with social, psychological, and cultural factors.

Biology, then, is not just determined, as noted earlier in this chapter, but rather is "softly assembled" in conjunction with culture, psychology, and everyday social life (Fausto-Sterling 2003: 128). And style-fashion-dress become part of the soft assemblage—bridging the boundary between the body and the social world, albeit ambiguously (Wilson 1985). Feminist theorist Judith Butler (1990) argues that gender is not a stable identity but rather "an identity tenuously constituted in time, instituted in an exterior space through a *stylized repetition of acts* [that comprise] the 'material basis of gender'" (Butler 1990: 126). Gender, again, is something we *do* in everyday life: what we wear, how we groom, how we carry ourselves, and the like. Our bodies and our clothes are key factors in our articulations and representations of gender as a subject position and as a mode of subjectivity. As we have seen, transgender theory helps to open up the possibility to think more flexibly about gender, in the interplay between the body and style-fashion-dress.

TRANSGENDER STUDIES THROUGH BODIES AND STYLE-FASHION-DRESS

Gender multiplies as we consider intersectionalities and possibilities for articulations through "stylized repetitions of acts." Historian Susan Stryker describes transgender as the "movement across a socially imposed boundary away from an unchosen starting place—rather than any particular destination or mode of transition" (Stryker 2008: 1). In its interrogation of the dominant binary sex/gender ideology in euromodernity, the field of transgender studies includes "anything that disrupts, denaturalizes, rearticulates, and makes visible the normative linkages" assumed to bridge among biological sex, social constructions and cultural discourses of gender, subjectively experienced gender identity, and "social expectations of gender-related performance" (Stryker 2006: 3).

Topically, the field of transgender studies pursues a wide and flexible range of gender possibilities: transsexuality; cross-dressing; some aspects of intersexuality (having biological characteristics of both sexes) and homosexuality; and cross-cultural, historical, and subcultural studies of human gender diversity. The terminology is frequently controversial or contested.

Typically, the term *transsexual* describes an individual who seeks medical assistance to modify the sex of their physical bodies, whereas those who merely want to change their gendered clothing cross-dress—a practice than can range from resisting or seeking temporary relief from one's assigned social gender to a theatrical performance, to the erotic pleasure of wearing "forbidden" clothing, to economic necessity (e.g., historically women have dressed as men in order to be able to work), to public celebrations or holidays (e.g., Mardi Gras, Halloween, Burning Man). Of course, both transsexuality and cross-dressing involve a wide range of body-modifying practices: from a change of clothing to hormonal therapy to surgery. The term *transgender* has the benefit of inclusiveness of a wide range of subject positions, subjectivities, and practices.

In euromodern cultures, the sex/gender binary only allows acceptance of, or movement away from, one's assigned sex/gender. There is neither a third nor an in-between option. Some other cultures, however, allow additional gender options beyond the binary. For example, a number of Native American cultures have a gender space for "two-spirit" people: individuals who articulate both masculine and feminine spirits and who play a special spiritual role in the culture.

Anthropologist Charlotte Suthrell (2004) conducted a comparative ethnographic study of male-to-female (MtF) cross-dressing between the United Kingdom and India, where there is a separate *hijra* gender culture. *Hijras* are initiated into a new life and join a community. Part of the community is based on a spiritual dimension; *hijras* bestow blessings at heterosexual weddings and before or during birth. *Hijras* come from both Hindu and Muslim backgrounds and frequently wear a sari or *salwaar kameez* (tunic and trousers), makeup, long hair, and jewelry like women; but often smoke, talk and curse like men (Suthrell 2004).

British MtF cross-dressers, in contrast, do not live in a separate physical community but are able to experience a sense of community online. Most often, they experience part of their lives in secrecy and often with great anxiety. It is evident that in euromodern cultures, it is much more difficult for biological males to "cross . . . gender barricades" than it is for biological females to do so. Men who choose to wear women's clothing are viewed as imitating the "inferior sex" (Suthrell 2004: 23), and perhaps this is why popular culture (e.g., films such as *Some Like It Hot*, *La Cage Aux Folles*, *Tootsie*) has found humor in men dressing like women. Elite men's organizations frequently have skits that involve cross-dressing—meant to be funny. Often, laughter has a nervous edge to it, and can be attributed to cultural anxiety. Literary scholar Marjorie Garber (1992) sees cross-dressing (or transvestism) as an indicator of a "category crisis" in cultural gender discourse. She sees cross-dressing as "a space of possibility" that structures and disrupts the idea of cultural categories (including, but not limited to, gender categories). She argues that it is important to look *at* rather than *through* cross-dressers in popular culture and everyday life: to consider cross-dressing as an additional (third or higher) space of gender possibility; it is a provocative space, because it generates and articulates cultural anxiety.

The majority of cross-dressers are heterosexual, but some groups within the gay and lesbian communities perform gender to subvert binary boundaries

(e.g., drag kings or drag queens, discussed further in Chapter 7) and to challenge the hegemonic, gendered system of looking ("men act, women appear").
This system has been a problem for men, as well—especially those who
choose to exert their agency and express themselves through style. Transgender studies (or indeed, trans fashion) remind us that gender is not fixed in
clothes; instead, symbols and meanings of gender *float* across appearances
and contexts. When and how symbols and meanings float within and across
genders can tell us a great deal about power relations. A feminist perspective
reminds us that there is a reason why girls and women may not agonize too
much about appropriating masculine symbols ranging from jeans or pants to
T-shirts, tailored wool jackets, and baseball caps.

Less typically, feminine symbols float from female- to male-identified bodies; often, it has to be in a context that is unusually flexible or free. The explanation for this tendency toward a one-way flow of influence can be explained
by differences in power. A feminine borrowing or appropriation of masculine
power seems to be more logical than a masculine borrowing or appropriation
of female power. Who has something to gain, and who has something to lose
(i.e., power)? The context of cross-dressing, in turn, seems to follow from
this principle of hegemonic masculine power. That is, MtF cross-dressing is
likely to arouse more attention and anxiety than female-to-male (FtM) cross-
dressing, due to gendered power relations that are in flux but obviously still
uneven.

MtF transgender experiences involving the body itself have received more
attention than FtM gender subject positioning, perhaps for some similar reasons: gendered power relations, along with related cultural obsessions and
anxieties. As noted above, there are some complicated politics as to choice
of adjectives in identity and subjectivity: transgender or transsexual, but the
terminology is also culturally shifting and personally chosen. Transgender is
generally used in a more inclusive way than transsexual, and is currently pre-
ferred by the activist community. Transsexual is a term that emerged from the
medical community, so it implies going through a physical and social transitioning process that is likely to involve hormones as well as surgery. However,
some individuals who have gone through all of these processes may still prefer the adjective transgender for personal, community, and political reasons.
So the choice of words is complicated.

The process of MtF medical transitioning first came to the attention of the
U.S. public in 1952, when George Jorgensen returned to the United States
from Denmark as Christine Jorgensen (1926–1989). Jorgensen had under-
gone hormonal therapeutic treatments, as well as a series of sex reassignment surgeries. A media frenzy ensued. One example was the headline, "Ex-GI
becomes blonde beauty: Operations transform Bronx youth," of an article run
by the *New York Daily News* on December 1, 1952. What was supposed to

be a quiet medical process had turned into a deluge by the press, along with an anxious public obsession with the idea of sex change. Jorgensen managed to turn the attention into an opportunity to tell her story from her own perspective. She became an entertainer, author of an autobiography, and frequent lecturer to college campuses around the United States, fostering public awareness about the MtF experience (christinejorgensen.org).

If we "fast forward" into the 2010s, MtF transgender and transsexual experiences have acquired greater visibility and yet still generate public fascination. More generally, transgender experiences include an array of gender crossings: some that are more about the body and some that are more about the style-fashion-dress, and many that involve both and navigate in between. Transgender practices include MtF cross-dressing (mostly involving heterosexual males, but "drag" is often associated with gay male culture, discussed further in Chapter 7), transsexual transitioning, and a whole array of MtF mind-body crossings. For example, MtF transgender subject positions and subjectivities include RuPaul, the famous male-identified drag queen, musical performer (with the *Supermodel* CD), author of *Workin' It! RuPaul's Guide to Life, Liberty, and the Pursuit of Style* (2010), and host of television and radio shows. In 2011, for example, the Brazilian supermodel Lea T. appeared on the *Oprah Winfrey Show* and described herself as a MtF transsexual woman.

In the last half of the twentieth century, FtM transgender and, more specifically, transsexual subjectivities received much less media attention than MtF. However, in the twenty-first century, there has been more academic interest, community building, and mainstream popular discourse on FtM transgender and transsexual experiences. (The choice of term depends on the individual and some complicated politics in connection with the medical community and political activism; the meanings of the terms are not fixed.) One highly publicized example of a FtM transgender experience is Chastity Bono's social and physical transition from a lesbian woman to a FtM transgender man (Chaz). Bono was assigned a female identity at birth and—as the daughter of Sonny and Cher, the famous singing duo and television stars of the 1960s and 1970s—frequently appeared on her parents' television variety show in the early 1970s. So the public came to know and adore her as a cute little two-year-old girl who charmed the audience when she spoke to open or close the show. Chastity came out as lesbian when she was 18 and appeared on the *Oprah Winfrey Show*, and then announced in 2009 that she was undergoing a transitional FtM process. As detailed in the documentary *Becoming Chaz* (2011, World of Wonder Productions), Chaz Bono's (2011) book *Transition: The Story of How I Became a Man*, and on his 2011 appearance on the final season of the *Oprah Winfrey Show*, Chaz explains how he had never felt comfortable in his own body as a female. Puberty was especially difficult when

Chastity developed breasts, and their surgical removal during Chaz's forties was one aspect of the transition process that was most satisfying. As an already public figure who was already widely known (by those old enough to remember the *Sonny and Cher Show*), Chaz made the decision to tell his story and to contribute to transgender awareness.

Similarly, transgender activist/scholar Jamison Green's (2004) book, *Becoming a Visible Man*, had chronicled his experience of the transition from a female assignment at birth, to his feelings of being a male in a female body, to his refusal to wear dresses as a child, to his lesbian identity and family relationships, to his decision to undergo the medical process with hormones and sexual reassignment surgery to become a FtM transsexual man. Although he does not talk very much about his clothing in the book, photos of him reveal his male-identified subject position with body modifications and other accoutrements (e.g., suit, beard) associated with upper middle class masculinity.

Interestingly, during this same period of time that FtM transgender experiences have received more public attention, the study of menswear and the possibility of men's fashion came out of the closet and became a hot academic topic of study. Regardless of the type of soft assemblage or gendered subject position involved, menswear itself seems to have become a topic that is finally being studied in greater depth, especially in the context of British men's tailoring.

MENSWEAR OUT OF THE ACADEMIC CLOSET

A few examples of works contributing to academic interest in menswear and the process of fashioning masculinity in the context of euromodernity include the following.

Christopher Breward's (1999b) book, *The Hidden Consumer: Masculinities, Fashion and City Life 1860–1914*, unpacks the unmarking of masculinity by challenging the tendency for the male population to be largely excluded from the history of the interplay among consumption, euromodernity, and urban life. He details the ways in which "an underlying insistence on the unmanliness of the whole clothing business" undermined the reality that men, too, were consumers and wore clothes (Breward 1999b: 2).

In *Sex and Suits*, Anne Hollander (1994) argues that the euromodern masculine suit represents a kind of evolutionary streamlining that has become lasting and hegemonic, in part, due to its visual form:

> I believe the staying power of male tailoring shows how visual form can have its own authority, its own self-perpetuating symbolic and emotional force. This is a modern belief; and the very way modern suits look expresses the thought. It is

expounded by their intrinsically abstract formal character, together with their abiding evolutionary character—their look of looking like themselves, even while their style keeps slightly changing. (4)

Hollander goes on to say that she believes that the history of (euro)modern women's wear has followed (after modern menswear) a similar evolutionary path. (As I write this, I wonder, why is menswear an acceptable and accepted single, compound word in English, whereas "women's wear" is a term that requires two words and seems almost redundant, as if "fashion" is all that is needed to "code" what women wear?) The flapper look of the 1920s, pants and pantsuits that had become a fixture in women's wardrobes by the end of the twentieth century, and jeans all represent examples of clothes that follow this pattern. There are some exceptions to this pattern of streamlining: wedding dresses, bouffant skirts, little girls' tutus, and so on. Overall, however, a pattern of euromodern streamlining does seem to prevail in what women, as well as what men, wear over time.

How does streamlining present itself through color? Again, there are exceptions and ambiguities, but arguably neutrality has become a dominant theme, especially in menswear. In his book, *Men in Black*, John Harvey (1995) analyzes the multiple meanings of black and how it became the dominant color of bourgeois menswear in the nineteenth century. We might say that blackness helped simultaneously and ambiguously to mark, unmark, and remark hegemonic masculinity.

Sociologist Tim Edwards published *Men in the Mirror: Men's Fashion, Masculinity, and Consumer Society* in 1997, and then *Cultures of Masculinity* with a chapter on men's fashion (Edwards 2006). His 2011 book, *Fashion in Focus: Concepts, Practices and Politics*, also includes a chapter on men's fashion. Throughout his books, he develops a nuanced argument that "men's fashion" is a contradictory space that needs to be unpacked and studied in greater depth. Based on studying masculine style-fashion-dress for several years, I agree with his argument, and I would further add that—consistent with the circuit of style-fashion-dress discussed in Chapter 2—it is a space that is fraught with ambivalence and anxiety.

By the late 2000s, men's fashion had become a hot topic in the field of fashion studies. In 2008 and 2009, two books of readings on men's fashions were published: one called *Men's Fashion Reader* (Reilly and Cosbey 2008) and the other called *The Men's Fashion Reader* (McNeil and Karaminas 2009). A number of factors may have contributed to the emerging academic interest in masculine fashion. One factor was probably the popular discourse on the "metrosexual" or "new" man in the 1990s and 2000s. Although not a completely new discourse (dating back to dandy discourse in the nineteenth century and the so-called colorful peacock revolution in the 1970s), the timing of the 1990s and 2000s discourse coincided with (a) heightened visibility of men in visual culture, including more media body exposure, as noted earlier, since the 1980s; and (b) the emerging field of masculinity studies. One of the major contributions of masculinity studies is a self-reflexive analysis of hegemonic masculinity, along with a conscious attempt to pluralize masculinity into *multiple* masculinities by way of intersectionalities with ethnicity, sexuality, national identity, class, and other subject positions (e.g., Connell 2005).

MULTIPLE MASCULINITIES

It is a myth that euromodern hegemonic masculinity *is* masculinity. Pluralizing masculinities, as well as femininities, opens up spaces for considering all kinds of intersectionalities and modes of articulation. Historically, a good example of a complex intersectionality among gender (masculinity), ethnicity, class, age, and musical preference (jazz) is the zoot suit, which represented a unique masculinity that articulated intersectionalities and resisted hegemonic masculinity.

ZOOT SUIT

In 1931 a *New York Times* reporter described some of the African American men in Harlem as "fashion plates who were several jumps ahead of the rest of the world" (Foster 1997: 235). In the 1940s Jelly Roll Morton, known as the father of jazz from New Orleans, proudly described African American men as "suit men from suit land" (White and White 1998: 262). Already identified as "different" in U.S. society and often denied access to its world of masculine privilege, African American men—along with Latino, Filipino, as well as some white U.S. men who were into jazz culture—used the zoot suit to highlight their differences from hegemonic masculinity while also appropriating the suit as a symbol of power. Young, urban men were especially drawn to the style. By the late 1930s, the term *zoot* was commonly used as a term within urban jazz culture, and it became attached to the "unmistakable style [a long coat with a drape-shape, pleats, and padded shoulders; full pants that could be gathered and pegged at the bottom]" (Cosgrove 1989: 34). By 1943, it had become a potent symbol of ethnic pride and jazz culture in cities ranging from New York to Detroit to Los Angeles (see Figure 6.2).

It is uncertain where and how the zoot suit was first created. There was a report on the front page of a June 1943 issue of the *New York Times* that the first zoot suit was purchased by a black bus worker, Clyde Duncan, from a tailor's shop in Gainesville, Georgia. Reportedly, he was inspired by the film *Gone with the Wind* (and Rhett Butler's style). Yet there are other reports, as

Figure 6.2   Jerome Mendelson models a zoot suit (the latest fashion) in a clothing store in 1942. Photo by Marie Hansen/ Time Life Pictures/Getty Images.

well. Some attribute the style to Harlem nightlife; others point to jazz culture more specifically, as noted above. Still another account focuses on the inspiration from British military uniforms. Alternative and independent newspapers at the time pointed to its potential evolution from the *pachuco* style of Mexican American young men. This style, it was said, reflected a particular Mexican masculine national consciousness—and yet one that articulated the ambivalence associated with being caught between two cultures (the United States and Mexico). The style was particularly popular among second-generation working class men (Cosgrove 1989: 5–6). It became a huge fashion trend among Mexican American young men in Los Angeles—a city where fantasy is a way of life and culture (e.g., the Hollywood film industry). It became a form of self-representation for these men, allowing them to articulate the connections and disconnections between two cultures:

In Mexico the pachuco was perceived as a caricature of the American, while in the United States the pachuco was proof of Mexican degeneracy. (Mazon 1984: 5)

Whatever the origins of the zoot suit—and no doubt they were multiple—it is evident that the zoot suit was "put into discourse" in U.S. society in the early 1940s. It was creating a kind of moral panic, cultural anxiety, and ultimately a series of riots in various cities around the country. Most often, these riots involved struggles between (predominately white) soldiers, often in uniform, and African American or Mexican American young men of about the same age. It became fairly common for groups of soldiers to ambush zoot suiters, strip them down to their underwear, and then leave them (feeling humiliated) in the streets (Cosgrove 1989: 10).

During World War II, the zoot suit was perceived by some in dominant U.S. society as an affront to American nationalism; it was apparent that racial tensions were a large part of the problem. But there was also a material dimension: fabric was rationed during the war effort, with a mandated 26 percent cutback in the use of wool, in particular. Still, young men were able to obtain zoot suits, sometimes through bootleg tailors:

[T]he polarization between servicemen and *pachucos* was immediately visible: the chino shirt and battledress were evidently uniforms of patriotism, whereas wearing a zoot suit was a deliberate and public way of flouting the regulations of rationing. (Cosgrove 1989: 9)

The tensions came to a head in a series of riots in Los Angeles between June 3 and June 13, 1943. There were no deaths, but a large number of zoot suiters were arrested, and "what the riots lack in hard incriminating evidence they make up for in a plethora of emotions, fantasies, and symbols" (Mazon 1984: 1), as well as sartorial ambiguity and cultural anxiety.

By the late 1940s (after World War II), the hegemonic business suit itself had become transformed into a toned-down version of the zoot suit: pleated trousers, a fuller jacket cut, and so on. One might say that the zoot suit was appropriated and neutralized through the course of hegemonic masculine fashion, which the zoot suit had earlier rejected yet appropriated in its own way. Figure 6.3 is a good example of the complex negotiation and mediation between the early zoot suit (especially the waistband and pegged pants legs in trousers in the man on the left) and the dominant suit cut in the late 1940s. The three men in Figure 6.3 are Jamaican immigrants to England; they are on the ship and about to arrive in Tilbury. They are also wearing what the British call trilby hats. They mark their transition from a former British colony to a hopeful engagement with Britain; masculinities are entangled (Kaiser and McCullough 2010).

Figure 6.3 From left to right, these three Jamaican men are in the process of immigrating to Tilbury, England: John Hazel (a twenty-one-year-old boxer), Harold Wilmot (thirty-two years), and John Richards Carpenter (a twenty-two-year-old carpenter). Wearing zoot-influenced suits and trilby hats, these men represent a sense of pride in the multiplication and entanglement of masculinities. Courtesy of Getty Images.

THREE GENERATIONS OF THE *LA SAPE* MOVEMENT IN CONGO

Another compelling case study of multiple, entangled masculinities is the *La SAPE* movement in Congo. The French concept *La SAPE* is an acronym for the Societé des Ambianceurs et des Personnes Elégantes (Society for Ambiencers and Persons of Elegance). La SAPE is also a slang word for clothing. Since the 1930s, around the time of the zoot suit's origins in the United States, la SAPE has been a tradition in the Congo, a former colony of France, and remains a vital part of visual culture in transnational, urban diasporas associated with the historical entanglements between France and Congo. In popular fiction (e.g., novels) as well as style-fashion-dress, la SAPE bases itself on a desire "to be 'honored,' to 'shine,' and to take part in celebrations" (Thomas 2003). Paris, as the former center of colonial power, still plays a hegemonic role in the narratives of *sapeurs* (individuals who participate in the la SAPE movement and tradition). As the prevalent popular narrative goes, sapeurs travel to Paris to work and to obtain designer clothes, and then return to their Congolese neighborhoods in their new looks. In fact, the designer clothes may be acquired in this way or in other ways (e.g., borrowed, acquired from a relative or friend or perhaps from some form of supply chain or another through various routes).

There has been a great deal of critique of poor or working class men spending so much on designer clothing. As Thomas (2003) notes, following critical theorist Homi Bhabha, it is important not to interpret la SAPE as mere imitation of colonizers' fashion. Rather, it is an express of colonial ambivalence and a strategy to decolonize the mind; there are entanglements, as with the zoot suit, but there is also a kind of distancing from both stereotypical impressions of African immigrants to France *and* dominant (French designer)

Figure 6.4 Firenze Luzolo (age twenty-six); Guy Matondo (known as "The Chinese from China"); and Ukonda Pangi (age twenty-two), pose in the Parc de Prince neighborhood of Kinshasa in Congo. They are striving to revive the *sapeur* tradition of dressing elegantly and expensively, despite harsh economic circumstances. Photo by Miguel Juárez, courtesy of the *Washington Post*/Getty Images, February 26, 2010.

Figure 6.5 In his Kinshasa neighborhood in Congo, Yannick "Mzee" Kindingo (age eighteen) shows off some of his favorite items of style-fashion-dress by the transnationally renowned, Japanese-born designer Issey Mikaye. Photo by Miguel Juárez, courtesy of the *Washington Post*/Getty Images, February 26, 2010.

fashion norms. In a way, it is an expression of masculinity that strives to beat the former colonizers at their own game.

The sapeurs in Figure 6.4 and Figure 6.5 articulate the principles of their movement in different ways. The men in Figure 6.4 strike poses in suits with unique twists. Note the NASCAR (car racing) black-and-checked pattern influences in the middle man's (Guy Matondo's) otherwise red jacket and his display of his jacket's red patterned lining. Yannick "Mzee" Kindingo in Figure 6.5 articulates a more transnational hip hop influenced style, combining yellow, red plaid, and black pieces designed by Issey Mikaye. The men in both of these images keep to the SAPE aesthetic of wearing no more than three different colors; together, these images illustrate how an aesthetic movement can carry on and change at the same time—both maintaining and transforming constructions of masculinity.

U.S. NATIONAL SURVEY OF MALE INTERSECTIONALITIES

To explore the variety of perspectives on men's fashion, I became involved in a U.S. national, multiyear and multimethod study of men's attitudes toward menswear, fashion, and media representations of masculinities. We began with a series of interviews with men representing different ethnic, age/

generational, class, sexual, and other subject positions and body types. One man summarized a lot of what we heard from men speaking from a diverse array of intersectional subject positions (as we all do):

> There's multiple men with different body types, and they're trying to achieve different things with what they're wearing. (Latino heterosexual male, 27)

We heard from many baby boom generation (born 1946–1964) men that there should be more men's body types (not just slim men in their early twenties with six-pack abs) in menswear advertising. Men of this age frequently talked about wanting to look current without looking like they're trying too hard to look young. One gets a sense of the negotiations of ambivalences at play: navigating deftly between youth and age; caring but not overdoing, looking nice but not *too* nice; and so on. They said they wanted to represent themselves as the following:

> "respectable yet casual"
> "sharp looking, not loose or wrinkled generally"
> "respectable yet casual"

The baby boomers' this-yet-that or this-not-that responses reveal the need to qualify, mediate, and navigate masculinities carefully. They also offered advice to menswear manufacturers and advertisers:

> Design the clothes so that they make me feel young again, but design them in a way so that I do not appear too young to others. (Caucasian male, aged fifty-six)
> Make clothes that are in between what the young people wear and the old styles . . . Have advertising that depicts men in that age bracket. (white male, aged fifty-seven)
> More emphasis on comfort and style rather than trying to sell sexuality. I think men my age would be more inclined to purchase a broader variety of clothes if there were more ad campaigns showing men my age in the clothes. (Middle Eastern American male, aged fifty)
> Stop treating men like sheep. We all don't like the same colors and designs. *Treat men like full time consumers.* Women get many choices and stores gear themselves to women shoppers. Men's clothes are drab and ugly . . . Men have been made to believe that using bold colors is not acceptable. (white male, aged fifty-one)

We also interviewed menswear company representatives, to get a sense—recalling the circuit of style-fashion-dress in Chapter 1—of production and distribution approaches to baby boom male consumers.

When we do our advertising, we will still check it against the older consumer to make sure we're not turning him off, but develop our strategy more so that it gets the younger consumer. It's really both; we don't want to do anything that would turn him off from the brand.

In general, men put more attention into their clothes, not because clothes are important to them per se, and not that they want to be trendy or very fashionable, but most guys put a lot of emphasis on being perceived as current or up to date, and having the right clothes—wearing the right outfit—is part of that, and that is very important to them.

In our analysis of these interviews, our research team pursued the dilemma of producing for and marketing to baby boom male consumers who have to navigate carefully to maintain just the right degree of unmarkedness. These men do not want to look as though they are trying to be too young, too trendy, or too slick; yet they do want to look good and want to be treated seriously—not ignored or taken for granted—as consumers (Kaiser, Looysen, and Hethorn 2008).

The larger research project on menswear and masculinities also revealed that men of various ethnic backgrounds shared some issues of particular concern. Asian American men of different ages told us that they often have a difficult time finding clothes that fit, because the standard U.S. sizing system tends to be too "large and tall" for them. We also heard from some Asian American men with relatives in China, Korea, Taiwan, and other locations in Asia that they stock up on clothing there when they travel every other year or so, partly due to the better fit and partly due to ethnic or national identity affiliations (Chen 2008).

We explored style-fashion-dress issues and intersectionalities further in an online, demographically balanced U.S. national survey, yielding 1,952 usable surveys. Using quotes from the previous interviews, we developed attitudinal statements to which the men responded. We identified the following factors (clusters of statements to which there were similar responses) and explored the theme of multiple masculinities by looking for differences among the men as a function of age/generation, ethnicity, and other factors such as sexuality and location, which are discussed further in Chapters 7 and 8.

1. **Interest in appearance through style-fashion-dress**
   I like to feel attractive in my clothing.
   I like shopping for clothes.
   There should be more fashion ads in non-fashion magazines.
   I wish there were more choices in menswear.
   I talk about clothes with my friends.

There were some significant differences in the ways that men responded to these statements, according to their subject positions of ethnicity, age, and sexuality. As age increased among the sample, there was less agreement with the cluster of statements. Younger men (e.g., in their 20s) were most likely to agree with the cluster of statements. Could these differences be explained by the developmental process of aging per se, or by generational differences (e.g., more emphasis on men's style-fashion-dress and changing attitudes in the last couple of decades)? We suspect the answer is "both/and," as suggested by changing cultural discourse. We will address age/generational issues in the context of time in Chapter 8.

We also found that white males were less likely than men of other ethnicities (e.g., African American men, Latino American men, Asian American men) to agree with the cluster of statements, indicating that white men expressed the least interest in appearance through style-fashion-dress. Further, straight men were least likely to agree with the statements. We will consider further the complicated way in which differences of sexuality and place (e.g., rural, urban) play out in Chapters 7 and 8.

2. **Desire to be unmarked**

I do not want my clothes to attract attention to me.
I do not think about how my masculinity is perceived based on how I dress.
I prefer clothes that are easy to mix and match.

Older men, we found, were more likely to agree with the statements, or they had a greater desire to be unmarked. Surprisingly to us, gay and bisexual men were more likely than straight men to agree with these unmarked statements, perhaps because they may be accustomed to "passing" in a hegemonic, heternormative world (more on this in Chapters 7 and 8).

3. **Participation in gendered risk taking**

I've been called derogatory names in public based on what I was wearing.
If I find a women's garment that suits my style, I will wear it.

Although intended to explore further some of the themes we heard in interviews with men who experiment with gender bending through style-fashion-dress (Green and Kaiser 2011), we found an interesting and troubling significant difference as a function of ethnicity. Among the different ethnic groups of men in the study, we found that Asian American men were most likely to agree with the statement. One explanation for agreement with the second statement most likely has to do with the fit of clothing items such as jeans and T-shirts, and the problem of the U.S. sizing system being too large for some Asian American men, as we found in previous interviews, noted earlier. With respect to responses to the first statement, we plan to pursue further research to understand the possibility of discriminatory experiences based on the intersectionality between gender and ethnicity.

As these factors indicate, navigating masculinities can be described as a process of negotiating the boundaries between what is "safe" and what is "dangerous." Based on his research with straight and gay Italian men, consumer behavior scholar Diego Rinallo (2007) developed a theoretical model in which men navigate across three zones: There are two kinds of "danger zones" in his model, and in between is the "safety zone." The middle, safety zone can be achieved through unmarked style-fashion-dress (Looysen 2008). But if a man moves too far toward more marked ways of dressing (on either side of the safety zone), he moves into marked territory. One can be in a marked danger zone because he represents too little care of, or attention to, his style-fashion-dress; he is perceived as sloppy or unclean, inappropriately dressed, or hopelessly out of style. The opposite danger zone is marked in a different way: Too much care of, or attention to, his style-fashion-dress labels him as too effeminate or too fashionable. He may be perceived as gay or as metrosexual, according to Rinallo (2007).

Of course, the extent to which there is danger depends on context, as well as the desires, pleasures, and identity issues associated with the boundaries of gender.

As part of our larger project on menswear and masculinities, fashion studies scholar Denise Green undertook an in-depth study of men who experiment with gender boundaries. She found that many of her interviewees identified a safe space/place for such experimentation: Burning Man, an annual (late August) festival and experimental, artistic project enacted in "Black Rock City," Nevada. In recent years, a desertous, blank space has been transformed into a city of 50,000 people. Green conducted ethnographic research at Burning Man in 2007 and 2008, and followed up with men before and after the events to see how gender experimentation may have influenced their style-fashion-dress in their everyday "default" lives. She learned that Burning Man functions like an "enlarged safety zone." Articulating the interplay between masculine and feminine style-fashion-dress, the men draw attention to the absurdity of hegemonic masculine norms. (Women, too, experiment with style-fashion-dress at Burning Man, but they are more likely to do so in a way that articulates a hyperbolic version of feminine sexuality, rather than to mix masculine and feminine signs.) Some examples of male gender experimentation includes the combination of bodily markers of maleness (e.g., beards, muscles, genitalia) or masculine dress (e.g., leather chaps) with tutus, pink spandex, lingerie, and faux fur. As one informant, "Kevin," expressed it, "I'm immensely glad that I'm here at Burning Man, because I get to kind of test all these things and try all these things, and it will absolutely inform and transform the way I dress when I get back to California." Indeed, many men did modify how they dressed in their everyday "default" lives, working in more gender-bending statements and crossing at least gingerly, if not directly, into "danger zones" (Green and Kaiser 2011).

The interplay between body and style-fashion-dress in gender constructions and reconstructions can be captured by the idea of performative, soft
assemblages, described earlier in this chapter. The interplay between biological and social factors, along with the ambiguities and anxieties that surround
gendered appearances, applies to the subject position of sexuality or sexual
orientation, considered in the next chapter.

Sexuality and Style-Fashion-Dress

> How can we ever define what turns people on? . . . [H]uman sexuality must be seen as a kind of theatre of the imagination and the body, a theatre in which many forces come together. (Horrocks 1997: 190)

This definition of sexuality—as *a kind of theatre of the imagination and the body*—is one that acknowledges the complexity and even the mystery that goes into trying to understand desire or what or who "turns people on." The body is central to the study of sexuality, but so are emotions and fantasies. Critical theorist Michel Foucault (1977) argued that sexuality was "put into discourse" in the late nineteenth century, and this discourse needs to be understood as exerting power as well as manipulating pleasure through an intertwining of bodies and psyches. The mind-body connection is central to sexuality, which has connotations of subjectivity; and to sexual orientation, which is a way of locating sexuality in a subject position. To be "oriented" in some way (or in multiple ways) typically means to be "going somewhere in space." This route is not necessarily a linear path, although a "straight and narrow" (heteronormative) path dominates hegemonic cultural discourse: from romantic comedies to "happily ever after" fairy tale narratives to fashion spreads. Yet there are a number of ways in which even hegemonic fashion toys with sexual desire in ways that are not strictly heteronormative. Since the 1980s, even men's bodies have been put into sexual discourse. Photographer Bruce Weber, for example, used sexual ambiguity and innuendo as themes in Calvin Klein underwear and jeans ads, exposing men's bodies and suggesting the possibility of homoerotic or bisexual desire.

Cultural theorist Marjorie Garber (1995: 30) asks: "[W]hat if we were to begin with the category 'sexuality' (or 'desire') rather than with a binary opposition between homosexual and heterosexual, or same-sex and opposite-sex partners?" A Möbius strip way of thinking about sexuality as a concept avoids the pitfalls of lapsing first and foremost into binary oppositions, especially in the context of studying style-fashion-dress, in which sexuality is a vital component for a number of reasons. First, fashioned bodies circulate in everyday life and in popular culture as sexual signs. The boundary between wanting to be attractive and wanting to be sexy is blurry; and it is hard to anticipate how an appearance style will be perceived. Second, clothes—even apart from bodies—can turn people on, because imagination plays such an important role in sexuality. Clothes, like bodies or appearance styles in general, can be turned into symbols that are desired or fetishized. Women's lingerie, high heels, leather, and men's ties or bowties, to name just a few articles of dress, and any part of the body can function as symbols of fetish that arouse the imagination. Third, sex "sells," so the fashion industry and other capitalist enterprises (e.g., films, television, magazines) use bodies and clothes strategically to foster desire. Fourth, sexuality becomes a critical and creative component of identity. Although sexual identities are most often framed in binary terms such as gay versus straight (or, through scientific and clinical discourse, homosexual versus heterosexual), systems of desire are much more complicated than this opposition suggests. Fifth, partly because the human imagination is involved, the boundaries between sexuality and other forms of identity (e.g., gender, class, ethnicity) become blurry when it comes to appearance style and how it is created and perceived.

The boundaries between gender and sexuality are especially tricky to navigate. Charlotte Suthrell (2004)—an anthropologist who has done comparative work on issues of sex, gender, and sexuality—observes that the tools of style-dress-fashion (e.g., clothes, accessories, makeup) are extremely helpful in analyzing the similarities and differences among these issues or subject positions. She notes that they allow for the temporary or permanent "play" of identity and self-image, across cultures. Sex, gender, and sexuality ultimately intersect in different ways in various cultural discourses; they form a knot that is "unusually difficult to unravel, partly because they are so seldom questioned, so integrated into societal structures" (Suthrell 2004: 2). She argues further, based on her research, that these three cannot be fully divided, "in the same way that a person cannot be divided" (Suthrell 2004: 160). We can imagine style-fashion-dress intimately intertwined with sex, gender, and sexuality, as well as other subject positions. Style-fashion-dress enables articulations of subjectivity, reminding us that clothes mark the boundary between the biological world (the body) and the social world (society, cultural discourse) ambiguously (Wilson 1985). We have to "mind" our appearances to sort through this ambiguity and to navigate through the knot of sex, gender, and sexuality. These three concepts have been debated as attempts to untangle them have generated cultural anxieties regarding nature versus nurture, boundary maintenance, and power relations.

We can consider the knot of sex, gender, and sexuality through the model's style-fashion-dress in Figure 7.1. She is wearing a jacket designed by Schquay Brignac of Studs Clothing and Dabonaire Fashion at the 2010 annual conference of BUTCH Voices, an organization with the mission "to enhance and sustain the well-being of all women, female-bodied, and trans-identified individuals who are masculine-of-center," according to the founder Joe LeBlanc. BUTCH

Figure 7.1   Butch fashion show curated by Tania Hammidi of
Invincible. Jacket designed by Schquay Brignac. Photograph courtesy of Melanie Aron.

Voices provides programs that "build community and positive visibility, inclusive of and beyond our gender identity and sexual orientation" (BUTCHVoices.
com). The fashion show was curated and staged by Tania Hammidi, scholar,
activist, performer, and founder of INVINCIBLE:

> **INVINCIBLE** is a state of mind: an unyielding spirit and a dream of an immediate
> future made manifest . . . where butch/stud/trans/masculine-of-center folks like
> us take our place as the hot fashion centerfolds that we are in everyday life. We
> pull in seasoned designers to share their latest line. We specialize in masculine
> modeling, and give modeling classes to masculine butch, gay, and trans guys
> about how to snatch up the runway. (taniahammidi.com/invincible.html)

The sex of BUTCH Voices participants may be female or FtM transgender or
transsexual. Gender identity can be described as butch or "masculine-of-center."

And sexuality is primarily queer or lesbian. Conceptually, sex, gender, and sexuality can be disentangled, but in the context of minding appearances and fashioning identities, they become re-entangled on an everyday basis. Further complicating matters are intersections with race and ethnicity; for example, "butch" usually refers to white masculine-of-center women, whereas "stud" is the term that is often used in the African American masculine-of-center community (Hammidi 2011).

The number and changing nature of terms for non-straight sexualities point to the multiple ways in which individuals can fashion their sexual identities in conjunction with communities, politics, and aesthetics. Acronyms such as LGBTQ (lesbian, gay, bisexual, transgender, queer) or LGBTIQQ (lesbian, gay, bisexual, transgender, intersex, queer, questioning) are meant to be inclusive. Probably the most inclusive single term is "queer": once used in a derogatory way but appropriated from homophobic discourse to capture the obliqueness of sexual paths and practices that are not exclusively straight. Queer theorist Sara Ahmed (2006) describes queer as not only a sexual, but also a political, orientation. It characterizes paths and practices that are "off-line," twisted, or "just plain whacky" (Ahmed 2006).

Terminology, however, like style-fashion-dress, varies cross-culturally. In a transnational context, queer theorists Lisa Downing and Robert Gillett (2011) note that the concept of queer itself has "problems of translation, transmission, transport, and dissemination" and needs to be understand locally and contextually—not just as a one-way influence from the United States (xv). In their book of readings, *Queer in Europe*, they describe Europe itself as a "queer kettle of fish" with its complicated array of cultural histories. Similarly, queer theorist José Quiroga (2000) argues that queer Latin America cannot just be understood as having imported U.S. versions of identity politics. And feminist scholar Jessica Horn (2006) points out how the European colonial project enforced "new cultural hegemonies" in Africa, including prudish and heteronormative beliefs. Now engrained culturally, she notes that political leaders often use homophobic rhetoric justified by their resistance to moral corruption from the West. In fact, homophobia is "less an 'African' tradition" than one that "has been hijacked into local discourses."

Also euromodern in origin is the binary opposition between homosexuality and heterosexuality. The next section pursues how this occurred and how it pertains to style-fashion-dress.

BINARY "BEGINNINGS" AND REVERSALS

The terms *homosexuality* and *heterosexuality* were coined in 1888. Historian Colin Spencer argues that these terms were created for scientific and clinical discourse because sexologists "needed them for their work in understanding human sexuality" (Spencer 1995: 11). The history of non-hegemonic sexualities go back much further in history, however. By the eighteenth century in Europe, cities such as London had developed small and yet secretive male sexual subcultures such as the "mollies." Many mollies wore women's clothing, for two different purposes: (a) to foster a sense of identification and community within the subculture, and (b) to signal non-hegemonic possibilities for attracting sexual partners. They met in safe inns and pubs, dressing in styles ranging from milkmaid to shepherdess costumes, riding hoods, gowns, and petticoats; some had painted faces (Cole 2010).

In the nineteenth century, only gender-based binary frameworks were available to understand sexuality. Sexuality either mapped with heteronormative gender roles, or it did not. Until 1888, when the terms homosexuality and heterosexuality were invented, the only term available to sexologists to describe nonnormative sexualities was *invert*. A sexual invert was described as a female soul in a male body, or a male soul in a female body. Preference for the "wrong" (same) sex was mapped onto, and confused with, gender identity (Spencer 1995). Invert-based thinking continued in scientific and clinical discourse, to the extent that homosexuality could only be viewed as a pathological inversion of the gender binary (Bristow 1997: 24).

In other words, there was a perceived disconnect between one's body and his/her object of sexual desire: whereas it was considered natural to desire the opposite gender, some kind of inversion led some people to desire their own gender. Sexologists such as Havelock Ellis made observations of gay men or male inverts to determine just what made them different; in case studies, he reported that they focused vainly on their own looks and patterns of adornment and seemed to prefer the color green (Ellis 1938). (The latter observation, it later became apparent, was subject to change in accordance with shifting signs and meanings within the gay community, as well as fashion.) Ellis also reported case studies of "sexually inverted" women who enjoyed wearing men's clothing, as well as those who were "indifferent to dress" and found sewing "distasteful" (Ellis and Symonds [1897] 1975): 88, 91).

Historically, there has been a great deal of uncertainty surrounding reports of women who have dressed like men. Many women needed to pass as men in order to survive economically (that is, to hold a job), to avoid physical abuse, or to enjoy other benefits of a man's world. It becomes very difficult, looking back, to attribute motivation, much less sexual or gender subjectivity. There were a variety of reasons women might have dressed like men, because gender was almost completely conflated with sexuality, and there was an obsession with gender opposition and biological explanations in clinical discourse.

HOMOPHOBIC DISCOURSE

Within scientific and clinical discourse, then, homosexuality was constructed and represented as deviant and unnatural. Once it was named as a psychiatric and psychological illness, it was "back filled" with heterosexuality as its opposite: the normal, healthy sexuality. Homosexuality became an identity, whereas previously the focus had been on the sexual acts themselves. Characteristics of homosexual men and women were exaggerated, overgeneralized, and stereotyped. It was not until the 1970s that gay and lesbian activists managed to get homosexuality removed from the list of diseases and disorders identified by professional psychologists and psychiatrists.

Popular media discourse also cast people who were labeled homosexual into the role of sexual deviant. In the 1890s in England, Oscar Wilde (1854–1900)—a famous author, playwright, social critic, and dandy—was put on trial, convicted, and vilified in the press for "gross indecency with other male persons" (Breward 2010: 728). The British press praised Wilde's guilty verdict for acts that "attack all the wholesome, manly, simple ideals of English life and set up false gods of decadent culture" (Spencer 1995: 286). The Wilde trials received quite a bit of publicity in the United States, as well, and public fears about homosexuality intensified. Media coverage of the trials drew public attention to the idea that homosexuality represented a type of identity, which became visually stereotyped as effeminate (Spencer 1995: 286). Wilde was one of the first public victims of the coining of the term "homosexuality" and became a symbol for homophobic anxieties (Spencer 1995: 20). The image of Wilde's velvet coats, knee breeches, silk stockings, long cape, and flowing ties became symbolic of how homosexuality was supposed to look. Effeminate, homosexual images such as these were to continue generating anxiety well into the twentieth and twenty-first centuries.

Unlike gay males, who can experience fashion as subversive pleasure in their resistance to hegemonic masculinity, lesbians have faced the dilemma of fashion as a sign of heterosexual conformity. Perhaps the most profound influence lesbian culture has had on dominant fashion has been the idea and image of women wearing pants, and being fashionable in the process. This practice is essentially a twentieth-century phenomenon in the United States and Western Europe. In nations such as Turkey and Pakistan, women had traditionally worn pants. Yet women who wore pants in the context of euromodernity were dressing "outside their sex"; it is virtually impossible to know how many women prior to the twentieth century "passed" as men for reasons of personal desire, economic survival, or personal safety.

Historian Gayle Fischer (1998) detailed a case study of a fascinating, nineteenth-century woman who refused to hide her biological sex but who wore pants: Dr. Mary Edwards Walker (1832–1919). Walker adopted the

short dress and pantaloons (bloomers) of the feminist dress reform movement and wore it in medical school and at her wedding. (She was briefly married to a man she had met in medical school but managed to get a divorce
when he was unfaithful; Katz 2010). When Dr. Walker became a contract sur-
geon during the Civil War, she wore a masculine military uniform but never
tried to disguise her sex. She was awarded the medal of honor by President
Andrew Jackson for her meritorious service during the war: She was the first
woman to receive such an honor. By the 1870s, her attire had evolved to
resemble that of a middle class gentleman. Fischer argues that Dr. Walker
represented a "living contradiction" in her blending of masculinity and femininity through her clothing. Gender and sexuality were still so intertwined in
medical, as well as popular, discourse, that in 1902, a medical journal called
her "the most distinguished sexual invert in the United States" (Katz 2010).
This labeling was undoubtedly based upon her style-fashion-dress.

In the late nineteenth and early twentieth centuries, some women lived
together in long-term relationships labeled "Boston marriages." The novelist
Henry James (1886) used the term in his novel *The Bostonians*. Lesbian identities became more fully articulated as communities began to form in large
cities. In the dress of lesbian couples, the interplay between sameness and
difference became an important symbolic theme. The dominant model of heterosexual difference in modern Western culture made the "pursuit of the
whole" very challenging for lesbians wanting to display their union. Lesbian
couples who dressed alike simultaneously emphasized their special close-
ness and their difference from the rest of society. Dress became a vehicle
to bind two women together, transforming them from separate individuals
into a united couple. Another alternative was to draw on gendered themes in
dress—highlighting differences between butch and femme roles—to highlight
the possibility of active masculine desire within the sameness that lesbianism
represents (Rolley 1992).

At the end of the nineteenth century, the ideas of Sigmund Freud (1856–
1939) were especially influential in contributing to homophobic anxieties,
within and beyond the scientific and medical communities. His ideas took a
while to filter to the general public because they were so complex and ambiguous. Initially, he viewed homosexuality as a disorder in human development,
but he changed his mind over the course of his career. In his earlier work,
Freud characterized homosexuality as an illness and an immature form of
sexual development. Freud postulated that infants begin life with an innately
bisexual disposition, and normal sexual development (presumably, including gender-specific clothing) led to heterosexuality. Many psychotherapists
followed this line of thinking and attempted unsuccessfully to cure homosexuality (in individuals who had not matured" sexually) well into the 1970s. Yet
in Freud's later work, he described homosexuality as a variation in sexual

development and "a matter of taste, of aesthetics." He also argued that the "mystery of homosexuality" was not a simple process of gender inversion (Freud [1920]1963: 157). In general, he regarded the roots of homosexuality as never being fully eradicated from the heterosexual adult. This assertion contributed to public anxieties, when there were also concerns about the "new woman" of the early twentieth century and, with a declining birthrate, concern about the future of euromodern nations.

The mainstream circulation of Freud's ideas may have contributed to creative community building among non-hegemonic sexual cultures in the years between the two world wars in Europe. In Berlin in the 1920s and 1930s, for example, vibrant gay, lesbian, transgender, cross-dressing, and bisexual communities flourished in a vibrant cultural scene. Experimentation with style-fashion-dress was part of this scene. Lesbian and bisexual women wore trousers and men's jackets with wing collars, and wore their hair short. Sometimes the look was topped off with a monocle (glass for one eye) or a top hat (Cole 2000).

Women who had sexual relationships with women were not subject to the same criminalization as men who had same-sex relations. (The rationale was that gay men were more subversive in their "threat" to German family life. It was assumed that gay women could be coerced to bear children.) Since 1871, the German Penal Code known as Paragaph 175 had been in force:

> An unnatural sex act committed between persons of male sex or by humans with animals is punishable by imprisonment; the loss of civil rights may also be imposed. (Epstein and Friedman 2000)

When the Nazi party came into power in 1933, the enforcement of this law intensified dramatically. Gay, lesbian, bisexual, and transgender pubs and gathering places closed down. Between 1933 and 1945, an estimated 100,000 gay men were arrested. Ten thousand were sent to concentration camps, where they were forced to wear pink triangle symbols on their prison garb. In addition to six million Jews who lost their lives in the concentration camps, an estimated 6,000 gay men died. Among the 4,000 gay men who survived, some were reimprisoned after World War II ended and the concentration camps were closed, because Paragraph 175 was still law. (It was finally eliminated in 1994; Epstein and Friedman 2000.)

Laws prohibiting sodomy (unnatural sex) were also on the books in many states in the United States; in 2003, a Supreme Court decision invalidated the laws in those states (about a dozen) where they still existed. Still today, it is illegal to engage in same-sex sexual relations in nations around the world. Hence, it is important to remember the extent to which intersectionalities—subject positions such as national identity and gender—influence sexuality as a subject position embedded in legal, as well as scientific discourses.

Scientific discourse had a strong, anxiety-generating impact on popular cultural discourse in the late 1940s and early 1950s in the United States, with the publication of the Kinsey Reports, based on studies that detailed diverse sexual practices. The 1948 publication focused on male sexualities, whereas the 1953 publication addressed female sexualities. These reports challenged existing assumptions about sexuality and indicated that homosexuality and bisexuality were more common than had been previously believed (Spencer 1995). Although the studies have been critiqued in terms of some technical details; there is no question that they intensified cultural anxieties in popular discourse, generated conversation on topics that had previously been taboo, and opened up possibilities for thinking about sexuality as a continuum rather than as a binary opposition. In her book on bisexuality, cultural theorist Marjorie Garber (1995) critiques the idea of the continuum, indicating that it (a) is too linear to capture the complex, multidimensional realm of sexual experience; and (b) locates bisexuality problematically at the middle of the continuum. Rather than simply being an in-between kind of sexuality, Garber argues that it is a both/and phenomenon. She uses the metaphor of a Möbius strip, introduced in Chapter 1 (and shown in Figure 1.1), to characterize how bisexual subjects may move through time and space in a continuous and circuitous way, without crossing edges.

In addition to the cultural anxieties generated by the Kinsey Reports, neo-Freudian psychoanalysts in the 1950s picked up on, and exaggerated, Freud's conservative interpretations of homosexuality in the earlier part of his career (interpretations, as we have seen, that he later reconsidered more openly and inclusively). Among some of the homophobic writings was a book entitled *Fashion and the Unconscious*, published in 1953 by the psychoanalyst Edmund Bergler. Using a link between fashion and homosexuality to condemn both, Bergler derided Oscar Wilde's clothing style (more than fifty years after Wilde's death) and that of the Harvard "wannabes" who had showed up in green ties (a sign of homosexuality at that time) at Wilde's lectures in the United States (Bergler [1953]1987). Bergler drew parallels among homosexuality, femininity, and infancy; and he asserted that male homosexual fashion designers' "infantile and repressed sexuality" was responsible for the "absurdity" of women's clothes (Bergler [1953]1987).

Also occurring in the early 1950s was political organizing for human rights for homosexual individuals. One of the founding members of the Mattachine Society, a homophile organization, in Los Angeles was the fashion designer Rudi Gernreich, who became famous in the 1960s for designing the topless bathing suit. Indeed, many top fashion designers (of menswear as well as women's wear) of the twentieth century were gay or bisexual: for example, Christian Dior, Cristobal Balenciaga, Yves Saint Laurent, Halston, Calvin Klein, and Gianni Versace (Cole 2000). They generally had to keep their sexuality private—until later in the century—in order to be successful. Although Bergler ([1953]1987) may have been correct in noting that many male fashion designers were gay, he certainly missed the mark in his analysis of their creative contributions to fashion history.

PROTRACTED COMING OUT OF HETEROSEXUALITY

Cultural anxieties about sexuality pervaded popular and scientific discourse between the 1890s and the 1950s, as homophobia became institutionalized in U.S. culture. Because dominant ("straight," white, middle class) masculinity was generally "unmarked," or assumed to be the norm without a lot of cultural visibility, in the nineteenth and twentieth centuries, it was male homosexuality (along with femininity) that seemed to define what was perceived as not manly. There was a stereotypical, visual image that was supposed to represent male homosexuality; and homosexuality was more fully defined and explained in scientific and clinical discourse than heterosexuality. Katz argues that heterosexuality had a "protracted coming out" well into the twentieth century (Katz 1995: 83). Part of the modern legacy of scientific and popular discourse of the late nineteenth century was a "tentative, ambiguous heterosexual" mystique (Katz 1995: 82). Hence, the cultural anxiety. Questions such as the following emerged with this ambiguity: What did male heterosexuality look like? How could one be sure? Although male heterosexuality was the dominant rule, it was unmarked (or not so visible; it was assumed or unmarked) in modern sexual clinical texts. It still had to be "invented."

Ahmed (2006) describes heterosexuality as a "field, a space that gives ground to, or even grounds, heterosexual action through the renunciation of what it is not, and also by the production of what it is" (558). In other words, it requires ongoing work that is not supposed to show. It is "not simply an orientation *toward* others, it is also something that we are oriented *around*, even if it disappears from view" (560). She goes on to say that compulsory heterosexuality functions hegemonically like "a straightening device" (562) in order to avoid the "slant" of queer desire.

Ironically, despite this distancing of heterosexuality from homosexuality, queer community styles have had a great deal of influence on mainstream fashion. In other words, mainstream fashion appropriates from queer culture. As a gay, white male architect indicated in an interview in the 1990s, "They rip us off. If we look fabulous, they take it away from us. It is true for disco, and it is true for all the great looks of our eras . . . It is fine with me, because we will come up with a new one. We are clever. We are fabulous. It will take me two seconds to come up with a new look" (Freitas, Kaiser, and Hammidi 1997).

1960S AND 1970S: SOCIAL MOVEMENTS AND SEXUAL FASHIONS

Political activism grew in the 1960s when police cracked down on the assembly of gay, lesbian, bisexual, and transgender individuals in clubs, restaurants, and other public sites. In 1965 the Mattachine Society and the Daughters of Bilitis (a lesbian organization) organized the first gay and lesbian protest in the United States. A small group of men and women marched with pickets in front of the White House in Washington, DC. They argued for civil rights, employment equality, freedom from police brutality, and a de-pathologization of homosexuality as a disease. To be safe, the men wore business suits (and some wore sun glasses to resist identification), and the women wore dresses, hose, and heels. They reasoned that they needed to look employable to make their case. Their picketing occurred without an incident and received very little media attention, but it did mark the desire and ability to engage in public protest (Kohler 2011).

The following year, in 1966, a riot broke out at Compton's Cafeteria in San Francisco between transgender customers and the police (Stryker 2008), and in 1969 the pivotal Stonewall Riots occurred in Greenwich Village (at the Stonewall Inn) in New York. In both cases, cross-dressing men and women of color were among the protesters who stood up to the police. (The alternative was to be arrested and possibly have one's name published in the newspaper—an outcome that was sure to wreak havoc with one's career or family.) Gay pride parades around the world still commemorate the Stonewall Riots, which are frequently cited as an impetus for the Gay and Lesbian Rights movements of the 1970s.

The 1960s and 1970s are known for spawning a number of social justice movements: civil rights, Black Power, Chicana Nationalism, feminist, and gay/lesbian rights. In the world of fashion, too, and related to the social justice movements, "revolutionary" changes occurred and challenged existing gender, ethnic, sexual, class and other boundaries.

The feminist movement brought to light a lot of the ambivalence that women experienced when facing traditional notions of femininity through fashion. For some lesbians, there were especially compelling reasons to be ambivalent: The differences between butch (masculine) and femme (feminine) fashion that had represented some lesbian communities' aesthetics were themselves being challenged by androgynous, gender-bending styles. Some writers have reported that there was a general shift in lesbian fashion from butch and femme styles to the "clone" look, featuring sameness, often in the form of flannel shirts and jeans (Wilson 1985). During this period, the butch-femme aesthetic of difference fell out of favor and was critiqued as reproducing heteronormative gender relations (Walker 1993). However, it may be argued that gendered roles within lesbian relationships (i.e., butch and femme roles), like masculine and feminine roles within heterosexuality, are "fugitive rather than fixed," changing contextually according to temporal, inter-personal, and identity dynamics (Rolley 1992).

Further, performance studies scholar Sue Ellen Case recalls and interprets lesbian articulations of style as having been more complex in the 1970s. She offers a personal, historical memoir of "making butch" in the 1970s in San Francisco lesbian bar culture, extending her previous work highlighting the inter-sections among class, race, and lesbian identity in the butch-femme aesthetic. Countering the commonplace assumption that lesbian feminism can be char-acterized unproblematically as "anti-fashion," Case describes the hippie butch look arising in the 1970s as stylistically combining (i.e., *articulating*) elements of the classical butch look with "hippie anti-masculine male fashions" (e.g., 1930s men's clothes and flowing Dietrich-style pants and silk bow ties). As hip-pie dykes dedicated themselves to new ways of being and appearing, the con-cept of style became conceptualized as a vehicle for lesbian self-representation. Case argues that the encounter between classic and hippie butches had more impact on new negotiations of style than the stereotypical image of the "clone" lesbian feminist that dominates characterizations of the 1970s (Case 1998).

The fashion and beauty industries profited from the appropriation of second wave feminism's and lesbian culture's anti-fashion, natural discourse. The cos-metic industry developed "natural look" makeup to appropriate the look of wearing no makeup in the 1970s. The practice of wearing jeans and pants also became widespread among women; this practice is a long-term trend with which lesbian and bisexual women and FtM transgender individuals had been experimenting for generations. When the apparel industry replaced the worn and ragged jeans of the late 1960s with the designer jeans of the mid- and late 1970s, the les-bian community had to develop some new looks to distinguish itself symbolically.

The late 1960s and early 1970s were also formative in terms of shifts in menswear. Cole (2000) contends that the cultural discourse linking fashion to homosexuality began to diminish with the "menswear" or "peacock" revo-lution, when menswear became more colorful and included a wider range of fabrics. Accordingly, gay men, as well as straight men, had more license to experiment with fashion. Cole (2000) begins his book, *Don We Now Our Gay Apparel*, with a quote from Andrew Holleran's 1978 novel, *Dancer from the Dance*. The quote describes the obsession of two gay men, living in New York in the 1970s, with clothes:

The Clothes! The Ralph Lauren polo shirts, the Halston suits, the Ultrasuede jackets, T-shirts of every hue, bleached fatigues and painters jeans, plaid shirts, transparent plastic belts, denim jackets and bomber jackets, combat fatigues and old corduroys, hooded sweatshirts, baseball caps, and shoes lined up under a forest of shoe trees on the floor; someone had once left the house and all he could tell his friends was that Malone had forty-four shoe trees in his closet . . . And then there were the clothes that Malone really wore: The old clothes he had kept since his days at boarding school in Vermont—the old khaki pants, button down shirts with small collars (for someone who ran around with the trendiest designers, he loathed changes in style), a pair of rotten tennis sneakers, an old tweed jacket. There was one drawer filled with nothing but thirty-seven T-shirts in different colors. (Cole 2000: 1)

This vivid description may be a bit unique, but it does point to a dominant representation of gay men in popular culture. It especially highlights how white, upper class males have dominated this representation, despite the involvement of a wide range of ethnic and socioeconomic groups in the gay or queer community. This tendency can be traced to the nineteenth century, and the white, upper class "aesthetic movement" associated with Oscar Wilde and his gay male followers at Oxford and Harvard Universities. It would also have been the case that upper class men had relatively more money and mobility to make contacts with other gay men. From a working class point of view, gay male culture often became associated with leisure class privilege. In the first half of the twentieth century, social class had a tremendous impact on the clothing choices of gay men. Wealthy gay men could buy some acceptance of their difference or afford to create safe private spaces such as the bohemian circles of San Francisco and New York. Middle and working class men could become socially mobile by associating with men of higher classes, often through artistic or theatrical circles. Remaining culturally invisible, or "passing" as straight, however, was the safest route for many gay men (Cole 2000).

Throughout the latter half of the twentieth century, working class culture had an influence on LGBTQ style. In the 1970s, as among lesbian and bisexual women, the clone look for gay men included jeans and flannel shirts, although there were other subcultural options (e.g., disco, S&M) available. Garber (1995) observes that the more borders there are to patrol, the more "border crossings" are likely to occur, and the role of clothing and fashion as political statements in this process should not be underestimated (23). She argues, citing the gay publication *The Advocate*, that style-fashion-dress has contained a more complex function for queer fashion than for heterosexual fashion since the 1970s or so. The straight community did not develop the same kind of complex coding system that was seen, for example, among gay men in the 1970s (prior to the HIV/AIDS pandemic). Color-coded handkerchiefs, body piercings, tattoos, and other symbols were used strategically to communicate not only male gayness, for example, but also specific sexual proclivities.

1980S AND BEYOND: QUEERING FASHION

The HIV/AIDS crisis in the early 1980s had a devastating effect on the gay male community. Yet the activism continued and, if anything, intensified in the wake of this crisis, fostering a queer consciousness through groups such as AIDS Coalition to Unleash Power (ACTUP) and Queer Nation. The LGBTQ communities fought for the recognition and visibility of the disease, in order to enact crucial, proactive policy making (e.g., funding for research, outreach) and the reduction of social stigma.

Lesbians participated actively in the political organizing associated with queer politics. Also in the 1980s, some lesbians in major cities in Europe (e.g., London, Amsterdam) and the United States created a new "subversive" style. Rather than rejecting fashion, they developed the controversial strategy of associating fashion with forbidden areas of sexual experience. Clothing styles included garter belts and bras as outwear, worn with boots and cowboy hats. By the 1990s, younger urban lesbians pursued a different discourse—one that exposed the constructedness of the natural flannel and denim look, for example, and used fashion as a site for female resistance and masquerade.

Experimentation with style and butch-femme roles resulted in "transgressive self-representations" that are in turn appropriated by capitalism into trendy and chic styles. The process of signaling sexual preference to other women becomes more complicated; yet subcultural knowledge in the form of the ability to read appearance codes provides a sense of pleasure that cannot be easily appropriated. Some pleasure, ironically, can be found in dominant fashion media, in which lesbian consumers manage to read subcultural codes (e.g., short-haired models, motorcycle iconography, man-tailored jackets and ties) into "lesbian window ads." Lesbians "in the know" can read and enjoy these ads subversively, challenging the reading practices of straight culture, while also reinforcing the dominance of heterosexual fashionability. Hence, appropriation "cuts both ways." The political edge of style becomes diffused when it enters the fashion world, but there also seems to be a realignment of butch-femme aesthetics within the lesbian community, based in part on a new femme, fashionable assertiveness (Clark 1991; Walker 1993).

To understand issues of lesbian style in greater depth, Freitas, Kaiser, and Hammidi conducted interviews with thirty-six lesbians in Northern California. Respondents discuss the increased visibility of lesbian culture as a result of media coverage of "lesbian chic." For example, a white Jewish female comments: "I think it is easier [now, as compared to twenty years earlier] to be out at a younger age. It is easier to ask questions at a time in your life when you are seeing styles and buying clothes." But most lesbians agree that it is *how* clothes are worn and how one carries her body that influences lesbian style; an African American lesbian comments: "Seems to me that lesbians tend to stand up a little straighter . . . Sort of like an assurance of where their toes are and an awareness of where their personal space is." Another African American female notes that "you are more welcomed [in the larger lesbian community] if you look like you identify." Somewhat similarly, a white lesbian expresses concern about the "lesbian police" and "the way in which fashion ideas are supposed to go together in a very limiting way . . . I don't want to meld myself into one metal. I want to stay all the different parts" (Freitas, Kaiser, and Hammidi 1996).

In a later analysis, fashion/performance studies scholar Tania Hammidi and I suggested that beauty has often been theorized as a singular image, system, or narrative. In our study involving interviews with lesbians from Northern California, however, we learned that they conceptualize beauty as more than prescribed, normative standards, femininity, and consumer culture; instead, they strive to open a meaningful space for reimagining beauty in the context of their diverse, visual negotiations in everyday life. In other words, the women we interviewed reframe and reclaim beauty as they navigate competing and contradictory discourses: hegemonic heteronormative beauty (i.e., fashionable femininity), dominant lesbian beauty in the 1990s (i.e., "looking butch"), inner beauty (i.e., antimaterialism and "feeling strong or powerful"), and political beauty (i.e., "natural" or comfortable expressions of resistance). Challenging notions of dominant lesbian beauty, for example, a South Asian woman comments, "Excuse me, but I don't have to have short hair to be a dyke. Okay?" Comfortable within the discourse of political beauty, a Puerto Rican non-bra wearer "hates to feel clamped." Hammidi and I argued that it is the negotiation of ambivalences associated with diverse discourses that allows lesbians to *do* beauty and style in everyday life (Hammidi and Kaiser 1999).

Heteronormative femininity tends to be more visible or marked than heteronormative masculinity, which defines itself primarily in terms of what it is *not* (gay, feminine). Interviews with heterosexual males in the 1990s indicated that "identity *not*" is a major theme. Some males made comments that were overtly homophobic. For example, one commented: "My dad . . . saw a shirt of mine hanging in the closet, and he thought a queer would wear it, so . . . " This male stopped wearing the shirt as a result (Freitas et al. 1997). As we saw in Chapter 6 in Diego Rinallo's model of safety (unmarked) and danger (marked) zones, male heterosexuality became constructed as "safe," but the boundaries between safety and danger were sufficiently tenuous and anxiety producing to require a continual process of unmarking—by styling-fashioning-dressing in ways that were *not* homosexual (Freitas et al. 1997). But how was it possible to gauge this, especially in a period when many gay or bisexual men necessarily, for the sake of safety, styled-fashioned-dressed their bodies in ways that enabled them to "pass" in heteronormative contexts? In this context of safety zones, being "in the closet" became more than a metaphor; it became an *epistemology*: a way of knowing, a kind of consciousness or subjectivity, or a way of looking at the world (Sedgwick 1990). Style-fashion-dress became an important part of this in-the-closet epistemology, because it was necessary for non-heteronormative individuals to know how to navigate safely from homophobia while simultaneously communicating and developing a sense of community with other LGBTQ individuals.

By the early 2000s, popular cultural discourse had begun to grapple more openly with LGBTQ themes—often in a comedic, anxiety-releasing way. In the United States, Ellen DeGeneres starred in the sitcom *Ellen* (1994–1998); DeGeneres made television history in 1997 when she "came out" as a lesbian personally, and then her character did as well on the sitcom (imdb.com/name/nm0001122/bio0). Oprah Winfrey played the role of her therapist in the episode.

Will and Grace (1998–2006) was another sitcom that featured a gay male lawyer (starring Eric McCormack) sharing an apartment with a straight female interior designer (co-starring Debra Messing); they are the closest of friends. Completing the cast are Jack (played by Sean Hayes), who is a flaming gay male neighbor; and Karen, who is Grace's assistant and has had a string of wealthy male husbands (played by Megan Mullally). The show challenged a number of stereotypes about the interplay between gay and straight relationships (imdb.com/title/tt0157246).

The reality show, *Queer Eye for the Straight Guy* (2003–2007) (imdb.com/title/tt0358332/plotsummary) depicted five gay men doing a makeover on a hapless straight guy in need of fashion and other lifestyle advice. In many ways, the show enacted the ideas behind David Simpson's concept of *metrosexual*: an urban man who cared about how he looked and had other fashion/lifestyle credits to his persona. His sexual identity was ambiguous, and that didn't matter as much as how he presented himself (marksimpson.com/metrosexy). The pairing of urban and sexual subject positions will be discussed further in Chapter 8. For now, it is helpful to know that the metrosexual label attempted to define a space in between gay and straight; hegemonic masculinity itself was in a state of flux. The fact that five gay men could make over a straight guy—as a positive outcome—was a step in that direction. This was not the first time such movement or decentering had occurred. (The dandy of the nineteenth century and the "New Man" of the 1980s [see Edwards 1997, 2006, 2011] had made such strides but to a less culturally visible extent.)

Meanwhile, since the 1980s, hegemonic heterosexual fashion had become increasingly blatant in its circulation of sexual imagery, leaving less and less to the imagination—even on men's bodies. Menswear (e.g., underwear, jeans) advertising had shown increasing amounts of skin on male fashion models between the 1980s and the end of the twentieth century (Thompson 2000). Accordingly, questions arose regarding the *homoerotic gaze* in mainstream fashion: Is the fashion gaze necessarily heterosexual? Calvin Klein and Abercrombie & Fitch ads featured topless men (with six-pack-abs, as we will see later in Chapter 8) in suggestive poses that can be interpreted as gay or bisexual, as well as straight. Similarly, hegemonic women's fashion magazines have represented female fashion models together in homoerotic poses. The issues of sexual pleasure via viewing are complex: Fashion imagery (popular discourse) and queer theory (academic discourse) alike have challenged the ideas that hegemonic (heterosexual) masculinity is the only viewing gaze that matters, and that hegemonic (heterosexual) femininity is the only object of a desiring gaze. There are multiple, flexible subjectivities of desire. Alongside the political activism, queer theory and sexuality studies have emerged as vibrant interdisciplinary fields aimed at complicating rigid or fixed sexual categories (e.g., gay versus straight). The study of style-fashion-dress has been important in doing so, because it is a system that brings to life the intersectionalities among sexuality, gender, and other subject positions that are performative—that individuals do and experience through subjectivity in everyday life (Butler 1990).

Historically, LGBTQ consumers have necessarily had to find their own ways of identifying and circulating sexual signs, and of interacting with fashion images. One of these ways has involved the creation of sexual signs and cultural discourses that are distributed within their own communities (e.g., magazines, videos, books). This community-based circulation of signs and discourses has intensified with Internet communications, cable channels, and other targeted media.

A second way LGBTQ consumers have interacted with fashion media is to direct homoerotic desire toward mainstream media images. Especially since the 1980s, as noted above, a general "queering" of hegemonic fashion—that is, a mainstream "flirting" with homoerotic desire—has made this more possible and has made options for subjective desire, overall, more flexible. Advertisers are aware that there are diverse kinds of desire and have often strategically included signs that would appeal to homoerotic desire in mainstream ads, while also being careful to avoid turning off the larger, mainstream and possibly homophobic market. Examples of this kind of *gay window advertising* in the past thirty years or so in the apparel industry include androgynous images of women in fashion ads (for example, women with short or spiky hair in pantsuits or black leather) and shirtless men in suggestive poses.

This general queering of fashion was not without its new challenges. A fundamental dilemma emerged: how to appear fashionable *and* signify one's own LGBTQ subject position or identity. In an increasingly problematic relationship between style and identity, fashion becomes both "a newly available playground and a danger zone of irrecognizability" (Lewis 1997: 108). Another dilemma has to do with what it means to be targeted as a consumer. In an interview in the 1990s, one gay male noted that "there is a kind of satisfaction" associated with his reading of Calvin Klein underwear and jeans ads.

Although he was aware of the obvious marketing motivation, he appreciated knowing "that they have to target us. We are not just going to buy. They need to ask for it" (Freitas, Kaiser, and Hammidi 1996). Similarly, historian Shaun Cole shares a comment from a gay man he interviewed:

> Straight men never [have to] question their identity, but growing up gay and realizing that one is different means a constant questioning of who you are. Experimenting with clothes is a way of exploring this difference, a way of showing or accepting your difference. (Cole 2000: 2)

Yet straight men also have challenges in the ways they interact with fashion media. Research shows that the desire to be "unmarked" (i.e., to avoid standing out because of appearance) is not only an issue for straight men. Bisexual and gay men, for example, may be at least, if not more, concerned than straight men about navigating fashion and unmarking themselves, as evident from their responses in the UC Davis masculinities study described earlier. It makes sense that bisexual and gay men would have to grapple with the consequences of their style-fashion-dress on a daily basis for reasons of safety, identity, and other issues.

This ambivalence associated with identity and difference, or being marked and unmarked in various ways, is not unique to sexual subject positions, as we have seen throughout this book. Complicating the simultaneous need for a sense of identity with others and a sense of social difference from some others are the intersectionalities among subject positions; the entanglements are everywhere and always emerging. And the system of style-fashion-dress is pleased to comply, with subjectivity as the site of agency that navigates entanglements— often ambivalently, at times optimistically, and at other times curiously.

SEXUALIZING AND GENDERING AMBIGUITY

Style-fashion-dress, like feminist theory and queer theory, challenges and destabilizes gender and sexual categories, respectively. Visually or otherwise, style-fashion-dress reveals that at least part of gender and sexuality involves active social construction; neither gender nor sexuality can be a complete biological essence, because each varies in its articulations across time and space. Cross-gender dressing, for example, challenges the gender binary. As we saw in Chapter 6, most cross-dressing individuals are heterosexual, but within queer communities, the concept of *drag* functions to represent that gender is not just something one *is* but rather something one *performs*. Anthropologist Esther Newton (1979) described how drag queens within the gay community use the abstract general epistemology of *camp*—a cultural sensibility based on irony, drama, and humor—to interrogate gender, as well as sexuality. She noted that camp *is* style, and it is through the theatrics of camp that the focus shifts from "what a thing *is* to how it *looks*, from *what* is done to *how* it is done" (Newton 1979: 107). Camp has functioned as a mode of resistance to homophobia and dominant culture. It signifies performance and a sense of community, rather than mere existence (Bergman 1993). Together, drag and camp reveal how gender is not just a natural occurrence; it has to be constructed and represented. Literary critic Marjorie Garber (1992) argues that drag represents cultural anxieties about sexuality, as it disrupts binary gender as well as racial and other codes.

In New York in the 1920s and 1930, for example, drag balls offered a vehicle for African American and Latino (mostly poor or working class) gay men, transgender, and some lesbian individuals to cross-dress (Cole 2010). The tradition of "vogueing" (striking poses) in elaborate competitions—organized by fashion houses has continued and was chronicled in a 1990 documentary called *Paris Is Burning*, by Jennie Livingston. Madonna appropriated elements of this scene in her song/video "Vogue," issued in the same year. Despite criticisms regarding who has profited (not the "voguers") from representing and/or appropriated drag ball culture, this culture can be seen as a helpful reminder that heterosexuality is itself a performance that is "perpetually anxious" (Butler 1993).

Some drag performances, such as the drag balls described above, rely on fashioning a feminine appearance on a male body (or a masculine appearance on a female body). Often, however, the irony and ambiguity of camp humor become represented through a mix of gendered symbols: both/and articulations and contradictions. For example, a popular Radical Faerie look for gay males articulates the "two spirits" of masculinity and femininity by combining work or combat boots with a tutu and no shirt. Together, the body and style-fashion-dress produce gender ambiguity. At the same time, they articulate a kind of spiritual sexual subjectivity that communicates connections with other men, as well as nature. In an interview in 2011, two Radical Faerie men discuss how the concept of drag, in their culture, is not simply a process of putting a tutu on a male body. Rather, it is a matter of rethinking everyday style-fashion-dress itself as drag:

> D: I wanna re-iterate, like, it's ALL drag. Everything that you put on, everyday. It's drag. It is all drag.
> B: You've got to think about your clothes like that. Once you make that click, it's like, "okay." I mean it's all a costume. Feel more at home in your body. Everything's an accessory. This shirt's an accessory; these shoes are accessories.
> D: It's all accessories to your body . . .

Much of the ongoing, performative, ironic nature of drag—as an intersectionality between gender and sexuality—aims to deconstruct rigid, binary oppositions between masculinity and femininity, and gay versus straight. Highlighting the extent to which gender and sexuality are socially constructed, drag complicates these binaries and simple conflations between them. Drag articulates ambiguity.

If there are ambiguities regarding sexuality per se, Marjorie Garber (1995) argues that bisexuality plays a special role in disrupting the binary opposition between homosexuality and heterosexuality. Using the metaphor of a Möbius strip, as noted earlier, Garber challenges a binary-oppositional approach to the study of sexuality and argues for more nuanced studies of sexuality and desire. Garber notes that it is very complex to articulate bisexuality in terms of style. As a result, it becomes a somewhat invisible or overlooked category of experience. There is a tendency to "look through," rather than at, bisexuality (Garber 1995: 25). This is consistent with the U.S. survey of men conducted at UC Davis; self-identified, urban bisexual men in the study were the ones who were most concerned with the idea of being unmarked (i.e., not standing out publicly). We will take this finding up further in Chapter 8, in the context of intersectionalities among gender, sexuality, and place/space. For now, it is helpful to think about bisexuality as an ambiguous space in terms of style-fashion-dress, to the extent that it is likely to require continual and, perhaps, disparate ways of unmarking appearances, navigating safety and danger zones, and attracting multiple potential audiences.

GAZING SUBJECTS: POSITIONALITIES

Issues of positionality come into play, then, as we think through sexuality in relation to style-fashion-dress. Sexual subjectivities involve dressing, gazing, and desiring. Recalling the metaphor of the Möbius strip, we can think about sexual subjectivity and subject position as two components of a united experience. Sexual subject positions bring intersectionalities to life: they clarify how sexual object choice may be "sticky" (Ahmed 2006), but is not necessarily fixed. Indeed, the complexity and proliferation of labels, looks, and communities used to identify sexual subject positions and subjectivities attest to the role that mind-body desires and fantasies play. Transnationally, colonial fantasies have historically influenced how and why certain bodies, clothes, and fabrics have been imagined and represented in dominant culture as sexually "exotic," for example.

Systems of looking, including the issue of the gaze, become intertwined with power relations. The question of which sexual signs circulate and whose fantasies are represented largely depends, of course, on who has control over the production and distribution of images and ideas. Perhaps it is not too surprising, then, that it has most often been women's bodies and clothing that have circulated as sexual signs in cultural discourse since the nineteenth century in euromodern cultures.

Explanations of fashion change have been developed, accordingly, in terms of heterosexual female sexuality. The theory of "shifting erogenous zones" is a case in point. The ideas behind this theory were first developed in the 1930s by the psychoanalytic psychologist J.C. Flugel. He based his explanation of sexual expression and, indeed, fashion change on human ambivalence regarding modesty and display of the body. He suggested that parts of the (female) body obtained erotic appeal through the use of clothing:

> [P]erhaps the most obvious and important of all the variations of fashion is that which concerns the part of the body that is most accentuated. Fashion, in its more exuberant moments is seldom content with the silhouette that Nature has provided, but usually seeks to lay particular stress upon some single part or feature, which is then treated as a special centre of erotic charm. But when modesty predominates these same centres of potential greater attractiveness become the objects of particular concealment and suppression. (Flugel 1930: 160)

Later, the British historian of clothing, James Laver, actually named the theory, using the phrase "shifting erogenous zone." Like Flugel, he focused almost exclusively on the female body, suggesting that fashion becomes a kind of game of "hide and seek"—first covering one part of the female body and then another. This game, he argued, kept those gazing (presumably, heterosexual men) at the female body by maintaining these gazing subjects' erotic interest:

> If the psychologists' theory of the Shifting Erogenous Zone can be accepted, once a focus of interest loses its appeal another one has to be found. In the early 1930s the emphasis shifted from the legs to the back. Backs were bared to the waist and, indeed, many of the dresses of the period look as if they had been designed from the rear. Even day dresses had a slit up the back, and the skirt was drawn tightly over the hips so as to reveal, perhaps for the first time in history, the shape of the buttocks. (Laver 1969: 241)

Fashion historian Valerie Steele (1989) has pointed out that the shift in emphasis in the early 1930s from the legs to the back probably had less to do with Flugel's and Laver's theories than with (a) the influence of swimsuit designs, cut to maximize sun tanning of the back; and (b) the censorship of Hollywood films in 1934, which prevented women's dresses from being cut too low in the front (and hence the shift to the back). Moreover, she has questioned Laver's idea that the "Erotic or Seduction Principle" governs women's clothes, whereas the "Hierarchical Principle" (dressing to indicate one's position in society) governs men's clothes:

> Do women dress to attract men? Certainly, women's clothing has frequently emphasized female sexual beauty, through selective concealment, exposure, exaggeration, and occasional titillating cross-dressing. But is it true that sex appeal is the *primary* purpose of women's dress . . . [F]ashion does more than say, Look at my breasts! Oh, are you bored with breasts now? Then look at my legs! No one has ever offered any convincing evidence that heterosexual men become bored with breasts. (Steele 1989: 42)

Similarly, sociologist Fred Davis raised some fundamental questions regarding erogenous zones:

> What are the erogenous zones? Are they, as the theory's implicit biological determinism would lead one to believe, the same everywhere? For all time? Questions of cultural relativism and gender stereotyping are almost impossible to accommodate in the shifting erogenous zone theory of fashion change. (Davis 1992: 85–86)

From a feminist cultural studies perspective, one of the major flaws in the shifting erogenous zones theory is its assumed subject position. The theory assumes a focus (gaze) on the female body and from the subject position, presumably, of heterosexual males who are turned on by the sight of body parts that have obtained erotic capital by being covered for a while. Where is the agency of anyone else (e.g., gay or bisexual men and women, heterosexual women, transgendered individuals) who interprets images of sexy women in ways that differ from hegemonic ways of thinking about sexualized being or desire? And what about the possibility of male or transgender bodies being perceived as erotic or seductive? Certainly, the proliferation of shirtless male fashion models since the 1980s cannot simply be explained by a Hierarchical Principle. Or, one might wonder, had the male body been covered up so long that it, too, had gained sufficient erotic capital to become an object of a desiring gaze? Had the male body become marked erotically? To the extent that male power (the Hierarchical Principle) sustains itself through unmarked style-fashion-dress, as discussed in Chapter 6, it makes sense to engage in critical analysis of those instances when male bodies become sexually marked—and how and why.

   The shifting erogenous zones theory does little to explain any subject positions outside of the presumed gaze of hegemonic masculine heterosexuality. Nor does it even begin to explore intersectionalities between sexuality and race, ethnicity, class, age, and so on. However, perhaps the theory could be updated, rehabilitated, and revised to analyze the marking and unmarking of multiple gender and sexual subjectivities as processes, rather than zones per se. Together, marking and unmarking—along the lines of a Möbius strip—would need to be analyzed through an understanding of multiple inter-sectionalities. Such a project is beyond the scope of this chapter but could be a fruitful area for future consideration at the interface between fashion studies and feminist cultural studies.

SEXUALITY THROUGH INTERSECTIONALITIES

In many ways, sexuality is a topic and process of subject formation (includ-ing subjectivity and subject position alike, Möbius style) that especially de-mands attention to intersectionalities. Years ago, when conducting research with Anthony Freitas and Tania Hammidi (Freitas, Kaiser, and Hammidi 1996) on appearance style and sexualities, we were all struck by the extent to which the gay and lesbian individuals we interviewed emphasized intersec-tionalities when they talked about sexuality and style. They volunteered in-formation about class, race, ethnicity, age/generational, issues, as well as sexuality and gender. Somehow sexuality seems to complicate and open up

Figure 7.2 LGBTQ community picketing for inclusivity and tolerance in San Francisco, 2005. Courtesy of Shades of San Francisco, the San Francisco Public Library.

intersectionalities. At the same time, hegemonic stereotypes persist; they are not fixed, but they are "sticky." Magazines such as *Playboy* and the annual *Sports Illustrated* Swimsuit Issue keep the heteronormative male gaze on primarily white women with specific body types wearing, at most, string bikinis. Romantic comedies perpetuate heteronormative narratives with young, fit, fashionably dressed male and female pairs. Stereotypes exist, too, about the "model gay consumer," who is represented as an affluent white male with fashionable taste as evident, for example, in *Out* magazine (Sullivan 2011).

At the same time, the LGBTQ community—with an array of complicated and sometimes contradictory politics that require ongoing negotiation—strives to be inclusive as it recognizes the importance of respecting multiple intersectionalities, beyond hegemonic stereotypes. Figure 7.2 depicts a demonstration for diversity and inclusivity in the LGTBQ community in 2005. Some African American men had experienced selective screening upon admission to a popular gay bar in the Castro District, especially when wearing Afrocentric or hip hop attire; they were asked to provide three forms of identification. They witnessed white men, on the other hand, being admitted in shorts, T-shirts, and flip flops. The San Francisco Human Rights Commission intervened, and the group And Castro For All picketed, and eventually some resolution was reached through mediation. Community organizing and the understanding of intersectionalities were key to addressing the need for inclusivity in a gay urban neighborhood (Buchanan 2006).

The concept of intersectionality can be applied to sexuality through the nexus of the body, the imagination, and community building, as well as multiple modes of subject formation. As noted throughout this chapter, dominant culture has put sex into discourse in a way that unmarks heterosexuality in an uncomplicated way. Further, the euromodern binary construction of heterosexuality versus homosexuality, emerging from scientific and clinical discourse, cannot capture the complexity of sexual desires and experiences. It is hard to anticipate, much less explain, what turns people on. Yet sexuality is much more than being turned on. It also includes a personal sense of agency and identity, and a need to belong and express connections with others through time and space.

–8–

Bodies in Motion through Time and Space: Age/Generation and Place

Gender, sexuality, class, race, ethnicity, nation and other subject positions do not happen "on the head of a pin" (Cresswell 2004: 27). Rather, they happen or, more accurately, we *do* them in the larger contexts of time and space. Intersecting, embodied subject positions are not just about *who* we are becoming; they are also about *when* and *where* we are becoming. Time and space are abstract and yet crucial—concepts that shape how we style-fashion-dress our bodies, and what we know (and how we know it) about ourselves in relation to others. Tying together how we look and how we think, time and space influence how we mind and manage our appearances (Kaiser 2001). This chapter begins with a consideration of the Möbius-like interplay between time and space, enabling us to place in contexts the intersecting subject positions discussed throughout this book. Then it proceeds to consider two subject positions introduced in the Venn diagram in Chapter 2 (Figure 2.2): age/generation and place, which constitute how we experience time and space as we move through them in our styled-dressed-fashioned bodies. Then, I offer some Möbius-like closing/opening thoughts regarding the future interplay between fashion studies and feminist cultural studies.

TIME AND SPACE

How do we make sense of both "where we are" and "when we are"? Style-fashion-dress supplies some strategies to do so. To the extent that resources allow, body fashionings articulate not only the intersectionalities across our various subject positions, but also the interface between time and space. Personal style enables a sense of subjectivity in a visual way—representing to those around us, and to ourselves—some tentative idea about who we are and are becoming. Ultimately, time (memories of the past, tentative ideas about the present, hopes and anxieties regarding the future) cannot be separated from space.

One of the problems with modern Western thought and history has been a tendency to think of time as linear: as a narrative or story that plays out from a beginning to the advanced present (toward an even more advanced future). As noted earlier in Chapter 2, the hegemonic Western narrative of fashion goes something like this: it "started" in proto-capitalist fourteenth-century Italian city states, as young men competed with one another through street styles (Steele 1988). Although rarely highlighted in the narrative, subject positions such as gender (masculinity), ethnicity, class, age, and location are important to the plot. As the narrative continues, the "rise" of fashion then occurred in major European capitalist cities (especially Paris) in the eighteenth and nineteenth centuries. The focus turned to upper class and bourgeois women, and Paris became the hegemonic center of feminine fashion, whereas London became the hegemonic center of menswear. Of course, as we have seen, style-fashion-dress has been historically located all around the world, but euromodern *representations* of hegemonic fashion have generally tended to emphasize bourgeois and upper class women's attire as the site of newness and "now-ness." In contrast, other nations/cultures/spaces were depicted as static and exotic—as fixed in past time.

By the end of the twentieth century, the hegemonic "center" of the euromodern narrative could not hold. By this time, cities around the world were vying to be included in the handful of top world fashion cities. Who were these cities? Paris, New York, Milan, London, and Tokyo were frequently cited, but one could also look to Shanghai, Mumbai, Moscow, Dakar, Los Angeles, and San Francisco for their contributions to the global fashion stage (Gilbert 2006). Formulaic checklists for urban development emerged to enhance cities' fashion reputations (Scott 2002), and fashion weeks became a common representational strategy. Recalling the circuit of style-fashion-dress, introduced in Chapter 1, however, systems of production (complicated by outsourcing), distribution, and consumption remained key to a city's vitality in the world of fashion.

The restructuring of the world economy in the 1980s had fostered globalization and digital technologies, ushering in new relations between production and consumption, human and machine, local and global, and present and future. In the process, time and space have become smashed together, so to speak, like compressed Möbius strips. Cultural theorist David Harvey (1990) argues that the significance of place increases, paradoxically, with globalization, which threatens place with the speed and flexibility with which money and goods flow across national boundaries. He and others have called this phenomenon *time-space compression*.

As globalization blurs and threatens national boundaries, new circuit of production-distribution-consumption relations ironically also offer new opportunities to articulate national and local identities. In the transnational, twenty-first-century context of digital design and communications, flexible manufacturing (e.g., the outsourcing of garment manufacturing) and time-space compression—key assumptions about fashion and space/place—face major challenges. Clearly, fashion does not only emerge from a limited set of world fashion cities; and, further, fashion is not necessarily only urban. If one wants to design, market, or purchase clothing, there is little reason to be confined to certain spaces. Digital technologies (e.g., computer-aided design/ manufacturing and Internet marketing and shopping) hasten and flatten processes of production, distribution, and consumption. Materials and garment labor, however, are tangible, and their flows and efforts also need to be understood within transnational circuits of style-fashion-dress. They have routes.

Feminist geographer and space theorist Doreen Massey (2005) argues that we need to explore thinking through time and space with open and multiple *routes*, not just singular *roots*. In other words, journeys of production, distribution, consumption, subject formation, and regulation involve navigations through space. These routes are not just linear or straightforward. Rather, they twist and turn, detour, and entangle with other routes, through and beyond certain world fashion cities.

The clothing company Moods of Norway (see Figure 8.1) represents a good example of new fashion routes and centers. Headquartered in the small rural town of Stryn, Norway (population 6,750), the company was founded by two local designers, Simen Stallnacke and Peder Børresen, after they had spent some time studying and traveling abroad. Together with Stefan Dahlkvist, CEO, they developed the company into a transnational firm with distribution in urban and smaller town boutiques in Norway, Sweden, Benelux, Switzerland, Spain, Japan, and the United States, among others. Moods of Norway has its own retail stores in cities throughout Norway and in Los Angeles: "If you come at the right moment you are more than likely to be offered a homemade Norwegian waffle that will tickle your culinary senses and give you enough carbs to take you through the night." The company's logo is a hot pink tractor; and rural, local, and Norwegian national themes permeate its branding and imagery. The Website (moodsofnorway.com) includes panoramic and picturesque scenes of the landscape surrounding the company headquarters. Male and female models wear bright, plaid, and playful clothing ironically ("camp-ily") cast in grassy rural settings with tractors, pitch forks, and other nonurban props, framed by stunning glacier-capped mountains in the background. Mood of Norway's website describes their mission as follows:

> Moods of Norway has been doing the hibbedy-dibbedy on the international fashion dance floor for 6 years now, the philosophy is still the same even though the Norwegian oil price is as flexible as a Bulgarian gymnast after 14 tequila shots. Our main goal, besides making our grandmas happy, is to make happy clothes for happy people around the world. (moodsofnorway.com)

Fashion studies scholar Lisa Skov (2011) indicates that in the first decade of the twenty-first century, new fashion sites such as Moods of Norway

Figure 8.1 Moods of Norway articulates time and space together by resituating fashion/rural. http://scandinavianfashion.net/2011/08/17/norways-happiest-fashion-brand-does-women/ (August 17, 2011).

emerged in small nations within Europe (as well as many other sites around the world). Using a model that is oriented more toward transnational validation than hegemonic power, Skov argues that companies such as Moods of Norway articulate new formulations with imagery that slides between local and national, and fashion and rural (folk) representations. We can also consider ways in which the fashion imagery in Figure 8.1 articulates gender, ethnicity, place, age/generation, class, and so on. Intersectionalities can be interpreted through an analysis of time and space together in a Möbius-like interplay.

The space theorist Henri Lefebvre (1991) emphasized the importance of thinking about time and space together. He indicates that "time is known and actualized in space, becoming a social reality by virtue of a spatial practice. Similarly, space is known only in and through time" (219). Time and space can be distinguished conceptually from one another, but they cannot be separated. The same—as we have seen throughout this book, and as represented in the Venn diagram in Figure 2.2 in Chapter 2—can be said of all of our subject positions. We move through time and space through our physical and perceptual, embodied experiences—in our style-fashion-dress—as we *become* through subjectivity.

From a feminist perspective, Massey (2005) agrees with Lefebvre's call for the need to think about time and space together, but she delves more deeply into the binary power relations. A fundamental part of the problem, she indicates, is the way binary oppositions have been used in modern Western thought to construct boundaries—rather than interconnections—between time and space, as well as global and local, space and place, urban and rural, and so on. Philosophical binary oppositional thinking about time and space has contributed to a complex "geometry of power" (Massey 2005) in which space becomes constructed as "second fiddle" to time. In this geometric formulation, time is seen as the dynamic stuff of history, whereas space is viewed as rather dead or lifeless. Euromodernity became a way of envisioning the process of evolving or getting better through time. "Other" spaces became constructed as those that were outside of this linear narrative of time; they were fixed or fossilized in the past. The same may be said about rural or folk dress, but images such as Figure 8.1 cause a rethinking of such fossilization and moves instead toward revitalization (Skov 2011).

Another example of revitalization is a Chinese luxury fashion firm, Shanghai Tang, which also addresses the theme of time/space. A Hong Kong entrepreneur, David Tang, founded the company in 1994. According to fashion studies scholar Hazel Clark (2009), Shanghai Tang used "a nostalgic and self-Orientalizing approach in its brand image, merchandise, and retail environment," playing off the imagery and imaginary of Shanghai in the 1930s during its heyday as a modern, international city—similar to Hong Kong in the 1990s (Clark 2009: 180). Actually a Hong Kong-based, rather than Shanghai-based, company, Shanghai Tang capitalized on the skills of the original Shanghai tailors who arrived in Hong Kong in the 1940s and 1950s as refugees, to a bespoke (custom made-to-order) tailoring service. Garments included the cheongsam or *qipao*, a popular dress that originated in Shanghai in the 1930s but became identified with Hong Kong in the 1950s and 1960s. Blending elements of the majority Han gown with euromodern dress, the cheongsam or qipao was itself a complex Chinese modern women's garment. Target customers were local expatriates and international tourists seeking representation of Chineseness.

Clark (2009) indicates that what "was being retailed was a playful, even theme-park, vision of China" (182). A similar, almost campy yet luxury-oriented play on time and space can be seen in Shanghai Tang's contemporary "Mandarin Collar Society." This society includes male members who (at least upon occasion) wear Shanghai Tang's collarless men's shirts in lieu of a collared shirt and tie. A typical Shanghai Tang collarless shirt features orange button-holing and stitching details that make a statement without the aid of a tie.

Shanghai Tang cites the mission of the society as follows:

"Reorient Yourself"

Instead of the traditional necktie, the Shanghai Tang Mandarin Collar Society champions the modern, chic alternative of the mandarin collar. Shanghai Tang Executive Chairman, Raphael le Masne de Chermont, said, "It is a club with the goal to promote an elegant Chinese-inspired style for men. It's an alternative that allows you to reorient yourself, to be stylish while being yourself."

The World's Leading Men United for One Mission

The timely, compelling and slightly cheeky initiative unites men who are shaping the world in diverse fields, such as sports, business, politics and the arts. To spearhead the effort, Shanghai Tang has appointed MCS Ambassadors, including British sprint champion Linford Christie, Michelin star chef Pierre Gagnaire, world renowned pianist Lang Lang, Gavin Newsom mayor of San Francisco among others. (shanghaitang.com/mcs, accessed September 16, 2011)

The Mandarin Collar Society's "slightly cheeky" challenge to euromodern hegemonic notions of bourgeois masculinity refuses to fix Chinese menswear in the past. Rather, it freshens and modernizes it, offering a Chinese modern alternative to a collared shirt with a tie. Shanghai Tang articulates time and space in a way that expands concepts of transnational modernity while revitalizing the Chinese modernity of the 1930s in Shanghai.

As the story of Shanghai Tang reminds us, stories of fashion are not only modern; they are also inevitably urban. In a euromodern context in the nineteenth century, sociologists such as Max Weber and Georg Simmel inextricably linked fashion with urbanization and euromodernity's "decisive break with the past" (Wilson 1985). As part of a larger European fascination with memory and history, a "cult of the past" led to an obsession with capturing "authenticity" (Tuan 1977: 194). Dress historian Lou Taylor (2004) indicates that between 1850 and 1914, European museums collected rural dress in order to document history and to "locate" the "country" in the past. Perhaps some of the fervor for cultural preservation could be attributed to cultural anxieties about losing authenticity in the context of industrialization and urbanization. Taylor argues, however, that rural peasant attire was never really static; rather, it constantly shifted as individuals (mostly women) modified their clothes slightly when they made new ones (201).

In addition to constructing time-space binary oppositions such as urban (dynamic) versus rural (static), euromodern history has had a tendency to represent time as linear (i.e., increasingly modern) since the original, "decisive break with the past" (Wilson 1985). But fashion—as flux in time—complicates this linear representation. Instead, it articulates cyclical or circuitous ways of thinking about time (Riello and McNeil 2010: 2–3). The circuit of culture through style-fashion-dress, discussed in Chapter 1, reminds us that production, distribution, and consumption are not part of a straight line but rather are part of a more complex and interdependent circuit.

A second way in which we can recognize how fashion time is circuitous is to consider how fashion plays with the past. Fashion studies scholar Heike Jenss (2004) studied the sixties scene in Germany and explored how/why people aged sixteen to their thirties relate so deeply to clothes, hairstyles, makeup, and accessories from the 1960s, which were before their time. Influenced heavily by the British mods (e.g., the Beatles) of the 1960s and larger international revivals since the 1970s, participants in the German sixties scene strive for a sense of authenticity in the cut and materials of their clothes. They either buy 1960s clothes from vintage sources or make their own using patterns derived from this decade. Jenss notes that contemporary bodies differ from bodies 40 years prior; bodies in the early twenty-first century tended to be taller and more muscular. However, individuals in the 1960s scene are able to incorporate an array of 1960s styles (e.g., op or pop art, psychedelics, hippie dress) into their everyday lives. Jenss (2004) explains that retro "epitomizes the idea of space/time compression in dress, evoked through globally circulating images of other times and places" (398).

Jenss's research is a helpful reminder that individuals experience time subjectively. Style-fashion-dress can function as a kind of retro recycling, as well as periodic punctuations in anticipation of the future. The cultural theorist Walter Benjamin (1968) referred to fashion's ability to make a "tiger's leap into the past" to grab and appropriate styles and somehow rearticulate them to appear fresh. How might individuals vary in their responses to these newly renovated, fresh styles through their overlapping subject positions?

AGE/GENERATION AND PLACE

Processes of subject formation are located in time and space in an embodied way, in the form of the subject positions of age/generation and place, respectively (recalling the Venn model in Figure 2.2 in Chapter 2). Time is the more abstract cousin to embodied *age/generation: when* one lives and develops/ages; space is the more abstract cousin to physical *place: where* one lives. Through interlocking, overlapping subject positions, we experience age/generation and place as they intersect with gender, ethnicity, class, and other subject positions. Age/generation locates different stages in life as we move through time with a cohort of others in the same generation (e.g., baby boomers, Generation X, millenials). The concept of place includes *where* we are geographically—in a city? In the country? Or a suburb? The cultural geographer Tim Cresswell describes place as "space invested with meaning in the context of power":

> This process of investing space with meaning happens across the globe at all scales and has done [so] throughout human history. It has been one of the central tasks of human geography to make sense of it. (Cresswell 2004: 12)

We experience age/generation and place, and their more abstract versions of time and space, respectively, together. Like other subject positions, age/generation and place need to be analyzed within the larger context of cultural discourse, along with everyday habitus. And age/generation and place—just as time and space—need to be contemplated together.

As an army brat, I totally connect time with space or, more personally, age/generation with the many places (in the United States and in France and Germany) where I lived growing up. To me, the question "What grade (i.e., when) was that?" cannot be separated from the question "Where was I?" Figure 8.2 comes from my first grade experience in San Antonio, Texas. One of my sisters recently came across the photograph and shared it with my sisters and me. It was 1959, and although we cannot place the exact month, I was almost or barely six and in first grade. My oldest sister Linda (far left) was in eighth grade, my younger sister Pam (held by my father) was nearly or barely one year old, and my sister Jeanette (in the red and white checked dress, and with my mother's arm around her) was in the sixth grade. I have a variety of memories from that year, but disappointingly, I don't recall the suspendered skirt and blouse I was wearing, although I really like it! What I do remember is Jeanette's red and white checked dress, because she wore it in a sixth grade elementary school presentation that my first grade class attended. She needed to represent a farm girl in a skit, and this dress became her costume. It was apparently the closest costume available in the marketplace at the time to do so. It made quite an impression on me; I loved that dress (and so did she). So much so, on my end, that when my first grade class was drawing and drafting thank you notes to her class, I recall focusing on her and her dress, diligently drawing in the red and white checks on her dress. This dress became invested with meaning in the context of places (e.g., our home's backyard; our elementary school; San Antonio, Texas) that were themselves invested with meaning. And this dress became a costume to represent a different, imaginary place (a farm) or its more abstract, spatial cousin (the country).

Figure 8.2   Benke family in San Antonio, Texas, 1959. Photo from author's family collection.

My sisters and I are all part of the baby boom generation, born between 1946 (after World War II) and 1964. However, our age differences contribute to our recollections of the same events when we lived in various places (despite our shared family background, gender, ethnic, class, and other subject positions). Our subjectivities and perspectives are "softly assembled," to use Fausto-Sterling's concept discussed in Chapter 6.

A photograph is a snapshot of a certain time and space, experienced in an embodied and meaningful way as the intersectionality between age/generation and place. Fashion becomes a factor in interpreting a photograph. In terms of mainstream fashion, my father's crew-cut hairstyle and the length of our skirts all point to the late 1950s. Skirt silhouettes at the time were full or gathered (especially for young girls) and either full or narrow for adult women. The boundaries between the 1950s and 1960s, as with any decades, are not clear cut. Sociologist Fred Davis (1984) wrote about how "decade labeling" (e.g., the 1960s, the 1970s, the 1980s) rarely captures the experience of time, which does not avail itself to easy delineation, nor to clean breaks in years ending with a zero.

Not everyone was dressing this way in 1959, however. What else was going on in terms of style-fashion-dress? A more bohemian alternative in the United States (especially New York and San Francisco) was the "beat" movement or subculture. Although the roots (or routes) of the movement or subculture date to the late 1940s, the original use of the term "beat generation" has been attributed to Jack Kerouac (1922–1969), who used it in his 1950 book, *The Town and the City*. The beat generation rejected elements of hegemonic masculinity and questioned the ideals of the American Dream. Their motto, according to Feldman and Gartenberg (1958) was "dig everything" and "implicitly want nothing." Claiming that life should be "authentic," they experimented with writing, drugs, sexuality, and Eastern religion. By the late 1950s, some of the beat movement's claims to authenticity—including appropriations of African American and working class culture—had been appropriated, in turn, by popular media discourse. In 1958 Herb Caen of the *San Francisco Chronicle* coined the label "beatnik" as a synthesis between the "beat" movement and the Russian satellite Sputnik. Now beatniks were caricatured as marijuana-smoking, coffee-drinking existentialists who wore only black: black jeans, black leather jackets, black berets, black tights for women (Kaiser and Looysen 2010). The popular television situation comedy, *The Many Loves of Dobie Gillis* (1959–1963), featured a beatnik character Maynard G. Krebs (played by Bob Denver) as the sidekick to the lead: the more straight-laced character Dobie. Krebs wore a goatee and generally had an unkempt or bohemian appearance and an aversion to the word "work."

What else was happening in 1959? Popular culture was replete with themes of gender, ethnicity, race, and class. Mattel introduced Barbie Doll No. 1, inspired by (appropriated from) a German doll introduced in 1956. The sexy Hollywood comedy *Some Like It Hot* was released in 1959, starring Marilyn Monroe, Tony Curtis, and Jack Lemmon. Curtis and Lemmon dressed in drag to pass as women so that they could join an all-female band to escape the mob. As noted in Chapter 7, there had been considerable cultural anxiety— and hence cultural humor as a release—regarding gender and sexuality in the late 1940s and early 1950s. Also in 1959, the African American singer Ray Charles (1930–2004) had a hit song, "What'd I Say," banned on some mainstream radio stations for what was perceived as sexual innuendo through lyrics, moaning, and wailing. The play *Raisin in the Sun* opened on Broadway; it was the first Broadway production to be written by an African American woman—Lorraine Hansberry. The play was based on the experience of an African American family in a Chicago community.

Also in 1959 in England, the physicist and novelist C. P. Snow (1905–1980) warned about how the "two cultures" in modern societies—the sciences and the humanities—were a problematic binary opposition that would make it more difficult to address complex world problems (Snow 1959). Meanwhile, also in Britain, literary scholars Raymond Williams (1921–1988) and Richard Hoggart (b. 1918) were in the process of developing the field of cultural studies, bridging the humanities and social sciences in critical studies of class, culture, and society, as well as political activism. Hoggart (1957) had published

The Uses of Literacy: Aspects of Working Class Life, in a class-conscious critique of mass, popular culture; Williams (1958) had authored *Culture and Society*, in which he detailed how culture is "ordinary" and everyday, not only for the upper classes.

World events in 1959 provide insights on space within time. Civil rights activists Martin Luther King Jr. (1929–1968) and Coretta Scott King (1927–2006) traveled to India. Invited by the Gandhi Peace Foundation, the Kings discussed Mohandas K. Gandhi's philosophy of nonviolence with Prime Minister Jawaharlal Nehru. Gandhi had used a nonviolent approach against British colonial rule, and the success of this approach influenced the course of the U.S. civil rights movement (King 1993). Meanwhile, in China, there was a famine and considerable starvation. The Tibetan people rebelled against the communist Chinese government, and the Dalai Lama fled to India (Chen 2006). Soviet forces entered Afghanistan, and the Cold War raged.

In 1959 U.S. vice president Richard Nixon went to the USSR and engaged in the "Kitchen Debate" with the Russian president Nikita Khrushchev. The debate was cultural, political, and economic: Whose standard of living was higher? Americans or Russians? At the American National Exhibit in Moscow, an appliance-saturated modern kitchen, along with fashion, toys, cars, and voting machines were all displayed in an attempt to convince the Russian people that democratic capitalism contributed to a higher quality of life, fostering a binary opposition between Western capitalism and Eastern communism. The argument in the Kitchen Debate was that American women were being "liberated" by modern kitchen conveniences. (Recall that this was before the feminist movement of the 1960s.) Russian visitors to the exhibit, however, were not uniformly positive. Their review of the exhibit included comments that the exhibit was designed for "bourgeois tastes," rather than "culture." Americans may be wealthier, some Russian reviewers argued, but Russians were more "cultured." Moreover, the reviewers resisted "the unrecognizable and unflattering ['backward'] subject position the exhibition assigned to them" (Reid 2008). On the other hand, in research with Russian women who had migrated to Canada between 1992 and 2004, there were frequent comments about the scarcity of products in the former Soviet Union:

> At our stores there was nothing. They were empty, or things were so ugly. Because mostly the budget of the whole country went to weapons in the Soviet Union, so there was nothing in the stores. (Katerina, age sixty-three, quoted in Korotchenko and Clarke 2010)

From San Antonio, Texas (a major center for the U.S. military) to Moscow, the "binary cold war epistemology" (Reid 2008) shaped and limited popular thinking about world problems in 1959. The issue came closer to home when

Communist Party leader Fidel Castro assumed power in Cuba that year (and a few years later, the Cuban Missile Crisis was to put the U.S. public into a state of panic).

Also in 1959, on the world stage, the famous Swedish diplomat Sverker Åström (b. 1915) was working on cold war international policies. I am indebted to fashion and queer studies scholar Dirk Gindt (2010) for his work on Åström, who at the age of eighty-seven on September 14, in 2003, came out publicly as gay. To announce the occasion, he wore a well-tailored business suit befitting his illustrious career. It was actually his socks that he used to announce his queerness: one red sock and one green sock. A number of explanations can be offered: as always, style-fashion-dress offers up ambiguities and ambivalences that require navigation and negotiation. Clearly, however, his articulation with the use of contrasting, complementary colors on the color wheel, represents some kind of both/and, ironic or even campy statement, rather than simply an either/or opposition. It seems that he was saying "I can be this (a well-respected Swedish diplomat representing the nation) *and* that (a gay man who is comfortable in his own skin, and given the times we live in and my age, "I'm now able to come forward"). This both/and articulation, without necessarily attributing any particular meaning to any particular color, helps us to think through the many shades and blendings that intersectionalities and complex transnational entanglements entail. As summarized by Åström himself:

> All my life, I lived a double life, but I have never been a security risk. [In an exclusive interview with *Svenska Dagbladet's* (reporter) Karin Thunberg, the diplomat Sverker Åström, 87, tells the secret of his life: that he is gay. Only his bosses at the Department of State were informed. They shrugged their shoulders. (Thunberg, quoted in Gindt 2010: 234)

As Gindt (2010) details so well, Åström's life story is a lesson in the secrecy of transnational, cold war politics as they intersected in a particular time and space with a gay sexual subjectivity and subject position. At the height of the Cold War, in which Communism and homosexuality were equated and feared in euromodern nations, Åström worked diligently to craft and enact Sweden's policy of neutrality through representative diplomatic positions in the Soviet Union and the United States, as well as France, England, and Sweden. During World War II, Åström was a member of the Swedish delegation in Moscow; he then held a number of positions in Swedish governmental agencies in Washington, DC; London; New York City (at the United Nations); Paris; and so on. In the interview in *Svenska Dagbladet*, Åström was about to introduce a new edition of his biography, with an updated afterword in which he acknowledged being gay and expressed some regrets about the times in which he has lived, which did not allow for him to be more open in his sexual subjectivity and subject position:

> I have exclusively loved men. Some happy relationships I have had, but sporadically and short-lived. The relationships never developed into the legitimate partnership which I could have legalized with the new legislation. (Åström, quoted in Gindt 2010: 235)

Gindt (2010) notes how Swedish sexual politics since the mid-1990s had enabled possibilities for registered gay partnership, and public discourse had included the coming out of a number of celebrities. Gindt observes, however:

> Unfortunately, while Sweden was busily affirming itself as a sexually liberated and tolerant state, this did not involve a critical reassessment of the country's post-war history—something that became very clear in the media discourse surrounding Åström's coming out. Dismissing the importance of the diplomat's public coming out would belie what this unique case can reveal about Swedish gay history and the political dimension of the proverbial closet. (Gindt 2010: 236)

A Norwegian study entitled "Reading Fashion as Age: Teenage Girls' and Grown Women's Accounts of Clothing as Body and Social Status" (Klepp and Storm-Mathisen 2005) also focused on age/generational issues in relation to gender and sexuality. Females in both age categories that they studied had to negotiate how they represented their sexuality in relation to age. Young teenage girls did not want to look too young or babyish ("sweet, asexual"); but at the same time, they often realized that they needed to be careful about looking too sexualized (like a "babe") for their age. They were ambivalent about the babe concept; it wasn't all bad, and they did want to be sexually attractive. By the age of forty or so, the grown women were also at a crossroad. They wanted not only to look respectable but also to show that they were still sexual beings. In other words, they did not want to look like they were "on the make"; nor did they want to look "over the hill" (Klepp and Storm-Mathisen 2005).

Sociologist Julia Twigg (2010) has remarked that age is "simply not fashionable or sexy" (475). As a topic and subject position in fashion studies (and to some extent feminist cultural studies), the process of aging becomes sublimated under a mythic ideal of "ageless style" in hegemonic fashion discourse (e.g., UK *Vogue*). Despite the fact that the older adult population is substantial and growing as a sector of the market, the fashion industry and academics alike tend to shy away from a topic that generates considerable anxiety and denial. It seems that fashion and age "do not fit easily, or happily together" (Twigg 2010: 472) in a discourse that revolves around imagery of young girls made up to look older and adult female models airbrushed to eliminate any signs of maturity. How do older women feel about seeing primarily young (even prepubescent) females representing what it means to be fashionable? Fashion studies scholars Kozar and Damhorst (2008) conducted research with 163 women in the United States, ages sixty through eighty. They found that the women perceived older-looking models to be more attractive and more fashionable than the younger-looking models, and the women studied indicated a higher preference to purchase the clothes the older-looking models were wearing.

We found somewhat similar results in the masculinities research conducted at UC Davis. Although our sample was not as old as Kozar and Damhorst's study of older women (ours ranged in age from eighteen to sixty-five), we did find that the older men we interviewed or surveyed were interested in seeing more male fashion models who had bodies and ages that were more reflective of their own experiences. They tended to be weary of sexualized images of young athletic men, with bodies they felt that were unrealistic for them to achieve.

As a case in point, consider the case of the opening of an Abercrombie & Fitch (A&F) store on the famous Champs-Élysées Boulevard in Paris in May 2011. Young men of a different (younger) generation gathered for the opportunity—as models—to shift from being unmarked to marked in a very visible way. The American apparel company A&F opened the store with tremendous fanfare. Known for and branded through the imagery of shirtless male models, A&F hired 101 male models to line the sidewalk outside the store and the upper levels of buildings across the street. All shirtless and well-toned, the models wore low-rise, distressed A&F jeans with wide belts and brown A&F flip flops. Needless to say, the publicity created quite a stir, as did the opening of the store itself: a beautiful old building with impressive wrought iron gates and with casual, luxury merchandise for young men and women. Hundreds of shoppers, mostly young women, lined up to enter the store and to have their photographs taken with the male "greeters" (Clifford and Alderman 2011).

An online video includes interviews with a few of the male models, as they stand shirtless along one of the most famous streets in the world. We get some sense of their subject positions and their subjectivities. As they speak, we are reminded that they are not just there to be looked *at*. They are subjects, as well as objects. Two are British; one is black and has been to Paris many times before. His mother is originally from Mozambique and is French speaking. When asked why he is in such great shape, he explains that he is on his university's track team and also rows. But even before being asked this question, he had already identified himself as a physics major. The second British model is white and explains that he stays in shape as a rugby player. He has never been to Paris before but really likes it; he talks about the beauty of the women and the buildings. A third model is Italian; he is a college student and a swimmer. All three of the models are quick to let us know that they are not primarily models—this is a "side job" with their other pursuits. They "all do something else (first)." They are all probably in their early twenties, at most. This would place them in the generation of millenials (born after 1983 or so). This locates them in time and in the ages of their bodies. Of course, what they have done to get their bodies in such shape has been largely of their own doing in their recent years of life, but they did not get to have any say with respect to *when* they were born. Neither did they have any control over *where* they were born (or into which family and its genealogy, including issues of race and class). Similarly, doctors assigned their genders (male or masculine) at birth based upon biological, embodied indicators. Their sexualities (or sexual desires) were something they probably began to realize during middle child-hood or adolescence. And then there is the issue of place: *where* are they currently? They're on a famous street that has a lot of historical meaning in Paris and beyond. They come from other places. But in terms of the more abstract concept of space, they can be seen as bodies in motion.

But what happens when a place has already been endowed with value, and then seems to become undifferentiated through globalization? The A&F opening is an interesting case study at the intersection of globalization, subjectivity, space, place, time, and age. Cultural anxieties arise in the face of encroachment from other nations. Subject positions such as age and generation intersect with Frenchness (nation) to influence responses to the splashy arrival of an American retailer in a special French place. We can get a sense of shoppers' and onlookers' subjectivities from the *New York Times* (Clifford and Alderman 2011) account. A French male and female couple in their late fifties paused as they walked past the A&F store on the opening day: "American culture is okay, but we still must safeguard the French culture," said the woman. "We have traditions that are very important." A seventeen-year-old French female shopper waiting in line had a different perspective: "Globalization might have been an issue for our parents, but it is not a problem for us," she said as she perused an A&F blog (in English). Transnational marketers are likely to agree with her assessment of generational differences. For example, the president of a Milan-based luxury goods and retail consulting firm indicates that young European consumers are "becoming more cosmopolitan, living contemporary lives that are in tandem and no longer as a continuous fight among cultures" (Clifford and Alderman 2011). Clearly there is a need to reimagine time and space as interconnected concepts in a transnational economy. Still, the importance of place needs to be affirmed in an ongoing manner.

At the same time, the need to think through issues of intersectionality is compelling. These issues require unpacking using a variety of methods and perspectives. The 2008 U.S. national survey among male consumers, conducted at UC Davis and described earlier, revealed some intriguing inter-sectionalities, some of which are counterintuitive. We looked first to see if there were any differences among the men we surveyed, according to age (and there were, as might be expected, with younger men, and of a more recent generation, being more interested in issues of appearance and fashion than their older counterparts, by and large). We also found a "main effect" for place, as self-identified by the men we surveyed: Urban men expressed the most interest in style-fashion-dress overall, followed by suburban and rural. The surprise factor in the findings occurred in the interactions/intersectionalities. Gay rural men expressed the most interest in style-fashion-dress issues, whereas urban bisexual men were most concerned about navigating how to be unmarked through their style-fashion-dress (i.e., not to stand out too much). We are pursuing these complicated intersectionalities further and see these findings as just an opening in a larger door opening to the intersectionalities between place and sexuality, as well as other possibilities. We had a relatively small number of men in our U.S. national survey (1,952 total) who self-identified as both rural and gay (17) and as both urban and bisexual (23), but the statistical significance of the interaction effects raises questions for further study.

Following are representative self-descriptions of the rural gay men's style; these were the men who were most in agreement with statements about being interested in style-fashion-dress. They described their own style as follows:

"Casual, neat, colorful" (twenty-seven-year-old white male in a committed relationship)
"Relaxed, stylish, comfortable" (thirty-eight-year-old single white male)
"Casual, traditional, comfortable" (thirty-nine-year-old single white male)
"Country boy" (forty-one-year-old white male in a committed relationship)
"Casual, coordinated, fashionable" (forty-seven-year-old white male in a committed relationship)
"Conservative, comfortable" (fifty-three-year-old single white male)
"Quality, conservative, colorful" (fifty-six-year-old single white male)
"Classic, ageless, modern" (fifty-six-year-old single white male)
"Relaxed shag" (fifty-nine-year-old male in a committed relationship)
"Business, social, sophisticated" (sixty-three-year-old single white male)
"Colorful, casual, comfortable" (sixty-five-year-old single white male)

Self-descriptions by the urban bisexual men are included below; these are the men who were most in agreement with statements about the need to be un-marked. They are more diverse and eclectic in nature, as might be expected in an urban setting, but they clearly desire not to stand out too much. So there is some irony—if not campy ambiguity—suggested in their representations of themselves:

"Alternative/indie" (twenty-one-year-old white male in a committed relation-ship)

"Sexy, thin, short" (twenty-one-year-old Asian American male)

"Comfortable, unique, very casual" (twenty-one-year-old white single male)

"Fetish, tight, urban" (twenty-four-year-old Asian American male)

"Modern, casual, sharp" (twenty-four-year-old Latino single male)

"Punk, goth, eclectic" (twenty-four-year-old white single male)

"Sporty, workout, fashionable" (twenty-four-year-old white single male)

"Fierce, daring, bold" (twenty-five-year-old white single male)

"Classic, own, unique" (twenty-seven-year-old black single male)

"Neat, casual, fun" (twenty-nine-year-old white single male)

"Random, eclectic, color-coordinated" (twenty-nine-year-old white single male)

"Casual farm chic" (thirty-year-old white male)

"Casual, serious, traditional" (thirty-three-year-old Asian American single male)

"Hip hop traditional mix" (fifty-three-year-old white single male)

"Casual, stylish but fairly conservative" (fifty-five-year-old white married male)

"Plain, old fashioned, neat" (fifty-nine-year-old white divorced male)

"Casual" (sixty-year-old white married male)

Although it is rarely possible (given time and money constraints) to document every intersectionality in a quantitative or statistical sense, the conceptual inter-play among subject positions and subjectivities requires ongoing investigation—qualitatively or otherwise. Clearly, something interesting is going on in the in-tersectionalities between sexuality and place.

As individual bodies plow through time, in various places, issues of style-fashion-dress help to ground where and when they are. Bodies develop and age. They go through stages, and the apparel industry is pleased to comply. The sociologist Daniel Cook (2004) has documented how the emerging children's wear industry in the 1920s and 1930s capitalized on age/stage development, and he and I have collaborated to extend issues of age and generation to the "tween" consumer—in between, and largely gendered and sexualized anxiously as female (Cook and Kaiser 2004). Age/size stages become especially complicated in the toddler and tween years, and require considerable navigation of ambiguities between the mind and body. The gendering of the subject positions in these and other stages is very clear, however; the binary opposition between masculine and feminine is alive and well (Paoletti 2012).

Why does the euromodern, at least, style-fashion-dress of children engender such a desire for certainty, when the world itself is complex and open ended in so many ways? As the Danish philosopher Søren Kierkegaard (1980) said over 150 years ago, cultural anxiety is future oriented, like "a feeling in the bones that a storm is approaching" (Kierkegaard 1980). The themes or topics that generate a great deal of cultural anxiety (and censorship) include explicit sexual content and violence; yet these are also the kinds of themes that sell. Because children represent the future, which is uncertain, and because there is generally strong cultural consensus both to prepare and to protect them, cultural anxieties abound when it comes to thinking about children. Kierkegaard (1980) described the close relationship between innocence and anxiety. Children become a metaphor for both, because they represent both the innocence of the past (as people recall their own childhoods and look back) and the anxiety of the future (as people anticipate uncertainty). Issues of gender (discussed in Chapter 6) and sexuality (discussed in Chapter 7) intersect with other subject positions, including age, to generate cultural anxieties regarding a "loss of innocence":

> Our children are sacrosanct. We do not think of them as sexual beings, yet we do think of them very distinctly as boys and girls. Their gender is important to us. We believe strongly that all children are innocent and must be kept that way for as long as possible. (Spencer 1995: 404)

The art historian Anne Higonnet (1998) notes how images of children are at once common, sacred, and controversial in cultural discourse. Contradictory cultural impulses play out on the bodies of young children: We want to preserve their childhood innocence, and yet we also want to prepare them for an uncertain adulthood, knowing as we do that the future will be different. Hence, both innocence and anxiety involve a variety of mixed emotions:

> bittersweet, nostalgic recollections of times gone by that coexist with symbolic detachments from the past in the name of progress and modernity; and a sense of anticipation or even hope that coexists with uncertainties and fears about the future; respectively. (Kaiser and Huun 2002)

Kierkegaard (1980) went on to say:

> This is the profound secret of innocence, that it is at the same time anxiety . . . The anxiety that is posited in innocence is in the first place no guilt . . . *In all cultures where the childlike is preserved as the dreaming of the spirit, this anxiety is found. The more profound the anxiety, the more profound the culture.* (41–42, emphasis added)

If childhood becomes a metaphor for nostalgia about the past and anxiety toward the future, then the question arises: How do cultures vary in their representations of children—including how adults dress their children? How do they vary in their representations of older adults? There is neither the time nor the space to delve deeply into this issue at this point, but let's leave the possibilities open to complicate the idea that childhood, older adulthood, and non-Western cultures alike can be "fixed" in the past.

To come back to issues of place/space as they intersect with time, the cultural geographer Yi-Fu Tuan (1977) describes space and place as interdependent concepts: They rely upon one another. Space is the more abstract and open concept; it is the geometric opening that makes movement and freedom possible. Place is part of space but can be considered a pause with reflection. Tuan suggests that what begins as "undifferentiated" space "becomes place as we get to know it better and endow it with value" (Tuan 1977: 6). Both Tuan and feminist geographer Massey argue for both/and connective thinking.

We cannot simply talk about place; we also have to talk about space—the idea of a cultural site that can be abstract and even transnational and that enables a sense of belonging and connection. So, hip hop style may be found—especially among urban youth—in a number of locations around the world. The music and the clothes associated with hip hop style may enable a sense of identification and belonging that transcends national, racial, and religious boundaries. Similarly, people of similar religious backgrounds, such as Islam, may express their identification with Islam in a number of ways (consider the differences in head coverings or veiling among Muslim women). Yet they share some common principles and ideas about what is appropriate and why. Processes of identity and difference are ongoing; complex; and generally fluid, not fixed.

It is in and through place, Tuan (1977) notes, that we are able to pause—at least temporarily—in our movements. Place is part of space, but place allows us to locate ourselves, knowing at the same time that there is still a larger space out there to explor. Place is where we reflect, and in the process abstract or undifferentiated space becomes a concrete place that becomes "filled with meaning" (Tuan 1977: 199). In personal experience, "space and time coexist, intermesh, and define each other" (130). If time is about "flow or movement," then place is a "pause" in that movement (198). And, abstract space becomes a concrete place with that. Yet as Massey (2005) argues, space is still open to be experienced in a variety ways through multiple subjectivities. In order for the future to be open, space, too, must be open; it involves an array of loose ends and missing links. It cannot be captured in a single hegemonic narrative, such as the euromodern story of fashion's beginnings.

In a number of locations around the world, a sense of space/place has shaped how people dress. In villages in Guatemala, for example, the woven patterns of the fabrics people have used in their clothing has represented a sense of social location. Similarly, in most high schools in the United States, there are subgroups—often with names that further help to categorize difference (e.g., punks, goths, skaters)—that differentiate themselves in terms of style. These groups may even have certain locations around the high school grounds that they use to mark their sense of space/place. So the concept of cultural belonging in terms of space/place may have long and deep roots that lie in clearly identified locations (for example, a village) and in the materials they use to dress themselves (and how they do this). But in a highly globalized world, when people can see, and even identify with, clothes as well as people in physical locations beyond their own, a sense of belonging can span beyond a given location.

OPEN INTERSECTIONALITIES: FURTHER SUBJECT POSITIONS

The Venn diagram in Chapter 2 opens up the possibility of a lot of circles (2-D) and globes (3-D). How do we know when to stop adding circles/globes? This question is open ended because subjectivity is embodied, knowing that there are multiple possibilities, as fashion studies and feminist cultural studies alike remind us. Fundamentally, the combination of these fields of study move us beyond hegemonic ways of thinking about subject positions and other topics in binary terms: together, these fields require us to resist either/or thinking in favor of both/and or, better, multiple ways of thinking about being and becoming. We can always add circles or globes, because subject positions and subjectivities are always emerging and changing. Like fashion, they are unfolding. Time and space, in the process, cannot be essentialized as static or fixed, because just as people grow and change across time and space, so does fashion—through bodies.

Religion, for example, is an important subject position for some individuals and deserves its own deeper analysis. It may be a salient subject position that intersects with national, ethnic, or gendered subject positions, for example, as we have seen. Especially helpful in exploring religion as a subject position in relation to dress are fashion studies scholar Linda Arthur's edited books of readings (1999, 2000) and anthropologist Emma Tarlo's (2010) recent multimethod, in-depth analysis of British Muslim women's style-fashion-dress.

Physical ability/disability or other bodily considerations (e.g., height, weight, facial or somatic features) might be another circle/globe that could be added. This, too, is an important area of scholarship at the interface between fashion studies and feminist cultural studies. We could easily add more and more circles for meaningful subject positions, and multiply intersectionalities in the process. Space does not permit here to pursue as many possibilities as I would like.

Style-fashion-dress is a complex right at the center of important debates about the body, subjectivity, and culture through time and space. Style-fashion-dress constitutes the bridge; styled-fashioned-dressed bodies are "soft assemblages" (Fausto-Sterling 2003). We are born into our bodies and cannot really choose some of our subject positions fully, but we do have the agency to explore other subject positions. Subjectivity cuts across this process of navigating subject positions.

Most of the time, most of us are probably somewhere in between subject positions. These are the spaces that we inhabit. That's how we make sense of who we are and how we are becoming. The issues will vary by context or situation, but the cultural anxieties and ambivalences associated with processes of becoming are likely to influence the everyday choices that we make—whether we are dressed to impress, dressed to be "unmarked," dressed to avoid looking someone else, or dressed to navigate in-between spaces critically and creatively. Perhaps it is the process of navigating or negotiating itself that compels us to connect dots that might not otherwise be joined. Such is the contribution of style-fashion-dress: subjectivities across subject positions.

As discussed throughout this book, feminist, fashion studies, and cultural studies scholars have contributed to deeper understandings of social life and power relations by breaking down binary oppositions (e.g., masculine versus feminine, gay versus straight, black versus white). The fashion studies scholar Joanne Entwistle (2000) rightfully notes how bodies are central to the cultural studies circuit of culture. Bodies are pivotal to production, distribution, consumption, and other processes within the circuit of culture. These bodies, whether they are producing, distributing, or consuming are styled-fashioned-dressed. In short, they both *do* and *appear*, across time and space.

In a contemporary world of digitized imagery, social networking, Internet shopping, and global retailing, in some ways it becomes easier to think about time and space together. On the other hand, there is a danger of losing sight of time and space altogether, and place may become especially endangered. Some fashion Websites, for example, offer little sense of *where* a company is located, where the clothes are produced, and how long they have been in business. So, we have a delicate challenge here: to think integratively about time and space, and space and place, but not so abstractly as to obscure our ability to perceive and analyze them at all.

It is through the styled-fashioned-dressed body that individuals subjectively experience and navigate time and space. Bodies are in motion, and they are located in time and space. How do bodies manage? I continue to submit that it is through a process of "minding appearances" (Kaiser 2001) that individuals bridge mind and body issues, and style themselves in ways that articulate their most recent thoughts about who they are (becoming). To the extent that resources allow (e.g., one's bank balance or credit limit, aesthetic know-how, or accessible shopping venues), the system of style-fashion-dress offers a way to bridge across subject positions, manage power relations, and sort through visual and material cultures to see what just might be the best possible articulation of self at the moment. "Moment"—the root word of momentum—has a certain energy implied in its framing. Hence, time is moving, and, if anything, the pace has accelerated with globalization. And, all of this movement happens within spaces that are located geographically. In a contradictory manner, style-fashion-dress is locally constructed but yet is global in its circuit of culture.

CLOSING/OPENING THOUGHTS

> To underrate clothing and fashion as political statements would be to refuse to look at history—and to deny ourselves a lot of fun. (Garber 1995: 23)

> The eternal, in any case, is far more like the ruffle on a dress than some idea. (Benjamin 2004)

These quotes address, in complicated ways, the idea of time. They both address how the material aspects of style-fashion-dress intersect or become entangled with the feminist cultural studies concept of articulation through ideas/concepts that are cultural, political, and social in nature.

Cultural theorist Marjorie Garber's quote articulates the connections between politics and pleasure, pointing out how style-fashion-dress is embedded in subject positions, cultural discourses, and power relations that need to be understood historically; yet there are also possibilities for creative resistance, subversion, and play. Such is fashion subject formation. As we have seen throughout this book, intersecting subject positions (structure) and subjectivity (agency) can be seen as one in the ongoing process of subject formation—like a journey along a Möbius strip (Figure 1.1 in Chapter 1). Subject formation through the styled-fashioned-dressed body has its political pitfalls, but it also offers opportunities for critical hope, as well as fun. We experience and enact the politics and pleasures of style-fashion-dress together as one convoluted (nonlinear) path through time and space.

The quote (written more than sixty years earlier) by cultural theorist Walter Benjamin emphasizes the articulation between (tangible) material culture and abstract ideas. Brilliantly, as well, he points out the ways in which textiles turn and twist upon themselves, creating ways of thinking about not only time, but also space. He recognizes that style-fashion-dress, as part of material culture, has a certain kind of staying power. But this staying power is not static or fixed; it is not an essence, but rather a flexible vehicle for articulation and representation. Benjamin also seems to be saying, as I see it, that the paths of cultural history and individual subjectivity are not linear or straight; they have detours, they twist, and they fold back on themselves.

As metaphors or models at the interface between fashion studies and feminist cultural studies, the Möbius strip, the ruffle, the Venn diagram, the circuit, and the knot all contribute different ways of thinking about style-fashion-dress. They all work against essentialist, binary oppositional, and linear frameworks. Each metaphor or model explains something, but each has its limitations—hence, the need for multiple metaphors or models, so that no single metaphor will need to be pushed beyond its limits.

Cultural discourses also have their limits, and they define or structure subject positions. However, individuals exercise agency as they articulate their subjectivities through (a) the intersectionalities among these subject positions, (b) the spaces in between subject positions, and (c) entanglements with other subjects.

Subjectivity, as we have seen throughout this book, becomes visual and material through style-fashion-dress. Individuals navigate within and across overlapping subject positions (e.g., gender, sexuality, nation, class, race, ethnicity, age/generation, place) to represent the process of *becoming* in everyday life. Together, fashion studies and feminist cultural studies enable us to understand how subjectivity becomes embodied and negotiates power relations as we move through time and space. These two fields of study, in tandem, remind us that power is complex, multilayered, and nuanced. Through style-fashion-dress, power tends to operate less like a hammer and more like ongoing intersections, entanglements, and flows. Mixing metaphors, working through ambiguities and anxieties, and moving through time and space in a nonlinear manner, styled-fashioned-dressed bodies tell political, creative, cultural stories whose endings escape our grasps and extend our reaches.

References

Abdullah, Kulsoom. 2011. www.liftingcovered. Accessed December 29, 2011.

Abraham, Tamara. 2011. "J. Crew Ad Featuring a Five-year-old Boy with Neon Pink Toenails Sparks Debate about Gender Identity in Children." *Daily Mail*, April 12. http://www.dailymail.co.uk/femail/article-1376105/J-Crew-ad-featuring-year-old-boy-neon-pink-toenails-sparks-debate-gender-identity-children.html#ixzz1JPfsauRT.

Addams, Jane. 1899. "The Subtle Problems of Charity." *The Atlantic*, February.

Agins, Teri. 1999. *The End of Fashion: The Mass Marketing of the Clothing Business*. New York: William Morrow and Company.

Ahmed, Sara. 2006. "Orientations: Toward a Queer Phenomenology." *GLQ: A Journal of Lesbian and Gay Studies* 12(4): 543–74.

Anderson, Benedict. 2006. *Imagined Communities: Reflections on the Origin and Spread of Nationalism,* rev. ed. London: Verso.

André, Maria Claudia. 2005. "Frida and Evita: Latin American Icons for Export." In *The Latin American Fashion Reader*, ed. Regina Root, 247–79. Oxford: Berg.

Andrews, Gloria. 1969. "It Isn't Enough Just to Wear an Afro." *Seventeen*, May, 248.

Ang, Ien. 1996. "Culture and Communication: Towards an Ethnographic Critique of Media Consumption in the Transnational Media System." In *What is Cultural Studies*?, ed. John Storey, 237–54. New York: St. Martin's Press.

Appiah, Kwame Anthony, and Gates, Henry Louis, Jr., eds. 1997. *The Dictionary of Global Culture*. New York: Alfred A. Knopf.

Arthur, Linda B., ed. 1999. *Religion, Dress, and the Body*. Oxford: Berg.

Arthur, Linda B., ed. 2000. *Undressing Religion: Commitment and Conversion from a Cross-Cultural Perspective*. Oxford: Berg.

Ashley, Kathleen M., and Plesch, Veronique. 2002. "The Cultural Processes of 'Appropriation.'" *Journal of Medieval and Early Modern Studies* 32(1): 1–15.

Banerjee, Mukulika, and Miller, Daniel. 2003. *The Sari*. Oxford: Berg.

Barber, Elizabeth J.W. 1994. *Prehistoric Textiles: The Development of Cloth in the Neolithic and Bronze Ages*. Princeton, NJ: Princeton University Press.

Barker, Chris. 2002. *Making Sense of Cultural Studies: Central Problems and Critical Debates*. London: Sage Publications.

Barnard, Malcolm. 2002. *Fashion as Communication*. 2nd ed. London: Routledge.

Bartlett, Robert. 2001. "Medieval and Modern Concepts of Race and Ethnicity." *Journal of Medieval and Early Modern Studies* 31(1): 39–56.

Benjamin, Walter. 1968. "Theses on the Philosophy of History." In *Illuminations*, ed. Walter Benjamin, with an introduction by Hannah Arendt, trans. Harry Zohn 253–264. New York: Schocken Books.

Benjamin, Walter. 2004. *The Arcades Project.* Translated by Howard Eiland and Kevin McLaughlin. Cambridge, MA: Harvard University Press.

Berger, John. 1977. *Ways of Seeing.* London: Penguin Books.

Bergler, Edmund. [1953]1987. *Fashion and the Unconscious.* Madison, CT: International Universities Press.

Bergman, David, ed. 1993. *Camp Grounds: Style and Homosexuality.* Amherst: The University of Massachusetts Press.

Blackless, Melanie, Charuvastra, Anthony, Derryck, Amanda, Fausto-Sterling, Anne, Lauzanne, Karl, and Lee, Ellen. 2000. "How Sexually Dimorphic Are We? Review and Synthesis." *American Journal of Human Biology* 12: 151–66.

Blumer, Herbert. 1969. "Fashion: From Class Differentiation to Collective Selection." *Sociological Quarterly* 10: 275–91.

Bono, Chaz. 2011. *Transition: The Story of How I Became a Man.* New York: Dutton, Penguin Group.

Bourdieu, Pierre. 1984. *Distinction: A Social Critique of the Judgement of Taste.* Translated by Richard Nice. Cambridge, MA: Harvard University Press.

Brekke, Linzy A. 2010. "Ideology and the Dangers of Fashion in Early National America." In *The Fashion Reader: Global Perspectives*, ed. G. Riello and P. McNeil, 263–65. London: Routledge.

Breward, Christopher. 1995. *The Culture of Fashion: A New History of Fashionable Dress.* Manchester, UK: Manchester University Press.

Breward, Christopher. 1999a. "Patterns of Respectability: Publishing, Home Sewing and the Dynamics of Class and Gender 1870–1914." In *The Culture of Sewing: Gender, Consumption and Home Dressmaking*, ed. Barbara Burman, 21–31. Oxford: Berg.

Breward, Christopher. 1999b. *The Hidden Consumer: Masculinities, Fashion and City Life 1860–1914.* Manchester: Manchester University Press.

Breward, Christopher. 1999. *The Hidden Consumer: Masculinities, Fashion, and City Life.* Manchester: Manchester University Press.

Breward, Christopher, and Gilbert, David. 2006. *Fashion's World Cities.* Oxford: Berg.

Bristow, Joseph. 1997. *Sexuality.* London: Routledge.

Buchanan, Wyatt. 2006. "Castro Group Settles Differences with Neighborhood Bar; Boycott had Been Contemplated over Race Bias Claims." *San Francisco Chronicle,* January 1. http://goliath.ecnext.com/coms2/gi 0199–9464285/SAN-FRANCISCO-Castro-group-settles.html.

Bundles, A'Lelia. 2001. *On Her Own Ground: The Life and Times of Madam C.J. Walker.* New York: Scribner.

Butler, Judith. 1990. *Gender Trouble: Feminism and the Subversion of Identity.* London: Routledge.

Butler, Judith. 1993. *Bodies That Matter: On the Discursive Limits of "Sex."* New York: Routledge.

Butler, Judith, and Spivak, Gayatri Chakravorty. 2007. *Who Sings the Nation-State? Language, Politics, Belonging.* London: Seagull Books.

Caldwell, Paulette M. 2000. "A Hair Piece: Perspectives on the Intersection of Race and Gender." In *Critical Race Theory: The Cutting Edge,* 2nd ed., ed. Richard Delgado and Jean Stefanic, 275–85. Philadelphia: Temple University Press.

Calhoun, Craig. 1997. *Nationalism.* Minneapolis: University of Minnesota Press.

Canclini, Néstor García. 2000. "The State of War and the State of Hybridization." In *Without Guarantees: In Honour of Stuart Hall,* ed. Paul Gilroy, Lawrence Grossberg, and Angela McRobbie, 38–52. London: Verso.

Case, Sue Ellen. 1998. "Making Butch: A Historical Memoir of the 1970s." In *Butch/femme: Inside Lesbian Gender*, ed. Sally R. Munt, 37–45. London: Cassell.

Chapman, Malcolm. 1995. "Freezing the Frame: Dress and Ethnicity in Brittany and Gaelic Scotland." In *Dress and Ethnicity: Change across Space and Time*, ed. Joanne B. Eicher, 8–28. Oxford: Berg.

Chen, Jian. 2006. "The Tibetan Rebellion of 1959 and China's Changing Relations with India and the Soviet Union." *Journal of Cold War Studies* 8(3): 54–101.

Chomsky, Noam. 1986. *Knowledge of Language: Its Nature, Origin, and Use.* Westport, CT: Greenwood Publishing Co.

Clark, Danae. 1991. "Commodity Lesbianism." *Camera Obscura*, 25–26, 180–201.

Clark, Hazel. 2009. "Fashioning 'China Style' in the Twenty-first Century." In *The Fabric of Cultures: Fashion, Identity, and Globalization*, ed. Eugenia Paulicelli and Hazel Clark, 177–93. Oxon, UK: Routledge.

Clifford, Stephanie. 2011. "Even Marked Up, Luxury Goods Fly off Shelves." *New York Times,* August 5. www.nytimes.com.

Clifford, Stephanie, and Alderman, Liz. 2011. "American Retailers Try Again in Europe." *New York Times,* June 15. www.nytimes.com.

Cole, Shaun. 2000. *Don We Now Our Gay Apparel: Gay Men's Dress in the Twentieth Century.* Oxford: Berg.

Collins, Patricia Hill. 1991. *Black Feminist Thought: Knowledge, Consciousness, and the Politics of Empowerment.* New York: Routledge.

Connell, Raewyn. 2005. *Masculinities,* 2nd ed. Berkeley: University of California Press.

Considine, Austin. 2011. "The Perched, the Frothy, the Fascinator." *New York Times,* May 6. www.nytimes.com

Cook, Daniel Thomas. 2004. *The Commodification of Childhood: The Children's Clothing Industry and the Rise of the Child Consumer*. Durham, NC: Duke University Press.

Cook, Daniel Thomas, and Kaiser, Susan B. 2004. "Betwixt and be Tween: Age Ambiguity and the Sexualization of the Female Consuming Subject." *Journal of Consumer Culture* 4(2): 203–27.

Cosgrove, Stuart. 1989. "The Zoot Suit and Style Warfare." In *Zoot Suits and Second-hand Dresses: An Anthology of Fashion and Music*, ed. Angela McRobbie, 3–22. Boston: Unwin Hyman.

Craig, Maxine Leeds. 2002. *Ain't I a Beauty Queen? Black Women, Beauty, and the Politics of Race*. Oxford: Oxford University Press.

Craik, Jennifer. 1994. *The Face of Fashion: Cultural Studies in Fashion*. London: Routledge.

Crane, Diana. 2000. *Fashion and its Social Agendas: Class, Gender, and Identity in Clothing*. Chicago: University of Chicago Press.

Cresswell, Tim. 2004. *Place: A Short Introduction*. Malden, MA: Blackwell Publishing.

Damhorst, Mary Lynn. 1985. "Meanings of Clothing Cues in Social Context." *Clothing and Textiles Research Journal* 3(2): 39–48.

Davila, Arlene. 2001. *Latinos, Inc: The Marketing and Making of a People*. Berkeley: University of California Press.

Davis, Fred. 1984. "Decade Labeling: The Play of Collective Memory and Narrative Plot." *Symbolic Interaction* 7(1): 15–24.

Davis, Fred. 1992. *Fashion, Culture, and Identity*. Chicago: University of Chicago Press.

de Beauvoir, Simone. 1947. *The Ethics of Ambiguity*. Translated by Bernhard Frechtman. Secaucus, NJ: Citadel Press.

Delgado, Richard, and Stefancic, Jean, eds. 2000. *Critical Race Theory: The Cutting Edge*. Philadelphia: Temple University Press.

Downing, Lisa, and Gillett, Robert, eds. 2011. *Queer in Europe: Contemporary Case Studies*. Surrey, UK: Ashgate.

Dublin, Thomas, ed. 1993. *Farm to Factory: Women's Letters, 1830–1860*, 2nd ed. New York: Columbia University Press.

DuBois, W.E.B. [1903]1997. *The Soul of Black Folks*. New York: Bedford Books.

du Gay, Paul, Hall, Stuart, Jones, Linda, Mackay, Hugh, and Negus, Keith. 1997. *Doing Cultural Studies: The Story of the Sony Walkman*. London: Sage Publications.

Dunn, Charles J. 1969. *Everyday Life in Traditional Japan*. New York: Putnam and Sons.

Dyer, Christopher. 1989. *Standards of Living in the Middle Ages: Social Change in England 1200–1520*. Cambridge: Cambridge University Press.

Dyer, Richard. 1997. *White*. London: Routledge.

Earnest, Leslie. 2004. "California; Forever 21 Settles Dispute with Garment Workers." *Los Angeles Times,* December 15, C2. http://bitbucket.icaap. org/dict.pl?term=CONTRADICTIONS%20OF%20CAPITALISM.

Edwards, Tim. 1997. *Men in the Mirror: Men's Fashion, Masculinity, and Consumer Society*. London: Cassell.

Edwards, Tim. 2006. *Cultures of Masculinity*. London: Routledge.

Edwards, Tim. 2011. *Fashion in Focus: Concepts, Practices and Politics*. London: Routledge.

Ehrenreich, Barbara. 1989. *Fear of Falling: The Inner Life of the Middle Class.* New York: Perennial.

Eicher, Joanne B. 2001. "Introduction: The Fashion of Dress." In *Fashion*, ed. Cathy Newman, 29–35. Washington, DC: National Geographic.

Eicher, Joanne B. 2010. "Introduction to Global Perspectives." In *Encyclopedia of World Dress and Fashion. Volume 10. Global Perspectives*, ed. J. Eicher, 3–10. Oxford: Oxford University Press.

Eicher, Joanne B., Evenson, Sandra Lee, and Lutz, Hazel A. 2008. *The Visible Self,* 3rd ed. Oxford: Berg.

Eicher, Joanne B., and Sumberg, Barbara. 1995. "World Fashion and Ethnic and National Dress." In *Dress and Ethnicity: Change across Space and Time*, ed. Joanne B. Eicher, 295–306. Oxford: Berg.

"Ellen DeGeneres." www.imdb.com/name/nm0001122/bio. Accessed December 15, 2011.

Ellis, Havelock. 1938. *Psychology of Sex: A Manual for Students*. New York: Mentor Books.

Ellis, Havelock, and Symonds, J. A. [1897]1975. *Sexual Inversion*. New York: Arno Press.

Emberley, Julia V. 1997. *The Cultural Politics of Fur*. Ithaca, NY: Cornell University Press.

Enstad, Nan. 1998. "Fashioning Political Identities: Cultural Studies and the Historical Construction of Political Subjects." *American Quarterly* 50(4): 745–82.

Entwistle, Joanne. 2000. *The Fashioned Body: Fashion, Dress and Modern Social Theory*. Cambridge, UK: Polity Press.

Entwistle, Joanne. 2009. *The Aesthetic Economy of Fashion: Markets and Values in Clothing and Modelling*. Oxford: Berg.

Epstein, Rob, and Friedman, Jeffrey. 2000. *Paragraph 175*. http://www.imdb. com/title/tt0236576/. Accessed December 15, 2011.

Erdbrink, Thomas. 2011. "Olympics 2012: FIFA Bans Headscarves for Iranian Women's Soccer Team." *Washington Post*, June 6. http://www.washington post.com/sports/united/olympics-2012-fifa-bans-headscarves-for-irans-women-soccer-team/2011/06/06/AGzT1JKH_story.html?nav=emailpage. Accessed June 25, 2012.

Esbenshade, Jill. 2004. *Monitoring Sweatshops: Workers, Consumers, and the Global Apparel Industry*. Phildadelphia: Temple University Press.

Evans, Caroline, and Thornton, Minna. 1989. *Women and Fashion: A New Look*. London: Quartet Books.

Factory Girls of an American City. 1844. *Mind Amongst the Spindles: A Selection from The Lowell Offering*. Carlisle, MA: Applewood Books.

Falasca-Zamponi, Simonetta. 2002. "Peeking under the Black Shirt: Italian Fascism's Disembodied Bodies." In *Fashioning the Body Politic*, ed. Wendy Parkins, 145–65. Oxford: Berg.

Farrell-Beck, Jane, and Gau, Colleen. 2002. *Uplift: The Bra in America*. Philadelphia: University of Pennsylvania Press.

Fausto-Sterling, Anne. 2003. "The Problem with Sex/Gender and Nature/Nurture." In *Debating Biology: Reflections on Medicine, Health and Society*, ed. Simon J. Williams, Lynda Birke, and Gillian A. Bendelow, 123–32. London: Routledge.

Feldman, Gene, and Gartenberg, Max. 1958. *The Beat Generation and Angry Young Men*. New York: The Citadel Press.

Fernandez, Nancy Page. 1999. "Creating Consumers: Gender, Class and the Family Sewing Machine." In *The Culture of Sewing: Gender, Consumption and Home Dressmaking*, ed. Barbara Burman, 157–68. Oxford: Berg.

Ferrante, J. 1995. *Sociology: A Global Perspective*. Belmont, CA: Wadsworth Publishers.

Fischer, Gayle Veronica. 1998. "A Matter of Wardrobe? Mary Edwards Walker, a Nineteenth-century American Cross-dresser." *Fashion Theory* 2(3): 245–68.

Flax, Jane. 1990. "Postmodernism and Gender Relations in Feminist Theory." In *Feminism/Postmodernism*, ed. Linda J. Nicholson, 39–62. New York: Routledge.

Flugel, John C. 1930. *The Psychology of Clothes*. London: Hogarth Press.

Foster, Helen Bradley. 1997. *"New Raiments of Self": African American Clothing in the Antebellum South*. Oxford: Berg.

Foucault, Michel. 1972. *The Archaeology of Knowledge*. New York: Pantheon.

Foucault, Michel. 1977. *The History of Sexuality, Volume 1: An Introduction*. Translated by Alan Sheridan. New York: Pantheon.

Frankenberg, Ruth. 1997. "Local Whitenesses, Localizing Whiteness." In *Displacing Whiteness: Essays in Social and Cultural Criticism*, ed. Ruth Frankenberg, 1–33. Durham, NC: Duke University Press.

Freitas, Anthony, Kaiser, Susan, and Hammidi, Tania. 1996. "Communities, Commodities, Cultural Space, and Style." In *Gays, Lesbians, and Consumer Behavior: Theory, Practice, and Research Issues in Marketing*, ed. Daniel L. Wardlow, 83–107. New York: The Haworth Press.

Freitas, Anthony J., Kaiser, Susan B., Chandler, Joan, Hall, Carol, Kim, Jung-Won, and Hammidi, Tania. 1997. "Appearance Management as Border

Construction: Least Favorite Clothing, Group Distancing, and Identity . . . Not!" *Sociological Inquiry* 67(3): 323–35.

Freud, Sigmund. [1920]1963. "The Psychogenesis of a Case of Homosexuality in a Woman." In *Sexuality and the Psychology of Love*, ed. P. Rieff, 133–59. New York: Collier Books.

Fulbright, Leslie. 2008. "Sad Chapter in Western Addition." July 21. www.sfgate.com.

Gans, Herbert J. 1999. "The Possibility of a New Racial Hierarchy." In *The Cultural Territories of Race: Black and White Boundaries*, ed. Michele Lamont, 371–90. Chicago: University of Chicago Press.

Garber, Marjorie. 1992. *Vested Interests: Cross-dressing and Cultural Anxiety*. New York: Routledge.

Garber, Marjorie. 1995. *Vice Versa: Bisexuality and the Eroticism of Everyday Life*. New York: Simon & Schuster.

Garrison, Michael. 1982. "The Poetics of Ambivalence." In *Spring: An Annual of Archetypical Psychology and Jungian Thought*, ed. J. Hillman, 213–32. Dallas, TX: Spring Publications.

Gilbert, David. 2006. "From Paris to Shanghai: The Changing Geographies of Fashion's World Cities." In *Fashion's World Cities*, ed. Christopher Breward and David Gilbert, 3–32. Oxford: Berg.

Gindt, Dirk. 2010. "Coming Out of the Cabinet: Fashioning the Closet with Sweden's Most Famous Diplomat." *Critical Studies in Fashion and Beauty* 1(2): 233–54.

Gramsci, Antonio. 1971. *Selections from the Prison Notebooks*. New York: International Publishers.

Graybill, Beth, and Arthur, Linda B. 1999. "The Social Control of Women's Bodies in Two Mennonite Communities." In *Religion, Dress, and the Body*, ed. Linda B. Arthur, 9–29. Oxford: Berg.

Green, Denise Nicole, and Kaiser, Susan B. 2011. "From Ephemeral to Everyday Costuming: Negotiations in Masculine Identities at the Burning Man Project." *Dress* 37: 1–22.

Green, Jamison. 2004. *Becoming a Visible Man*. Nashville, TN: Vanderbilt University Press.

Grewal, Inderpal, and Kaplan, Caren. 1994. "Introduction: Transnational Feminist Practices and Questions of Postmodernity." In *Scattered Hegemonies: Postmodernity and Transnational Feminist Practices*, ed. Inderpal Grewal and Caren Kaplan, 1–33. Minneapolis: University of Minnesota Press.

Gronow, Jukka. 1997. *The Sociology of Taste*. London: Routledge.

Grossberg, Lawrence. 2010. *Cultural Studies in the Future Tense*. Durham, NC: Duke University Press.

Guidroz, Kathleen, and Berger, Michele Tracy. 2009. "A Conversation with Founding Scholars of Intersectionality: Kimberlé Crenshaw, Nira Yuval-

Davis, and Michelle Fine." In *The Intersectional Approach: Transforming the Academy through Race, Class, and Gender*, ed. Michele Tracy Berger and Kathleen Guidroz, 61–79. Chapel Hill: The University of North Carolina Press.

Halberstam, Judith. 2005. *In a Queer Time and Place: Transgender Bodies, Subcultural Lives (Sexual Cultures)*. New York: NYU Press.

Hall, Stuart. 1990. "Cultural Identity and Diaspora." In *Identity: Community, Culture, Difference*, ed. Jonathan Rutherford, 222–37. London: Lawrence and Wishart.

Hall, Stuart. 1991. "Old and New Identities, Old and New Ethnicities." In *Culture, Globalization, and the World System*, ed. Anthony D. King, 41–68.

Hall, Stuart. 1996. "For Allon White: Metaphors of Transformation." In *Stuart Hall: Critical Dialogues in Cultural Studies*, ed. David Morley and Kuan-Hsing Chen, 287–305. London: Routledge.

Hall, Stuart. 1997. *Representation: Cultural Representations and Signifying Practices*. London: Sage.

Halter, Marilyn. 2000. *Shopping for Identity: The Marketing of Ethnicity*. New York: Schocken Books.

Hammidi, Tania. 2011. *Judgement Day: Fashioning Masculinities*. www.tania hammidi.com.

Hammidi, Tania N., and Kaiser, Susan B. 1999. "Doing Beauty: Negotiating Lesbian Looks in Everyday Life." *Journal of Lesbian Studies* 3(4): 55–63.

Hancock, Joseph. 2010. *Brand/Story: Ralph, Vera, Johnny, Billy, and Other Adventures in Fashion Branding*. New York: Fairchild Books.

Harvey, David. 1990. *The Condition of Postmodernity*. Oxford: Blackwell Publishers.

Harvey, John. 1995. *Men in Black*. Chicago, IL: The University of Chicago Press.

Hebdige, Dick. 1979. *Subculture: The Meaning of Style*. London: Methuen & Co.

Heller, Sarah-Grace. 2010. "The Birth of Fashion." In *The Fashion History Reader: Global Perspectives*, ed. Giorgio Riello and Peter McNeil, 25–39. London: Routledge.

Higonnet, Anne. 1998. *Pictures of Innocence: The History and Crisis of Ideal Childhood*. London: Thames and Hudson.

Hoggart, Richard. 1957. *The Uses of Literacy: Aspects of Working Class Life*. London: Chatto and Windus.

Hollander, Anne. 1994. *Sex and Suits: The Evolution of Modern Dress*. New York: Alfred A. Knopf.

Holleran, Andrew. 1978. *Dancer from the Dance: A Novel*. New York: William Morrow and Company.

hooks, bell. 1990. *Yearning: Race, Gender, and Cultural Politics*. Cambridge, MA: South End Press.

hooks, bell. 1992. *Black Looks: Race and Representation*. Cambridge, MA: South End Press.

hooks, bell. 2000. *Where We Stand: Class Matters*. New York: Routledge.

hooks, bell. 2009. *Belonging: A Culture of Place*. New York: Routledge.

Horn, Jessica. 2006. "Re-righting the Sexual Body." *Feminist Africa* 6. www.feministafrica.org/index.php/re-righting.

Horn, Marilyn. 1965. *The Second Skin*. Boston: Houghton-Mifflin.

Horrocks, Roger. 1997. *An Introduction to the Study of Sexuality*. New York: St. Martin's Press.

Huehls, Mitchum. 2010. "Structures of Feeling: Or, How to Do Things (or Not) with Books." *Contemporary Literature* 51(2): 419–28.

Hunt, Alan. 2010. "A Short History of Sumptuary Laws." In *The Fashion History Reader: Global Perspectives*, ed. Giorgio Riello and Peter McNeil, 43–61. London: Routledge.

James, Henry. 1886. *The Bostonians*. London: Macmillan.

Jenss, Heike. 2004. "Dress in History: Retro Styles and the Construction of Authenticity in Youth Culture." *Fashion Theory* 8(4): 387–403.

Kaiser, Susan B. 1997. *The Social Psychology of Clothing: Symbolic Appearances in Context,* 2nd ed., revised. New York: Fairchild Publications.

Kaiser, Susan B. 2001. "Minding Appearances: Style, Truth, and Subjectivity." In *Body Dressing*, ed. Joanne Entwistle and Elizabeth Wilson, 79–102. Oxford: Berg.

Kaiser, Susan B. 2008. "Mixing Metaphors in the Fiber/Textile/Apparel Complex: Toward a More Sustainable Fashion System." In *Sustainable Fashion: Why Now?*, ed. Janet Hethorn and Connie Ulasewicz, 139–64. New York: Fairchild Publications.

Kaiser, Susan B., and Huun, Kathleen. 2002. "Fashioning Innocence and Anxiety: Clothing, Gender, and Symbolic Childhood." In *Symbolic Childhood*, ed. Daniel Thomas Cook, 183–208. New York: Peter Lang.

Kaiser, Susan B., and Ketchum, Karyl. 2005. "Consuming Fashion as Flexibility: Metaphor, Cultural Mood, and Materiality." In *Inside Consumption: Consumer Motives, Goals, and Desires*, ed. S. Ratneshwar and David Glen Mick, 122–43. Oxford: Routledge.

Kaiser, Susan B., and Looysen, Ryan. 2010. "Antifashion." In *Encyclopedia of World Dress and Fashion: Volume 3. The United States and Canada*, ed. Phyllis G. Tortora, 160–70. Oxford: Oxford University Press.

Kaiser, Susan B., Looysen, Ryan, and Hethorn, Janet. 2008. "Un(mark)eting Hegemonic Masculine Fashion: On the Politics of Cultural (In)visibility." In *Gender and Consumer Behavior*, ed. Shona Bettany, Susan Dobscha, Lisa O'Malley, and Andrea Prothero (online version, n.p.). Boston, MA: Association for Consumer Research.

Kaiser, Susan B., and McCullough, Sarah Rebolloso. 2010. "Entangling the Fashion Subject through the African Diaspora." *Fashion Theory* 14(3): 361–86.

Kaiser, Susan B., Nagasawa, Richard H., and Hutton, Sandra S. 1990. "Fashion, Postmodernity and Personal Appearance: A Symbolic Interactionist Formulation." *Symbolic Interaction* 14(2): 165–85.

Kaiser, Susan, Rabine, Leslie, Hall, Carol, and Ketchum, Karyl. 2004. "Beyond Binaries: Respecting the Improvisation in African American Style." In *Black Style*, ed. Carol Tulloch, 48–67. London: Victora and Albert Museum Press.

Kang, M. Agnes, and Lo, Adrienne. 2004. "Two Ways of Articulating Heterogeneity in Korean American Narratives of Ethnic Identity." *Journal of Asian American Studies* 7(2): 93–116.

Kaplan, E. Ann. 1983. *Women and Film: Both Sides of the Camera*. London: Methuen.

Kaplan, E. Ann. 2000. "Is the Gaze Male?" In *Feminism and Film*, ed. E. Ann Kaplan, 119–38. Oxford: Oxford University Press.

Katz, Jonathan N. (1995). *The Invention of Heterosexuality*. New York: Dutton/Penguin Books.

Katz, Jonathan. 2010. "Mary Edwards Walker: November 26, 1832–February 21, 1919." January 14. http://outhistory.org/wiki/Mary_Edwards_Walker:_November_26,_1832-February_21,_1919. Accessed August 4, 2012.

Kennett, Frances. 1995. *Ethnic Dress*. New York: Facts on File.

Kierkegaard, Søren. 1980. *The Concept of Anxiety*. Edited and translated with introduction and notes by Reider Thomte in collaboration with Albert A. Anderson. Princeton, NJ: Princeton University Press.

Kilbourne, Jean. 2010. *Killing Us Softly IV*. Northampton, MA: Media Education Foundation.

King, Charles W. 1963. "Fashion Adoption: A Rebuttal to the 'Trickle Down' Theory." In *Toward Scientific Marketing*, ed. S. A. Greyser, 108–25. Chicago, IL: American Marketing Association.

King, Coretta Scott. 1993. *My Life with Martin Luther King, Jr.*, rev. ed. New York: Henry Holt and Co.

Klein, Jordan. 2008. "A Community Lost: Urban Renewal and Displacement in San Francisco's Western Addition District." http://jordanklein.us/files/WA_Paper.pdf.

Klepp, Ingun Grimstad, and Storm-Mathisen, Ardis. 2005. "Reading Fashion as Age: Teenage Girls' and Grown Women's Accounts of Clothing as Body and Social Status." *Fashion Theory* 9(3): 323–42.

Kohler, Will. 2011. "46 Years Ago Today: First Lesbian and Gay Protest at the White House." April 17. http: www.bilerico.com//2011/04/46 years ago today 1st lesbian gay protest at the.php.

Korotchenko, Alexandra, and Clarke, Laura Hurd. 2010. "Russian Immigrant Women and the Negotiation of Social Class and Feminine Identity through Fashion." *Critical Studies in Fashion and Beauty* 1(2) 181–202.

Koshy, Susan. 2001. "Morphing Race into Ethnicity: Asian Americans and Critical Transformations of Whiteness." *boundary 2* 28(1): 153–94.

Koyen, Jeff. 2008. "Steal This Look: Will a Wave of Piracy Lawsuits Bring down Forever 21?" Sit-back-relax.popsugar.com/interesting-story-Forever-21–1074976. Accessed June 23, 2010.

Kozar, Joy M., and Damhorst, Mary Lynn. 2008. "Older Women's Responses to Current Fashion Models." *Journal of Fashion Marketing and Management* 12(3): 338–50.

Kuchta, David. 2002. *The Three-Piece Suit and Modern Masculinity: England, 1550–1850.* Berkeley: University of California Press.

LaBarre, Polly. 2007. "Sophisticated Sell." www.fastcompany.com/magazine/65/sophisticated.html. Accessed July 6, 2010.

Lancaster, Roger N. 1992. *Life is Hard: Machismo, Danger, and the Intimacy of Power in Nicaragua.* Berkeley: University of California Press.

Lancaster, Roger N. 2003. *The Trouble with Nature: Sex in Science and Popular Culture.* Berkeley: University of California Press.

Latour, Bruno. 2005. *Reassembling the Social: An Introduction to Actor-Network-Theory.* Oxford: Oxford University Press.

Laver, James. 1969. *A Concise History of Costume and Fashion.* New York: Scribner's.

Lefebvre, Henri. 1991. *The Production of Space.* Translated by Donald Nicholson-Smith. Malden, MA: Blackwell Publishing.

Lemire, Beverly. 2010. "Fashioning Cottons: Asian Trade, Domestic Industry and Consumer Demand, 1660–1780." In *The Fashion Reader: Global Perspectives*, ed. Giorgio Riello and Peter McNeil, 194–213. London: Routledge.

Levinson, Jeff, ed. 2007. *Mill Girls of Lowell.* Boston: HistoryCompass.

Lewis, Reina. 1997. "Looking Good: The Lesbian Gaze and Fashion Imagery." *Feminist Review* 55: 92–109.

Lipovetsky, Gilles. 1994. *The Empire of Fashion: Dressing Modern Democracy.* Translated by Catherine Porter. Princeton, NJ: Princeton University Press.

Looysen, Ryan. 2008. *Unmarked Men: Anxiously Navigating Hegemonic Masculinities.* Master's Thesis. University of California, Davis.

Lowe, Lisa. 2000. "Heterogeneity, Hybridity, Multiplicity: Marking Asian American Differences." In *Asian American Studies: A Reader*, ed. Jean Yu-wen Shen Wu and Min Song, 423–42. New Brunswick, NJ: Rutgers University Press.

Lynton, Linda. 1995. *The Sari: Styles-Patterns-History-Techniques.* New York: Harry N. Abrams.

Maira, Sunaina. 2000. "Henna and Hip Hop: The Politics of Cultural Production and the Work of Cultural Studies." *Journal of Asian American Studies* 3(3): 329–69.

Majtenyi, Cathy. 2010. "Kenyan 'National Dress' a Work in Progress." October 22. http://www.voanews.com/english/news/africa/Kenyan-National-Dress-a-Work-in-Progress-105576078.html. Accessed February 26, 2011.

Mama, Amina. 1995. *Beyond the Masks: Race, Gender and Subjectivity:* London: Routledge.

Manlow, Veronica. 2011. "Creating an American Mythology: A Comparison of Branding Strategies in Three Fashion Firms." *Fashion Practice* 3(1): 85–109.

Marx, Karl, and Engels, Friedrich. 2002. *The Communist Manifesto.* London: Penguin Classics.

Massey, Doreen. 1993. "Power-geometry and a Progressive Sense of Place." In *Mapping the Futures: Local Cultures, Global Change*, ed. Jon Bird, Barry Curtis, Tim Putnam, George Robertson, and Lisa Tickner. London: Routledge.

Massey, Doreen. 2005. *For Space.* London: Sage.

Mazon, Mauricio. 1984. *The Zoot-suit Riots: The Psychology of Symbolic Annihilation.* Austin: University of Texas Press.

McClintock, Anne. 1995. *Imperial Leather: Race, Gender and Sexuality in the Colonial Contest.* New York: Routledge.

McNeil, Peter, and Karaminas, Vicki. 2009. *The Men's Fashion Reader.* New York: Berg.

McRobbie, Angela. 1989. *Zoot Suits and Second-hand Dresses.* Oxford: Routledge.

McRobbie, Angela. 1991. *Feminism and Youth Culture.* Oxford: Routledge.

McRobbie, Angela. 1994. *Postmodernism and Popular Culture.* London: Routledge.

Mei, Hua. 2005. *Chinese Clothing.* Translated by Yu Hong and Zhang Lei. China Intercontinental Press.

Miller-Spellman, Kimberly, Damhorst, Mary Lynn, and Michelman, Susan. 2005. *Meanings of Dress,* 2nd ed. New York: Fairchild Publications.

Mohammad-Arif, Aminah. 2000. "A Masala Identity: Young South Asian Muslims in the US." *Comparative Studies of South Asia, Africa and the Middle East* 20(1): 67–87.

Möser, Justus. [1775]2004. " 'The Benefits of a National Uniform, Declaimed by a Citizen' from Patriotic Fantasies (1775)." In *The Rise of Fashion*, ed. Daniel Leonhard Purdy, 87–92. Minneapolis: University of Minnesota Press.

Mulvey, Laura. 1975. "Visual Pleasure and Narrative Cinema." *Screen* 16(3): 6–18.

Naukkarinen, Ossi. 1998. *Aesthetics of the Unavoidable: Aesthetic Variations in Human Appearance.* Series, Volume 3. Lahti, Finland: International Institute of Applied Aesthetics.

Newton, Esther. 1979. *Mother Camp: Female Impersonators in America*. Chicago: The University of Chicago Press.

Newton, Judith, Kaiser, Susan B., and Ono, Kent. 1998. "Proposal for an MA and PhD Programme in Cultural Studies at UC Davis." *Cultural Studies* 12(4): 546–70.

Oliver, Simone. 2010. "The Head Wrap Comes Back, Again." *New York Times*. November 10.

Omi, Michael, and Winant, Howard. 1994. *Racial Formation in the United States: From the 1960s to the 1990s,* 2nd ed. New York: Routledge.

O'Neal, Gwendolyn S. 1998. "African American Aesthetic of Dress: Current Manifestations." *Clothing and Textiles Research Journal* 16: 167–75.

O'Neal, Gwendolyn S. 1999. "The African American Church, Its Sacred Cosmos, and Dress." In *Religion, Dress, and the Body*, ed. Linda B. Arthur, 117–34. Oxford: Berg.

Ong, Aihwa. 1999. *Flexible Citizenship: The Cultural Logics of Transnationality*. Durham, NC: Duke University Press.

Ortiz, Renato. 2003. "Notes on Religion and Globalization." Translated by Fabio Durão. *Nepantia: Views from South* 4(3): 423–48.

Oxford English Dictionary. 2010. Oxford: Oxford University Press. www.oed.com.

Paoletti, Jo B. 1985. "Ridicule and Role Models as Factors in American Men's Fashion Change, 1880–1910." *Costume* 19: 121–34.

Paoletti, Jo B. 1987. "Clothing and Gender in America: Children's Fashions, 1890–1920." *Signs* 13(1): 136–43.

Paoletti, Jo B. 2012. *The Pink and the Blue: Telling the Boys from the Girls in America*. Bloomington: Indiana University Press.

Paoletti, Jo B., and Kregloh, C. L. 1989. "The Children's Department." In *Men and Women: Dressing the Part*, ed. Claudia B. Kidwell and Valerie Steele, 22–41. Washington, DC: Smithsonian Institution Press.

Parkins, Wendy. 2002. "Introduction: (Ad)dressing Citizens." In *Fashioning the Body Politic*, ed. Wendy Parkins, 1–17. Oxford: Berg.

Paulicelli, Eugenia. 2010. "Mapping the World: Dress in Cesare Vecellio's Costume Books." In *The Fashion History Reader: Global Perspectives*, ed. Giorgio Riello and Peter McNeil, 138–59. London: Routledge.

Perry, Pamela. 2002. *Shades of White: White Kids and Racial Identities in High School*. Durham, NC: Duke University Press.

Pesotta, Rose. 1944 (1987). *Bread Upon the Waters*. Ithaca, NY: ILR Press, Cornell University.

Phelan, Peggy. 1993. *Unmarked: The Politics of Performance*. London: Routledge.

Puar, Jasbir. 2007. *Terrorist Assemblages: Homonationalism in Queer Times*. Durham, NC: Duke University Press.

"Queer Eye for the Straight Guy." www.imdb.com/title/tt0358332/plotsummary. Accessed December 15, 2011.

Quiroga, José. 2000. *Tropics of Desire: Interventions from Queer Latino America*. New York: NYU Press.

Rabine, Leslie W. 2002. *The Global Circulation of African Fashion*. Oxford: Berg.

Reid, Susan E. 2008. "Who Will Beat Whom? Soviet Popular Reception of the American National Exhibition in Moscow, 1959." *Kritika: Explorations in Russian and Eurasian History* 9(4): 855–904.

Reilly, Andrew, and Cosbey, Sarah. 2008. *Men's Fashion Reader*. New York: Fairchild Books.

Reinach, Simona Segre. 2010. "If You Speak Fashion You Speak Italian: Notes on Present Day Italian Fashion Identity." *Critical Studies in Fashion and Beauty* 1(2): 203–15.

Reuters. 2012. "FIFA Lifts Ban in Hijab for Women Footballers." *The Express Tribune*, July 6. http://tribune.com.pk/story/404321/fifa-lifts-ban-on-heads carves-for-women-footballers/. Accessed August 3, 2012.

Riello, Giorgio, and McNeil, Peter. 2010. "Introduction." In *The Fashion Reader: Global Perspectives*, ed. G. Riello and P. McNeil, 1–14. London: Routledge.

Rinallo, Diego. 2007. "Metro/Fashion/Tribes of Men: Negotiating the Boundaries of Men's Legitimate Consumption." In *Consumer Tribes*, ed. Bernard Cova, Robert Kozinets, and Avi Shankar, 76–92. London: Butterworth-Heinneman.

Roach, Mary Ellen, and Eicher, Joanne B., eds. 1965. *Dress, Adornment, and the Social Order*. New York: John Wiley & Sons.

Roach, Mary Ellen, and Eicher, Joanne B. 1973. *The Visible Self: Perspectives on Dress*. Englewood Cliffs, NJ: Prentice-Hall.

Rock, Chris. 2009. *Good Hair*. http://www.imdb.com/title/tt1213585/. Accessed November 25, 2011.

Rolley, Katrina. 1992. "Love, Desire and the Pursuit of the Whole." In *Chic Thrills: A Fashion Reader*, ed. Juliet Ash and Elizabeth Wilson, 30–39. Berkeley: University of California Press.

Rosaldo, Michelle Z. 1974. "Woman, Culture and Society: A Theoretical Overview." In *Woman, Culture, and Society*, ed. M. Z. Rosaldo and L. Lamphere, 17–42. Stanford, CA: Stanford University Press.

Rosencranz, Mary Lou. 1950. "Sociological Aspects of Clothing Studied." *Journal of Home Economics* 42(3): 206.

Rosencranz, Mary Lou. 1962. "Clothing Symbolism." *Journal of Home Economics* 54: 18–22.

Rosencranz, Mary Lou. 1965. "Social and Psychological Approaches to Clothing Research." *Journal of Home Economics* 57(1): 26–29.

Russell, Kathy, Wilson, Midge, and Hall, Ronald. 1992. *The Color Complex: The Politics of Skin Color among African Americans*. New York: Anchor Books.

Ryan, Mary S. 1966. *Clothing: A Study in Human Behavior*. New York: Holt, Rinehart & Winston.

Said, Edward. 1978. *Orientalism*. New York: Vintage Books.

Scott, Allen. 2002. "Competitive Dynamics of Southern California's Clothing Industry: The Widening Global Connection and Its Local Ramifications." *Urban Studies* 39: 1287–1306.

Scott, David. 2005. "Stuart Hall's Ethics." *Small Axe* 9(1): 1–6.

Sedgwick, Eve Kosofsky. 1990. *Epistemology of the Closet*. Berkeley: University of California Press.

Sharpe, Jenny. 1993. *Allegories of Empire: The Figure of Woman in the Colonial Text*. Minneapolis: University of Minnesota Press.

Shryock, Andrew. 2010. "Introduction: Islam as an Object of Fear and Affection." In *Islamophobia/Islamophilia: Beyond the Politics of Enemy and Friend*, ed. Andrew Shryock, 1–25. Bloomington: Indiana University Press.

Simmel, Georg. 1904. "Fashion." *International Quarterly* 10: 130–55.

Simmel, Georg. 2004. "Fashion." In *The Rise of Fashion*, ed. Daniel Leonhard Purdy, 289–309. Minneapolis: The University of Minnesota Press.

Skov, Lise. 2011. "Dreams of Small Nations in a Polycentric Fashion World." *Fashion Theory* 15(2): 137–56.

Snow, C. P. 1959. *The Two Cultures*. Cambridge: Cambridge University Press.

Spencer, Colin. 1995. *Homosexuality in History*. New York: Harcourt Brace.

Spivak, Gayatri. 1999. *A Critique of Postcolonial Reason: Towards a History of the Vanishing Present*. Cambridge, MA: Harvard University Press.

Steele, Valerie. 1988. *Paris Fashion: A Cultural History*. Oxford: Oxford University Press.

Steele, Valerie. 1989. "Clothing and Sexuality." In *Men and Women: Dressing the Part*, ed. Claudia Brush Kidwell and Valerie Steele, 42–63. Washington, DC: Smithsonian Institution Press.

Stiglitz, Joseph E. 2011. "Of the 1%, by the 1%, for the 1%." *Vanity Fair*, May. www.vanityfair.com/society/features/2011/05/top-one-percent-201105.

Stone, Gregory P. 1969. "Appearance and the Self." In *Dress, Adornment, and the Social Order*, ed. Mary Ellen Roach and Joanne B. Eicher, 216–45. New York: John Wiley & Sons.

Stryker, Susan. 2006. "(De)Subjugated Knowledges: An Introduction to Transgender Studies." In *The Transgender Studies Reader*, ed. Susan Stryker and Stephen Wittle, 1–17. New York: Taylor & Francis Group.

Stryker, Susan. 2008. *Transgender History*. Berkeley, CA: Seal Press.

Sullivan, Kelly. 2011. *Gay Masculinity through the Lens of Fashion Theory*. Master's Thesis. University of California, Davis.

Suthrell, Charlotte. 2004. *Unzipping Gender: Sex, Cross-Dressing and Culture*. Oxford: Berg.

Tabili, Laura. 2003. "Race Is a Relationship, and Not a Thing." *Journal of Social History* 37(1): 125–30.

Takeda, Sharon Sadako, and Spilker, Kaye Durland. 2010. *Fashioning* Fashion: *European Dress in Detail 1700–1915*. Los Angeles County Museum exhibition. Munich: Delmonico Books.

Tarlo, Emma. 2010. *Visibly Muslim: Fashion, Politics, Faith*. Oxford: Berg.

Taylor, Lou. 2004. *Establishing Dress History*. Manchester, UK: Manchester University Press.

Tesfay, Saba. 2009. "Wearing Gypsy Identity in a Gábor Gypsy Community in Tîrgu Mureş." *Romani Studies* 19(1): 1–17.

Thomas, Dominic Richard David. 2003. "Fashion Matters: La SAPE and Vestimentary Codes in Transnational Contexts and Urban Diasporas." *MLN* 188(4): 947–73.

Thompson, Mary J. 2000. "Gender in Magazine Advertising: Skin Sells Best." *Clothing and Textiles Research Journal* 18(3), 178–81.

Tokatli, Nebahat. 2008. "Global Sourcing: Insights from the Global Clothing Industry—The Case of Zara, a Fast Fashion Retailer." *Journal of Economic Geography* 8: 21–38.

Tremlett, Annabel. 2009. "Bringing Hybridity to Heterogeneity in Romani Studies." *Romani Studies* 19(2): 147–68.

Tseëlon, Efrat. 1995. *The Masque of Femininity: The Presentation of Woman in Everyday Life*. London: Sage Publications.

Tseëlon, Efrat. 2010. "Is Identity a Useful Critical Tool?" *Critical Studies in Fashion and Beauty* 2(2): 151–59.

Tsui, Christine. 2010. *China Fashion: Conversations with Designers*. Oxford: Berg.

Tuan, Yi-Fu. 1977. *Space and Place: The Perspective of Experience*. Minneapolis: University of Minnesota Press.

Tulloch, Carol. 2010. "Style-Fashion-Dress: From Black to Post-black." *Fashion Theory* 14(3): 361–86.

Twig, Julia. 2010. "How Does Fashion Negotiate Age? Fashion, the Body, and the Older Woman." *Fashion Theory* 14(4): 471–90.

Vainshtein, Olga. 2010. "The Dandy." In *The Fashion Reader: Global Perspectives*, ed. G. Riello and P. McNeil, 329–31. London: Routledge.

Valania, Jonathan. 2003, "Clothes Make the Man." June 11. http://www.philadelphiaweekly.com/news-and-opinion/cover-story/clothes_make_the_man-38368134.html?page=4&comments=1&showAll=#ixzz1EpEDasoL. Accessed February 23, 2011.

Veblen, Thorstein. 1899. *The Theory of the Leisure Class*. New York: Macmillan.

Vesselinov, Elena. 2010. "Citizenship and the Nation-state." *Women's Studies Quarterly* 38(1–2): 335–49.

Vollmer, John E. 2010. "Cultural Authentication." In *Berg Encyclopedia of World Dress and Fashion*, ed. Joanne B. Eicher, 69–76. Oxford: Oxford University Press.

Walker, Lisa M. 1993. "How to Recognize a Lesbian: The Cultural Politics of Looking Like What You Are." *Signs* 18(4): 866–90.

Wronska-Friend, Maria. 2010. "Miao/Hmong in Australia." In *Encyclopedia of World Dress and Fashion*, ed. Jasleen Dhamija, vol. 4, 459–65. Oxford: Oxford University Press.

Warner, Patricia Campbell. 2006. *When the Girls Came Out to Play: The Birth of American Sportswear*. Amherst: University of Massachusetts Press.

Weber, Caroline. 2006. *Queen of Fashion: What Marie Antoinette Wore to the Revolution*. New York: Henry Holt and Co.

Weber, Max. 1974. "Class, Status, Party." In *Social Stratification: A Reader*, ed. Joseph Lopreato and Lionel S. Lewis, 45–54. New York: Harper & Row, Publishers.

Weinraub, Marsha, Clements, Lynda P., Sockloff, Alan, Ethridge, Teresa, Gracely, Edward, and Myers, Barbara 1984. "The Development of Sex Role Stereotypes in the Third Year: Relationships to Gender Labeling, Gender Identity, Sex-typed Toy Preferences, and Family Characteristics." *Child Development* 55, 1493–1503.

White, Shane, and White, Graham. 1998. *Stylin': African American Expressive Culture from Its Beginnings to the Zoot Suit*. Ithaca, NY: Cornell University Press.

Wild, Oliver. 2011. "The Silk Road." http://www.ess.uci.edu/~oliver/silk.html. Accessed February 25, 2011.

Williams, Raymond. 1958. *Culture and Society*. London: Chatto and Windus.

Williams, Raymond. 1977. *Marxism and Literature*. Oxford: Oxford University Press.

Williams, Raymond. 1980. "The Magic of Advertising." In *Problems in Materialism and Culture*, ed. Raymond Williams, 170–95. London: Verso.

"Will and Grace." www.imdb.com/title/tt0157246/. Accessed December 15, 2011.

Wilson, Elizabeth. 1985. *Adorned in Dream: Fashion and Modernity*. London: Virago Press.

Wilson, Elizabeth. 2007. "A Note on Glamour." *Fashion Theory* 11(1): 95–108.

Winakor, Geitel. 1969. "The Process of Clothing Consumption." *Journal of Home Economics* 61(8): 629–34.

Witte, Samuel Simon. [1791]2004. " 'An Answer to the Question: Would It Be Harmful or Beneficial to Establish a National Uniform?' (1791)." In *The Rise of Fashion*, ed. Daniel Leonhard Purdy, 72–78. Minneapolis: University of Minnesota Press.

Wright, Erik Olin. 2005. *Approaches to Class Analysis*. Cambridge: Cambridge University Press.

Wronska-Friend, Maria. 2010. "Miao/Hmong in Australia." In *Encyclopedia of World Dress and Fashion, Volume 4: South Asia and Southeast Asia*, ed. Jasleen Dhamija, 459–465. Oxford: Oxford University Press.

Wu, Juanjuan. 2009. *Chinese Fashion: From Mao to Now*. Oxford: Berg.

Yan, Yunxiang. 2009. *The Individualization of Chinese Society*. Oxford: Berg.

Zahedi, Ashraf. 2007. "Contested Meaning of the Veil and Political Ideologies of Iranian Regimes." *Journal of Middle East Women's Studies* 3(3): 75–98.

WEBSITES

www.friniggi.com. Accessed December 15, 2011.

www.manishmalhotra.in. Accessed December 15, 2011.

www.marksimpson.com/metrosexy. Accessed December 15, 2011.

www.state.gov/secretary/rm/2011/09/171860.htm. Accessed December 15, 2011.

Index